A LEGACY IN
PEANUTS

A Legacy in Peanuts

TOM'S FOODS AND THE TRANSFORMATION OF THE TWENTIETH-CENTURY SOUTH

Haisten Willis

NewSouth Books
AN IMPRINT OF
The University of Georgia Press
Athens

NSB

Published by NewSouth Books,
an imprint of the University of Georgia Press
Athens, Georgia 30602
www.ugapress.org
https://ugapress.org/imprints/newsouth-books/

Designed and set in Warnock Pro by Lindsay Starr

Printed digitally

EU Authorized Representative
Easy Access System Europe—Mustamäe tee 50, 10621 Tallinn,
Estonia, gpsr.requests@easproject.com

Library of Congress Control Number: 2026020624
ISBN 9781588385901 (paperback)
ISBN 9781588385925 (epub)
ISBN 9781588385918 (PDF)

To my family.

CONTENTS

A LEGACY IN PEANUTS

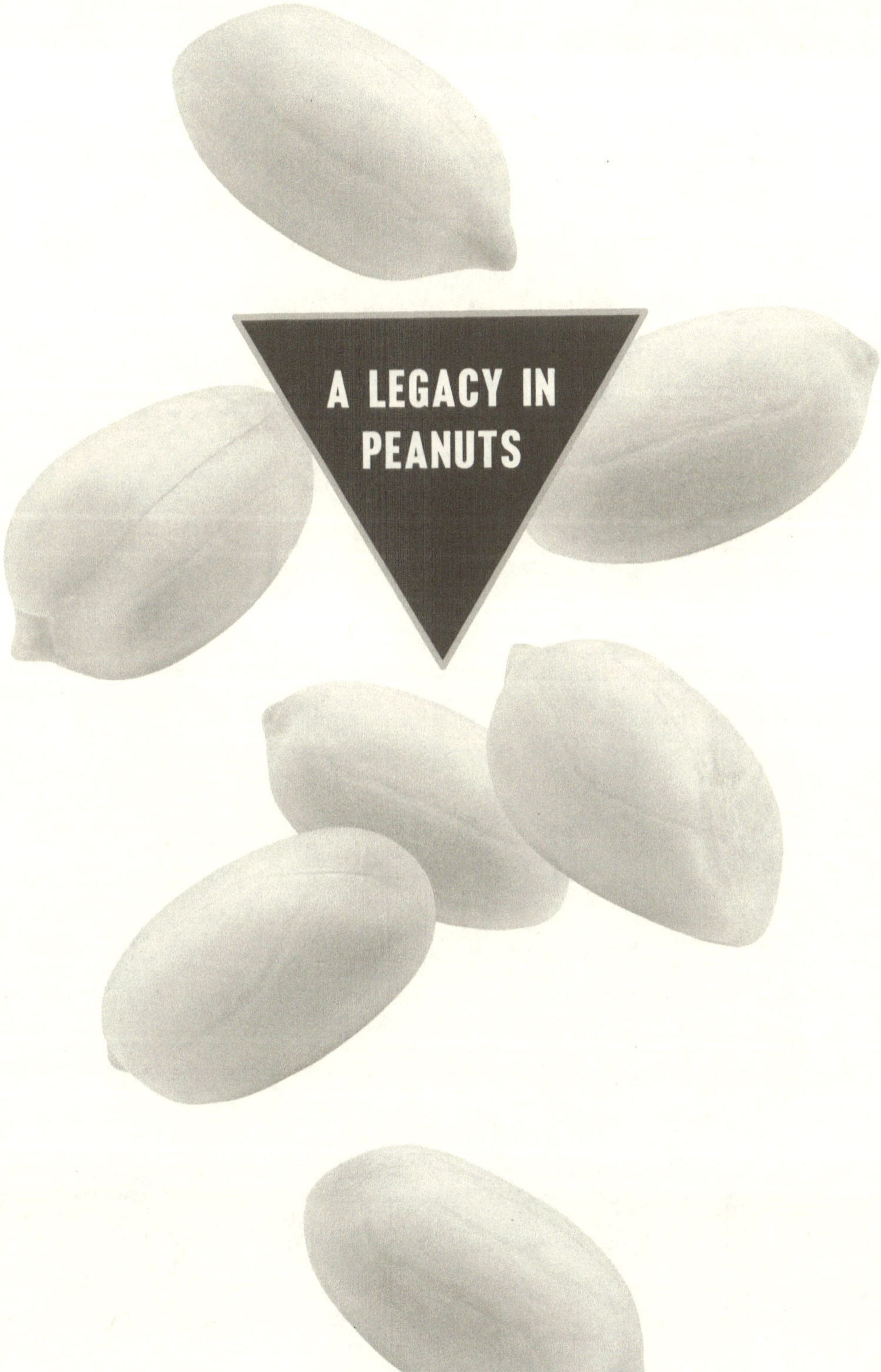

Introduction

"Tom's," meaning the Tom Huston Peanut Company or, later, Tom's Foods, was an entity I grew up acutely and yet vaguely aware of. It was something the adults would mention from time to time in their sky of conversation as I was off playing with toys or daydreaming. Sometimes there was a tone of annoyance or tedium when it came to "Tom's," it being, as I later learned, a place where so many of them labored day in and day out. That work wasn't usually glamorous, but coming at the end of the twentieth century as my childhood did, it looked a lot different, and most would agree a lot better, than work did at the beginning of that century.

"Tom's" in my childhood meant lots of little snacks in various shapes and sizes wrapped in colorful plastic packaging and stacked away in boxes: salted peanuts, of course, but also brownies, potato chips, hard and rolled candies, fig bars, butterscotch, peanut butter logs, candy coconut slices—all little goodies wrapped behind the familiar red triangle. These were presented to me as treats on occasion, or were something I begged for until my parents gave in and let me grab one. Mostly, though, they were packed up in enormous quantities in my dad's warehouse, which always smelled of damp cardboard and cold concrete, and then on his box truck, which bore a similar smell, only with the concrete replaced by unpainted wooden shelves.

These were snacks for other people, though exactly who I did not know. My dad, it turned out, was part of the company's army of independent contractors slinging Tom's products across the country. We were just up the road, relatively speaking, from the company's Columbus, Georgia, headquarters, in Douglasville, where we moved after my dad took a distributorship with Tom's in 1986. At a tender age I would ride with him along his route, so young at first that I once got in trouble for unwrapping and biting into a lollipop right in the middle of a store. In time, I learned that many of my other relatives worked for the same firm.

My story begins at the tail end of the twentieth century, or the end of the line for Tom's, and as I grew older it dawned on me that something was not right. To be frank, hardly anyone who wasn't directly involved with Tom's seemed to really want its snacks. Goliath competitor Frito-Lay was all over television with commercials—some of which aired during the Super Bowl—featuring Chester Cheetah or Miss Piggy, while Tom's appeared to have no marketing budget whatsoever. It was obvious to me, even as a child, that things must have been different at some point in the past. This must have been a stronger, healthier venture at an earlier time; otherwise we wouldn't be where we were. Once I reached that conclusion, a second question gradually crystallized in my mind: What happened?

Before getting fully into that topic, which of course is the question this entire book seeks to answer, I should lay out in detail my many personal ties to Tom's Foods. Doing so serves two purposes. First, it informs just why I've felt compelled to write a full-length manuscript on a historic but long-gone entity. Second, and more to the point, detailing these ties provides transparency about my perspective and bias as it relates to this project, for it cannot be said that I am a distanced observer of events described herein.

The first member of my family to work at Tom's was my great-great-aunt Ruth Davis, who briefly joined the sandwich cracker production line in the late 1940s after moving to Columbus from Blakely, Georgia. There's a bit of tragedy involved here. Her only child had died at the age of three, and the family suspects she moved to help get her mind off that terrible reality. In any case, Aunt Ruth quickly "employed" a second relative—my grandmother, Bobbie Goodwin, who was a small child at the time. Bobbie lived next door and washed Aunt Ruth's dishes while Ruth was at work. Bobbie's payment? A pack of Tom's crackers straight from the factory. Aunt Ruth soon returned to Blakely, but in 1952 my great-uncle began a thirty-three-year run with the company, followed by my maternal grandfather, who started working there fresh out of high school in 1957. My other grandfather joined Tom's in 1970 following a personal bankruptcy and stayed until his death twenty-five years later. A few months after I was born, my dad was laid off from a Columbus cotton mill and subsequently became a Tom's distributor (my mom joined him briefly in this venture). As I write this, he still peddles the few remaining products bearing a Tom's logo, now exclusively chips and pork rinds, stacking them in vending machines and on convenience store shelves across the western Atlanta suburbs.

My dad's older brother worked at Tom's, also as a "route man," from the late 1970s until his death in 2021, and my other two uncles, along with another great uncle and a great aunt, enjoyed shorter stints before moving elsewhere. In total, that's eleven relatives (twelve if we include my dishwashing grandmother) who dedicated some portion of their working lives to this company. Five of them stayed on for decades. Obviously, this wasn't the career path I chose. It couldn't have been, since the company went bankrupt in 2005 while I was still in college. But I did continue riding along with my dad as I grew up, for weeks at a time during summers in middle school, and on occasion thereafter. In fact, I spent a full year working a route myself after finishing graduate school in the middle of the Great Recession of 2007–9, though Tom's was by then simply a brand owned by Lance Inc. That gig ended when my journalism career started; I got my first full-time reporting job after sending out more than a hundred résumés over twelve months.

Can someone with such close ties to a company write an accurate account of it? I think so. For one, there is no getting around the fact that the company failed and that, with all factors considered, the failure was earned. Related to that, my family members suffered financially and otherwise from the wobbly state of affairs as things slowly unraveled at Tom's, just as they benefited in earlier years when the company was healthy. There are as many painful memories as happy ones.

Why write a book, then?

The idea pulled at me relentlessly for a full eighteen months before I finally gave in. It started in early 2021, when Campbell Soup Company, owner of the Tom's brand, announced it would close the Columbus headquarters for good. Tom's hadn't been a going concern in its own right since 2005, but the factory continued operating under outside owners throughout the ensuing years, and some products still bore the red Tom's triangle, providing a measure of continuity. The closing of the factory, the last physical link to the original company, was for me like a giant sinking ship that finally strikes the bottom of the sea, stirring up silt that had sat undisturbed for eons. All those old memories came rushing back, fresh again, as they tend to do when something or someone familiar passes. At the time I was a self-employed freelance journalist. The factory closing elicited only minor coverage in local media, and knowing so much of the background, I thought I could drum up interest in some deeper reporting. The story seemed like a good fit for *The Atlanta Journal-Constitution*; I pitched it as a Sunday feature, and the paper accepted.

Writing that story dug up even more of the undisturbed silt. I had a vague outline of how Tom's started and had heard a few times that George Washington Carver was involved. Researching the piece taught me that Tom Huston launched something of a revolution in 1925, one with national implications, and that Carver was heavily involved too, seeing the peanut venture as a way to rescue Black farmers from the scourge of cotton sharecropping. Carver once said that Tom Huston's plan "interests me more than anything that I have come in contact with."

Tom's was indeed a major firm in its heyday, thanks to Huston and to later innovations in mechanical vending machines. In the early 1980s, just a few years before my earliest memories of a snack-filled warehouse, Tom's hosted a homecoming celebration for its employees that brought singer Ray Charles, economist and future Presidential Medal of Freedom recipient Arthur Laffer, and the Florida State University marching band to Columbus—all on the same weekend. The company operated factories in Tennessee, Virginia, Florida, Texas, California, and Maine in addition to Georgia.

After the *Journal-Constitution* piece ran, I heard from dozens of people. They told me stories about eating Tom's snacks on trips to the beach as small children in the 1950s and 1960s and shared which candy bar was their favorite; some remembered touring the headquarters factory on school field trips. Many shared that their older relatives worked there too. Casting further out, a few people told me that their own hometown had a big factory that dominated the local economy, a center of community life that was so much more than just a place to work. The strength of the feedback was encouraging, and the hints of a wider archetype opened the idea that perhaps something bigger was at play.

The idea of turning the story into a book sprang up pretty quickly. Still, my hope was that the desire would simply fade away with time. Months went by, and then, in the fall of 2021, one of my uncles passed away unexpectedly. He had worked for Tom's since the late 1970s, and sure enough, there was an antique glass Tom's jar displayed at his funeral. The opportunity to tell the story in full, I realized, would not be around forever. The book idea became a constant presence in my daydreams. I imagined what went on in the break rooms and the boardroom during those eighty years when the company was a going concern. Most of all, that central question remained: What happened? It all seemed so far from my own life and my experience of digital labor in the twenty-first century: smartphones, tablets, remote work. On the one hand, this was a big reason not to pursue writing about Tom's, since the project wouldn't really align with my day job, but it also was a reason my curiosity remained so strong. The world of snack foods and factories, boiling ovens and confections, peanuts and seasonings, roasting aromas and churning conveyor belts, seemed so different, and more authentic in some nebulous way.

On a more concrete and more widely impactful level, my research for the newspaper story showed me that Tom's was part of an underreported segment of Southern history. The unfortunate parts of the South's past, including slavery, the Civil War, the cotton gin, Jim Crow, and to some extent the decades-long economic struggle for the region to do something, anything, other than produce cotton after the war, are well chronicled, as they should be. But the South's emergence from all of that has never seemed to captivate the public imagination in the same way.

Tom's represented the marriage of several vogue ideas of the early twentieth century. The company sprang up as the boll weevil completed its devastating march across the South. This was a ruinous development at the time but eventually proved a blessing thanks to the innovations it fostered, necessity being the mother of invention. Many prominent people were eager for change; they just weren't sure how to make it happen. The New South "boosterism" movement was alive and well, as it is in many respects today. Booker T. Washington's Tuskegee Institute was in its heyday. Tuskegee taught practical education in the areas of agriculture and industry, and its most famous professor, George Washington Carver, was beginning to focus on the peanut as a means to help Black farmers move beyond the cotton monoculture.

That Tom Huston's peanut venture succeeded so spectacularly is one of the great stories of the era and, dare I say, of the twentieth-century South. Huston's is part of the lesser-told story of the region, when it finally integrated economically with the rest of the nation and made tremendous strides with industries of its own that eventually, though unevenly, uplifted citizens of all stripes. True equality has still not arrived, racially or regionally, but the South progressed considerably between 1900 and 2000.

At some point, those big strides forward began to leave Tom's behind. Huston lost control of his own company rather quickly, in a manner similar to many other inventors. It then fell into the hands of Walter A. Richards, who stabilized and grew Tom's before handing it over to his son-in-law, J. W. "Bill" Feighner. These two men led Tom's from roughly 1930 to 1980, a period of steady growth and stable employment for thousands of people, not just in Columbus but throughout the distributor network and at a growing series of factories in other states. Things got wobbly in the 1980s, a decade in which Tom's was sold twice—first from longtime parent company General Mills to a British firm known as Rowntree Mackintosh, and then just four years later to a group of Tom's executives and managers. A final sale, in 1993, was to Chicago billionaire Michael Heisley, a self-described "turnaround guy." But he couldn't turn around Tom's, and the company filed for bankruptcy in 2005.

Tom's and its industrial cousins brought people out of the fields and into the cities, a national phenomenon that coincided with the automation of farming and allowed people to work higher-paying factory and, for some, office jobs. But just as that revolution swept Tom's into its heyday, so too did the wheels of innovation spark its decline. Tom's fell from prominence due to a number of factors, perhaps most notably its existence as a regional player in the increasingly national business and media landscape, and the general employment shift away from manufacturing jobs and toward the service sector. New Columbus businesses rode that next wave to prominence and remain dominant as I write this. These firms include insurance giant Aflac, banking firm Synovus Financial Corp., and credit card processor Total System Services (now a subsidiary of Atlanta-based Global Payments Inc.). These companies have taken the mantle of business and community leadership from Tom's and the old cotton mills and operate in decidedly postindustrial sectors.

What's left, then? What kind of book chronicles a venture that ultimately failed? Certainly, most of what we read and talk about daily involves success. Politicians who lose elections don't get a lot of press afterward. No one commemorates mediocre football and baseball teams with rings or trophies. But when a venture earns runaway success, only to lose it, there does tend to be a lingering fascination. I am reminded of Percy Shelley's 1818 sonnet, "Ozymandias." Exploring the fate of man and the destructive waves of time, the poem tells of a fictional empire long since vanished. It begins by describing an abandoned land where "two vast and trunkless legs of stone" arise from the desert, above a sculpted message:

"My name is Ozymandias, king of kings:
Look on my works, ye Mighty, and despair!"
Nothing beside remains. Round the decay
Of that colossal wreck, boundless and bare
The lone and level sands stretch far away.

Yes, but thank God for the inscription! At least we know something was there. Fragments of the Tom's story exist in many places, ranging from newspaper clippings and old company swag to promotional books commissioned by the company itself. Yet no full-length history has ever been written that attempts to tell the whole story, warts and all.

This, then, is my attempt to write such an inscription on the Tom Huston Peanut Company, complete with as many relevant voices alive today as possible. Beyond that, my aim with this work is to highlight a more recent, more hopeful American South marked by entrepreneurship and a closer approximation of racial harmony, leading to a more prosperous future for this fevered corner of the world.

John Haisten Willis Jr.
September 30, 2023

CHAPTER 1

Peanuts Before Tom

For Tom Huston, shelling always came at the wrong time. Huston enjoyed the hobbies of a typical farm boy of his day, and he especially loved to go squirrel hunting when he could find the time. The best time to hunt squirrels came when it rained. That's where the peanuts came in. Huston's efficiency-minded, Scottish-descendant farmer father, Ernest Huston, wanted something productive done at all hours. Rain cut out the opportunity to do much true farmwork, but there was always a pile of peanuts in the barn waiting to be shelled. Huston, the oldest of ten children, was put to the task on rainy days, cracking open the grainy shells by hand.

"It wasn't the goobers I hated so much as it was the shelling," he said later, in one of many accounts he gave to newspaper and magazine writers. "Many a night I've gone to bed with fingers feeling as if they had been held against an emery wheel."

Rather than feasting on rich squirrel meat after a big afternoon of hunting, Huston nursed sore fingers at night. The task pained all his digits but particularly the thumb, against which the shells were crushed by the others. The smaller fingers could be rotated, but not that poor thumb, and its throbbing, reddened rawness kept young Huston awake. This type of pain wasn't necessarily unusual for a boy of Huston's time and place. What was unusual was his reaction.

Huston's circumstances were in many ways typical of his generation of Southerners. Born John Thomas Huston on September 24, 1889, he spent his earliest years on a farm near Wilsonville, Alabama, in the southern part of Shelby County. According to the U.S. census of 1900, he was born in the Yellowhammer State, as were both of his parents, and was still living there the year of his eleventh birthday. The area in which the Huston family lived later became a relatively prosperous suburb of Birmingham, but it was a rural outpost of farms during Huston's childhood. Around the time Huston entered adolescence, his family moved to Henderson in the eastern part of Texas, which had a climate and landscape similar to that of the Southeast. The move happened sometime between 1900 and 1903, when Huston was between eleven and fourteen years old, as reflected in the 1910 census. He didn't seem particularly fond of the area, recalling that the family moved there when he was "still young enough to get excited about going to Texas."

Many accounts of Huston's story say that he grew up on a peanut farm. The truth is more nuanced. Huston's father ran a cotton farm that used peanuts as an insurance crop against the boll weevil. The dreaded bug entered the United States from its native Mexico in the early 1900s, traveling about fifty-five miles a year to the north and east and leaving agricultural and financial disaster in its wake. Because Henderson, Texas, is roughly six hundred miles west of the Alabama/Georgia state line, Huston's family encountered the boll weevil much earlier than did farmers to the east, giving them familiarity with its devastation and experience rotating peanut plants into the fields years earlier than if they'd remained in Alabama. Either way, the very idea of running a peanut-only farm would seem out of place at the turn of the last century, which is part of what makes Huston's story so remarkable. The peanut, history shows, had been a global snack food for centuries, but for a number of reasons it had never become a mass-market cash crop.

For a crop that sprouts up only to bury its seeds right back into the soil from which it came, the peanut plant is an amazingly well-traveled organism. Peanuts, which are actually part of the legume or pea family rather than being a true nut, are grown all over the world, with only slight variation, in dozens of different countries and cultures. For centuries it remained a mystery just where the peanut originated due to its globetrotting abundance.

This homebody of a plant became so well traveled in prehistoric times the same way peanuts travel today: through humans. Recent research has found that the peanut is the combination of two ancient species, carrying essentially the complete chromosomal imprint of each one. The pair merged some 9,400 years ago when human transport brought one genome species into contact with the other, enabling their hybridization.

Peanuts carry several key attributes that have benefited humans and, in turn, kept the plant itself thriving for millennia. Peanuts are now tended to gingerly by farmers and studied by university researchers every year, important as they are for business, agriculture, and sustenance. The peanut is filling and nutritious, high in protein, and relatively easy to harvest and grows in a reasonable variety of climates and soil types. Peanuts held a long shelf life even before the development of airtight packaging, since the edible portion comes prepackaged, in a sense. They are widely consumed across the world, growing well in portions of North and South America, Africa, and Asia. In Europe, peanuts and peanut oil are widely consumed, though much of that continent is too chilly for domestic growth.

It was only in the mid-twentieth century that research pinpointed the earliest origin of peanut cultivation to the eastern portion of modern Bolivia. History shows that ancient snackers loved peanuts and ate them basically the same way modern people do: cooked and seasoned, either inside or outside the shell. Centuries-old gravesites in Peru include jars filled with peanuts, and one twentieth-century naturalist, A. Hyatt Verrill, claimed they were still edible hundreds of years later. How did he know? He ate some himself. European explorers searching South America in the sixteenth century found peanuts being prepared as a candy, another role we still see today. Peruvian women covered roasted peanuts with a sugar mixture as a confectionery, and the Incas added honey to toasted peanuts, with the poor collecting the nuts and presenting them to the rich and powerful.

However, that state of affairs, in which the less well-off served peanuts to the elite, is an inversion of historic and modern norms. In *Peanuts: The Illustrious History of the Goober Pea*, author Andrew F. Smith outlines what he describes as three dichotomies of the peanut that date to early colonial history and remain true today. The first is that the peanut is a legume but looks, tastes, and is prepared like a nut. The second is that peanuts are fine to eat cooked but not raw. The third is that peanuts taste good but are not considered a proper food for high society.

From its origin point in South America, the peanut crisscrossed the globe. Some accounts have peanut plants traveling directly to Europe, where they grew well in sunny, sandy Spain, then to Africa, and finally to North America aboard slave ships. Peanuts can certainly be found in all those places, but the points of travel may not have been so neat and orderly. For example, early European explorers found peanuts in the Caribbean, a much shorter throw to North America than the fish-shaped circuit described above, and also in Africa, in Southeast Asia, and even on remote Pacific islands.

Narrowing our focus to the American South, there are two main kinds of peanuts that thrive in the region. A relatively small variety known as the Spanish peanut thrives in southeast Alabama, northern Florida, Georgia, and parts of the Southwest. The name comes from the simple fact that this variety also thrives in Spain. A larger variety known as the Virginia or Jumbo peanut thrives in Virginia and North Carolina. Georgia, however, is far and away the nation's largest peanut producer, growing some 772 billion peanuts a year as of 2022, good for more than half of the total U.S. output. While the peach is a symbol of Georgia and the designated state fruit, peanuts are Georgia's official state crop.

If one gets the impression that peanuts have always been a popular snack food, that's partially true and partially not. The crop has always been practical and fun to eat on a small scale, but its use for mass consumption didn't take off until the early twentieth century. Before then, peanuts were generally grown on a few acres of larger farms dedicated to something else—in the American South that "something else" was almost always cotton—and they had a variety of lesser uses. Peanuts could be a "cover crop," meaning one used to secure and replenish the soil rather than for harvesting, and a snack for children, slaves, or the very poor, all of whom shelled them by hand. Hogs were actually the biggest peanut consumers, with one variety of peanut even named the "hog runner" because pigs rooted them right up out of the ground. Peanut-fed hogs drew a premium at the market. Peanut-fed humans were another story.

There are several reasons for the limited success of peanuts before the twentieth century. As we've seen, one reason was the need for shelling, which can be fun with a small bagful of peanuts at a baseball game but is painstaking at scale. The other big issues were related to packaging and transportation. While peanuts remained edible for long periods of time even before the days of plastic seals, they quickly grew stale or even rancid, rendering them less than desirable when other options were available. For that reason, peanuts tended to thrive only in times of necessity. It's unclear whether slave ships were the first vessels to bring peanuts to the land that would become the United States, but it is undisputed that the ships were packed with peanuts to feed to those making the treacherous voyage. Slaves were among the first peanut consumers and the first peanut merchants of the South, selling them from homemade mule carts in the decades before the Civil War. The slang term "goober" comes from the African word for the crop. Africa seemed to have an early leg up on growing peanuts commercially as well, with expeditions sent to the continent in the 1840s to ship them westward. The African trade even posed a threat to Southern growers, who successfully lobbied Congress to impose a one-cent-per-pound tariff on imported peanuts in 1842, though imports continued to thrive even with the tariff in place. Africans also likely brought the custom of eating boiled peanuts to the United States.

Just as the confines of slave ships brought peanuts to the fore, so too did the ravages of war. Peanut consumption surged during the Civil War amid a brutal Northern blockade of goods coming into and out of the South. In the North, the supply of peanuts from Southern areas was cut off, leading to another surge in peanut imports from Africa, which reached 11.5 million pounds in 1868. They were eaten with some regularity in peacetime, though the shells, apart from the damage they caused to the consumer's hands, were considered a public nuisance once discarded. Washington Irving, author of the famous short stories "Rip Van Winkle" and "The Legend of Sleepy Hollow," used a pen name to complain about the litter of peanut shells on city streets. Throughout the nineteenth century, peanuts were sold roasted inside the shell, making a lot of noise when they were cracked open and littering the ground and getting stuck in the bootheels of pedestrians once discarded.

For the child Huston on a rural farm, peanuts were a constant torment as well, always looming in the barn, keeping him from his beloved squirrel hunting and leaving his hands painfully raw as an added insult. But Huston was an unusual child and would grow into an unusual adult. In an era before the widespread adoption of public education, he became a self-taught engineering marvel without ever graduating from high school. As his younger brother, newspaper editor Cleburne Huston, later wrote:

> He used to be as full of ideas as the hound dawg was of fleas when we were boys together on a sandy, stumpy hillside farm in East Texas. Tom had so many ideas and invented so many fool contraptions that the neighbors sometimes poked fun at him. However, this writer didn't laugh at him, for Tom was some five years bigger and in those days could thrash the present editor with one hand. Anyway, Tom had grit enough until he could chuckle quietly at the ignorance of

> those who laughed at him. He worked on his "fool notions" at night when the rest of us were asleep and in the daytime when other people were fishing or loafing around town.

It was a pattern that Tom Huston kept up the rest of his life. His childhood is not particularly well documented, but it is known that he first got the idea of inventing a peanut sheller after seeing a corn-shelling device that was on the market. Peanut-shelling machines also existed already in other parts of the country, though it is possible that Huston was not aware of prior models given the communication limitations of the time, the lack of a commercial market for peanuts, and the surprisingly long distance between himself and those machines.

The earliest reference to a peanut-shelling machine dates to 1879, ten years before Huston was born, when Henry Loomus built a shelling plant in Philadelphia. The Northern city may seem an unlikely location for such a facility given its vast removal from peanut-growing areas of the Southeast, even the relatively close regions of North Carolina and Virginia. The juxtaposition speaks again to the vast gap in economic development and industrialization between the North and the South in this period. Loomus at first trucked whole peanuts, shells and all, from Southern farms to Philadelphia for processing and distribution, but he eventually gave in to common sense and moved his equipment to Suffolk, Virginia, capital of the North Carolina/Virginia peanut industry. The Columbia Peanut Company was formed in 1896 in neighboring Norfolk, Virginia, and in 1916 another entrepreneur, Harvard Birdsong, launched a nearby operation to compete with Loomus. Yet all of these companies were located at least twelve hundred miles from Huston's Texas home, and furthermore, they were designed to shell the big peanuts that thrived in Virginia rather than the smaller versions that grew in the Deep South.

In any case, Huston spent years working on the peanut-shelling problem and had invented his first functional shelling machine by 1912, the year he turned twenty-three. This was likely a rotating, hand-operated model that churned peanuts into a choke point and then crushed them by force of the machinery. To separate shells from kernels, the peanuts were crammed against a grate through which the shells would fall, separating them from the kernels and hopefully leaving the kernels intact, along with the fingertips of the operator. It took a few more years, but rapid and painless shelling would open new frontiers across the South for the humble legume, which was already starting to make modest inroads into commercial use.

A sort of recreational use of peanuts had picked up toward the end of the 1800s, when they were sold in two ways that remain ensconced in the popular imagination. The first was the hawking of peanuts at carnivals, and the second was their sale at baseball games. The 1908 Tin Pan Alley song "Take Me Out to the Ball Game" immortalized the latter point of sale with its lyric "Buy me some peanuts and Cracker Jack." In fact, the line plugs peanuts twice, since peanuts are also an ingredient in Cracker Jack. But the peanuts sold at baseball games were not freshly rotated or sealed and were frequently stale.

Peanut butter began to take off around the turn of the last century as well. A common myth is that George Washington Carver invented peanut butter, though that is not the case. Peruvians made a crude form of peanut butter at least as far back as the 1500s, when Europeans first entered South America. The truth is that the process of making peanut butter, which involves grinding peanuts down to the point where the oil mixes seamlessly with the rest of the nut, is probably too simple for any one person to have invented. Carver played a hugely significant role in promoting peanut butter during his lifetime, but even here his influence pales in comparison to that of another man, John Harvey Kellogg.

Peanut butter was promoted as a health food around 1900 and grew into something of a fad. Kellogg grew up in the Seventh-day Adventist Church, a denomination that endorses vegetarianism, and his father had run a health clinic specializing in that diet. Kellogg become famous in his day for food inventions, among them corn flakes and granola, and he lauded peanut butter as a miracle worker. Kellogg gave thousands of presentations on peanut butter, including one at Carver's Tuskegee Institute in Alabama. Carver later became a "peanut butter priest" himself. Annual production of peanut butter had reached roughly six million pounds by 1916, and thousands of grocery stores installed peanut grinders to make it fresh in-house.

Huston helped accelerate the trend. In 1915, while still living in Texas, he filed his first two patents, one for a hand-operated sheller and one for a floor model, and set off to manufacture and market his inventions. They were designed to accept various sizes of peanuts, especially the small white Spanish peanut variety that flourished in the sandy soils of the Deep South. If there were other peanut shellers on the market that could do this, they weren't available in the region, weren't of a high quality, or simply weren't advertised well, as the young Huston found a reliable market for his invention and grew to dominate it in the lower peanut belt. The first spate of models was imprinted with "Tom Huston Pea Nut Sheller" and spelled out that they were manufactured in Henderson, Texas. But he soon moved to Columbus to set up operations.

There were two reasons for his move to the Southeast. The first is that Huston set up a manufacturing contract with the Columbus Iron Works, a firm that was known to work with young businessmen. The second reason was that Columbus sat in the dead center of the Spanish peanut belt (consisting of southwest Georgia, southeast Alabama, and northern Florida), providing huge potential for the young, ambitious Huston to grow his business. Columbus, as history shows, attracted from the outset "men of a speculating disposition," and it landed one of the biggest speculators of the era when Tom Huston arrived.

The Georgia General Assembly created Columbus in 1828 as a "trading town on the Chattahoochee" River. Although the exact definition and manner of trade has changed in the ensuing years, this foundational slogan remains an apt description of the city nearly two hundred years later, with the soul of Columbus still wrapped up in its location on the river and the big employers that drive its economy.

Its status as a "trading town on the Chattahoochee" made the city unique, even if its name didn't. Columbus, Georgia, is one of more than two dozen cities, towns, and counties in the United States named for controversial Italian explorer Christopher Columbus. More specificity was given to its location, as Columbus was founded not merely "on" the Chattahoochee River but at its northernmost navigable point. At its founding, Columbus was also located on the Federal Road, a mail delivery route through the Muscogee (Creek) Nation that ran from Washington, D.C., to New Orleans. The same road would later be used to expedite the tragic removal of the Creek Indians from the Southeast, though a link to this part of the story remains via the name of the county, Muscogee, in which Columbus is located.

River travel has been a crucial form of trade throughout history and was a chief consideration in the foundation of many Georgia cities. Macon and Augusta, cousins to Columbus in many respects, were also located atop the navigable portion of the rivers on which they lie. Columbus, being further west and further inland, was founded a bit later, at a crucial period in the development of industry and transportation. Steamboat technology advanced significantly during the 1810s and 1820s, with the machine-powered ships carrying up to twenty-five times the freight capacity of older keelboats or flatboats. This would be revolutionary on its own, but steamboats also made upstream travel economically feasible, reducing transportation costs and travel time significantly and opening the door to increased trade between the South, the crucial Northern states, and England.

Of course, for Columbus, the steamboat initially helped facilitate trade in cotton, a crop that would be woven deeply into the fabric of the South's economic and cultural life for another 150 years after the city's 1828 founding. Because Columbus was surrounded by low-lying, nutrient-rich, hot, flat earth, it was a natural gathering place for the cotton crop from nearby farms and plantations. Eli Whitney's 1793 invention of the cotton gin exponentially increased the amount of cotton that could be harvested, which had the unfortunate side effect of reinvigorating and retrenching slavery in the South.

Most of the South's cotton was shipped north for processing, as the antebellum slavery system was ill-equipped for industrialization. Columbus bucked the regional trend somewhat by developing an early reputation for textiles, thanks mostly to hydropower created by the rushing waters of the Chattahoochee. The city's early entrepreneurs used the river to power a series of industrial mills, some of which still stand, though they've long since been converted into office buildings or condominiums.

The mills helped Columbus stand out among Southern towns, and it was sometimes called the "Lowell of the South," a favorable comparison to Lowell, Massachusetts. Columbus industry also boosted Georgia's self-appellation as the "Empire State of the South." Over time, the cotton mills grew to dominate the city's economic, political, and social life, and by the 1860s Columbus was Georgia's third-largest city. The mills, the river, and trade attracted new investment and new people to Columbus.

The city's first settlers were middle- and upper-class entrepreneurs, "men of a speculating disposition" seeking commercial opportunities. This led to vast fortunes for some, but also to a top-heavy culture in which a select few leaders and their families held outsized sway. The members of the city's upper crust were typically more concerned with profit than class distinction, however, and they were willing or even driven to take risks to make it.

Textile mills were typically the leading edge of industrialization in any region, and the South was no different. Almost as soon as the city was founded, the river's hydropower was being used by mills, some to grind corn and flour and the larger ones to spin cotton. The Columbus City Council first looked into damming the river for hydropower in 1841, and by 1850 the five-story, river-fed Eagle Mill was in operation. Its owner, William H. Young, came to Columbus specifically because of the river and the nutrient-rich soil surrounding it. He found success right away and eventually became the city's top businessman of his generation, with his mill becoming the largest in the entire South by the 1880s. But cotton wasn't everything. Iron foundries were another early industry, including one founded by William R. Brown in 1849 that became known as the Columbus Iron Works. These businesses beget others throughout the city's history.

The Civil War boosted Columbus, as the city proved useful to the Confederacy. Unlike Atlanta, it was mostly spared the harshest ravages of the war until the conflict's final days, when one of the last battles of the war—local lore says it was the very last battle, though this is disputed—was fought largely on the Alabama side of the Chattahoochee before spilling over into Columbus. (One notable casualty of the battle was the Eagle Mill, which was burned by Union forces; the mill was rebuilt a few years later and renamed the Eagle & Phenix Mill.) Yet even relative wartime prosperity brought with it problematic speculation. Cotton prices surged during the war with so many farmers off fighting, and shrewd planters ignored official decrees to limit their production in order to take advantage. They smuggled the product to the North or circumvented the naval blockade to England, a phenomenon that inspired the character of Rhett Butler in Margaret Mitchell's *Gone with the Wind*. This practice was hugely controversial and eventually spilled onto the pages of local newspapers.

The end of the Civil War brought a host of new issues to Southern cities, Columbus included. While Black citizens were freed of chattel slavery, by the end of the 1890s the system of customs and laws known as Jim Crow placed them back into a tremendously compromised position politically, economically, and socially. White Southerners endured struggles of their own. The late nineteenth-century South is largely remembered for its boosterism of what proponents such as Henry W. Grady dubbed "the New South." Left unsaid is that such promotion was needed chiefly because the South found itself so far behind the North, and businessmen were desperate to advance the region's economy beyond its reliance on cotton. Georgia in the postbellum period was one of the nation's poorest states.

There was innovation in this period, however, with much of it fueled by necessity. Two stories in particular have entered local Columbus lore. The first is the tale of John Stith Pemberton, a pharmacist who was wounded at the Battle of Columbus in 1865 and spent the rest of his life seeking cures for his ailments. This led him to invent a drink with extracts of kola nut and damiana, which he dubbed Pemberton's French Wine Coca, later renamed

Coca-Cola when he created a nonalcoholic version. Pemberton and the drink wound up in Atlanta, but Columbus men were heavily involved with Coca-Cola through the end of the twentieth century, and the company's vast success helped seed the prominent Bradley and Turner families, plus many lesser names who bought stock shares during Coke's early days. Furthermore, Columbus was also home to a local Coke competitor, Royal Crown (or RC) Cola, which was founded by pharmacist Claud A. Hatcher and produced the Nehi line of flavored sodas as well.

The other story of local innovation and success begins with a female mill worker at the Eagle & Phenix who had her savings stuffed into the hem of her dress. One day her clothes became entangled in the mill's machinery, spilling the money onto the ground. A mill executive then offered to keep the cash in a company vault and pay her interest, a service he expanded to all mill workers in 1888. This eventually led to the formation of Columbus Bank and Trust, now known as Synovus. A spinoff, the credit card processor Total System Services, or TSYS, began as a side project for the bank in the 1950s and eventually grew to become a Fortune 1000 company in its own right before merging with Atlanta-based Global Payments Inc. Both TSYS and Synovus thus trace their origins directly to the cotton mills.

Yet in the post–Civil War period, Columbus and the South lagged the North significantly. William H. Young, owner of the mighty Eagle & Phenix Mill, said in 1883 that the rest of the country and even the rest of Georgia considered Columbus "outside of civilization," with the dominance of cotton again playing a factor in the city's lack of economic diversification. The mills crowded the riverfront, leaving little space for other industries to blossom and preventing further investment in railroads to connect the relatively isolated city with the rest of the nation. Columbus scored a few non-textile wins over the years—convincing Congress to establish Fort Benning in 1918, for example. Yet even this victory may have signaled desperation among city leaders, as some scholars have argued that military forts were typically placed in "god-forsaken" parts of the South selected for cheap land and cheap labor.

The view of the South as a backward swamp was widespread in the North circa 1900 and is still held to some extent today. Others say it's an unfounded stereotype with little basis in fact. "The presumption that Southerners saw little or no value in pursuing new technologies and innovations in their industries at any point in the past is an entirely false one," Susanna Delfino and Michele Gillespie write in their book *Technology, Innovation, and Southern Industrialization*. "Southerners from the early nineteenth century onward were as eager to embrace technology and innovation as any other Americans; they, too, viewed technology as the path to profit and modernity."

They definitely did so when old paths to profit were threatened. The powers that be in Columbus embraced Fort Benning in part due to an agricultural depression and the arrival of the boll weevil. But textile mills still ruled the day when Tom Huston first traveled to Columbus in the 1910s. Mill work was preferable to toiling in the fields and generally paid more, as farmwork set a kind of price floor that textile jobs had to exceed. An added benefit was that the mills often employed multiple family members in the same plant, providing wages that when combined could lift a household out of poverty. Mill hands were insulated from some of the more crushing aspects of agriculture in the postbellum South. This included overproduction of cotton due to a lack of viable alternatives, which drove down the price and drained the soil of nutrients; this in turn forced the heavy use of fertilizer, which was often bought on credit, triggering a debt cycle from year to year. Scores of farmers lost their land and became tenants throughout the postbellum era, and even the landowners were constantly in debt. Even when cotton prices fell, or there was a bad yield, or there were just too many other people doing it, these farmers grew cotton anyway, having no other options for their livelihood. The situation was immortalized in the Erskine Caldwell novel *Tobacco Road*, in which a family of poor white farmers pursue a hopeless cotton crop in the "west-central part of Georgia" even into the Great Depression, knowing no other way to live.

Still, wages in the Southern mills were a fraction of those in the North and were not improving in the early twentieth century. For example, mill owner W. C. Bradley cut workers' wages after busting a strike in 1921, writing that the best deal for his stockholders would have been to shut the place down altogether. That may have been hyperbolic, but it is true that the Southern monoculture of cotton landed on especially hard times in the early 1920s. As University of North Carolina history professor Peter A. Coclanis writes, "It has almost become a truism amongst agricultural historians to argue that for farmers the 'depression' actually began in the early 1920s, when farm prices for most American staples fell significantly and in some cases, such as that of cotton, precipitously."

Even this was not enough to cut the stranglehold of cotton on the South. Cotton and textiles represented more than half of Georgia's agricultural output into the 1920s, Southern per capita income remained just over half of the national average, and the South was not fully integrated into the wider U.S. labor market until after the Second World War. Indeed, in Columbus the captains of industry often actively resisted diversifying the economy.

It was this state of affairs that met Tom Huston as he looked to create an entirely new industry in Georgia. Roughly 26.5 million pounds of peanuts were grown in Georgia in 1910. That may sound like a lot until you learn that by 1970 the state's annual output topped 1 billion pounds, meaning that 1910 production was less than 3 percent of 1970 production. By 2020, Georgia fields were growing over 3 billion pounds of peanuts each year, more than one hundred times the 1910 figure.

Cotton remained king, or perhaps dictator, of the early twentieth-century Southern economy, a fact that fellow peanut man George Washington Carver noted keenly in his first trip down to Tuskegee, Alabama, in 1896. As he recalled years later:

> My train left the golden wheat fields and the tall green corn of Iowa for the acres of cotton, nothing but cotton. . . . The scraggly cotton grew close up to the cabin doors; a few lonesome collards, the only sign of vegetables; stunted cattle, boney mules; fields and hillsides cracked and scarred with gullies and deep ruts . . . not much evidence of scientific farming anywhere. Everything looked hungry: the land, the cotton, the cattle, and the people.

Cotton grew "close up" to the cabin doors because nearly every square inch of land on many Southern farms was dedicated to the crop. The cotton harvest was crucial to paying off debts and buying anything a farmer might need, though more often than not it became a source of more debt, with a poor season seeing many Southerners lose control of their land. This was especially true of Black farmers, who faced the daily realities of the Jim Crow system along with the economic monoculture.

But the cotton stranglehold wasn't merely an economic issue. Carver's word "hungry" was apt for all the reasons he described and more. Despite romantic notions of vegetable-rich farm diets prior to the advent of "processed" foods, the Southern cotton farmer's diet could not be described as healthy then or now. It had three main ingredients that became known as the "3 Ms"—meat, meal, and molasses—to which the addition of the humble peanut could add invaluable nutrients and protein. Well into the twentieth century, many Georgians suffered from a disease called pellagra, which gave its victims a painful skin rash and was often fatal. A doctor named Joseph Goldberger discovered that pellagra was caused by dietary protein deficiency.

Thus Carver, separately from Huston, had become determined to get other crops onto those hungry cotton fields, and he knew the task would be colossal. Carver was a plant whisperer from childhood, and his fascination extended to all plants, ranging from vital cash crops to roadside scrub trees. Over time he narrowed his focus to soybeans, sweet potatoes, and especially peanuts. Carver's main goal was to diversify farmers, particularly Black farmers, out of cotton's grasp. Peanuts proved up to the task.

Because cotton was so ingrained in the Southern economy and the Southern mind, Carver at first promoted peanuts as a cotton booster. The two plants thrived in different seasons, meaning peanuts could be grown on the same acreage as cotton without harming the coveted white cash crop. More to the point, Carver discovered that peanuts added nitrogen to the soil, which in most of the region had been badly depleted from the lack of crop rotation. The scientist toured Georgia and Alabama aboard something he called the Jessup wagon, a horse-drawn laboratory and classroom of sorts that he used to demonstrate soil chemistry to cotton farmers. Thus, peanuts could be viewed as the mere byproduct of a soil replenishment technique. A separate obstacle for Carver was convincing farmers that peanuts themselves were worth having around, as many didn't know what to do with them after the harvest.

In fact, neither did Carver. This dilemma is what set him on his quest to identify and cultivate uses for peanuts, a list eventually totaling hundreds of items. Less well known is the event that rocketed Carver to stardom. Domestic peanut farmers faced stiff competition from Africa, with peanuts imported from the continent as early as 1835, especially to the industrial Northern states. By 1841 the African peanut trade had developed into a decent business with a value of £8,127, with shipping expeditions all the way to and from West Africa for the express purpose of obtaining legumes. A modest tariff was imposed in 1842, but it did little to slow the trade. Europe also thrived on African peanuts in the 1800s, with England, Germany, and especially France importing shiploads of peanuts that were converted into peanut oil for use in margarine, soap, bread, cakes, cattle feed, salad oil, and even grease for industrial machinery. Tragically, this demand led to the continuation of de facto slavery on the African continent for decades after the practice was officially banned by European powers.

How does all of this involve Carver? Because he played a direct and outsized role in ending peanut imports into the United States, aiding domestic growers in the process. The commercial use of peanuts surged during World War I, providing a boon to peanut-growing areas. In 1919, shortly after the war, the city of Enterprise, Alabama, famously erected a statue to commemorate "Billy Boll Weevil" for helping it diversify into peanuts. That progress was threatened the very next year, however, when foreign peanuts from Africa as well as China and Japan flooded the domestic market. American farmers demanded a heavy tariff to protect their nascent peanut profits. Foreign import tariffs largely fell out of favor in the late twentieth century due to a prevailing economic theory favoring free trade and value to the consumer, though they've made something of a comeback in the Trump and Biden administrations. But tariffs were common between the end of the Civil War and World War II, seen as a tool to protect domestic industry from foreign competition and save American jobs.

In 1921, the House Ways and Means Committee held hearings on a potential peanut tariff, inviting a host of industry experts, Carver included, to testify. His appearance was expected to be a rather sleepy affair before a staid congressional committee, but it instead played out like something from an inspirational film. Carver was the only Black speaker and was scheduled to speak last. The committee was bored with peanut talk by the time he appeared, and the chairman reminded Carver that he had just ten minutes to present. Carver then calmly laid out his "pandora's box" of 101 different uses for the peanut. He faced some harsh initial questions from the chairman, including rude asides likely related to his race, but Carver responded not only with grace but with wit and humor as well. When his ten minutes were up, he was instructed to continue.

And so he did—for another hour and forty minutes. Carver pulled out chocolate-covered peanuts, peanut candy bars, peanut ice cream, peanut cakes, peanut flour, and peanut meal, taking bites of some items to show off how delicious they were. He displayed for the committee five breakfast foods made from peanuts, plus peanut-based livestock feed, peanut milk, peanut-based mock meat, peanut soy sauce, and peanut Worcestershire sauce. There were peanut-based face creams and powders, wood stains, and ink. Carver got a standing ovation when it was all over, and Rep. John Nance Garner, a Texas Democrat who would later serve as Franklin Delano Roosevelt's first vice president, described it as the most wonderful exhibition he had ever seen before the committee.

Remarkably, Carver did not ask for a tariff during his nearly two hours of demonstrations, or not directly, anyway. He was questioned on the topic by one of the congressmen and responded, "Tariff? This is all the tariff means—to put the other fellow out of business." The quip drew plenty of laughter, yet Carver reiterated the point in a letter he sent the committee afterward, writing, "My appearance was not to discuss the tariff. I have nothing to sell; I will manufacture nothing. I simply came to add my little bit if possible." He then added, tongue in cheek, "I feel sure you gentlemen will guard and put proper restrictions upon every interest that arises in harmful competition with ours without any suggestions of mine."

America's peanut growers got their tariff—and at three cents a pound for unshelled peanuts and four cents a pound for shelled peanuts, it was the highest the industry had ever seen. Peanut farmers lavished praise on Carver in their trade magazines, and the scientist promptly hit the lecture circuit, speaking about peanuts in Chicago and New York City en route to becoming one of the most famous figures of his day and a fixture of school history lessons for at least another century.

A peanut farmer in the 1920s.

The peanut harvest, 1920s.

With the tariff in place, the stage was set for massive growth in the American peanut industry, which aided farmers in all directions surrounding Columbus. The impact on the city itself was less obvious, at least initially. The challenge remained finding practical, everyday uses for the crop that could be consistently and repeatedly sold. Carver found three hundred different uses for the peanut, but he never commercially produced any of them at scale. The legendary scientist was a demonstrator, an educator, a booster even. He was not a businessman, however, celebrating the potential of non-cotton crops rather than developing that potential himself. He was glad to help when asked, though.

The tariff was tremendously well timed, coming as it did at the beginning of the agricultural depression of the 1920s. Georgia farmers lived mostly in unpainted shacks, traveled in wagons over unpaved roads, lit their homes with oil lamps, and drew water by hand from wells. Cotton prices fell by half from 1919 to 1920 and did not recover at any time during the next two decades. For Columbus, the death grip of cotton largely remained in the form of cotton mills that dominated the city's skyline, its riverfront, its employment landscape, and its politics. Competing employment opportunities were scarce, and the city was geographically isolated from the industrial North and even from most of the South. Columbus mill hands earned half the wage of their New England counterparts, and they'd learned through a series of unsuccessful and often violently repressed organizing efforts that union drives were not going to bring a quick remedy. But change was coming, if slowly and gradually, thanks to new technology, entrepreneurship, the protection of the tariff, and a spirit of progressivism following the Allied victory in the Great War. Carver found kinship with Huston, another innovative mind locked inside a shy personality, and with a plan he'd later describe as the most interesting he'd ever seen.

CHAPTER 2

Enter Huston

By 1918 Huston was living in Columbus and operating his own peanut-shelling operation, the Tom Huston Manufacturing Company, in the North Highlands neighborhood of Columbus. The company built big industrial-grade shellers that could churn through one ton of peanuts per hour. Following up on his initial patents, he filed three more in May 1919, continuing what would become a lifelong pattern of correspondence with various patent offices and research services. These and other patents proved to be a crucial aspect of his success, and he focused on patents manically from this point forward. The three he filed in 1919, under the name "J. T. Huston," were for a hand-operated peanut digger, a hand crank peanut sheller, and a larger industrial-grade sheller. The key selling point of the digger, which was used to cut the peanut crop out of the soil, was that its blade ran parallel to the ground and was thus self-sharpening, easily slicing through roots in the first step of the harvest. Little is written about this product other than the patent itself.

The other two patents represented improvements to his shellers, the source of Huston's first success. Huston found a reliable, even eager market for them, which brought a lot of business from nearby farmers and shelling concerns alike. The boll weevil had arrived in Georgia by this point, and an early 1920s agricultural depression left many cotton planters growing peanuts as an insurance crop, just as Huston's father had a decade earlier. While peanuts were not yet a reliable cash crop, they helped replenish the soil with nitrogen and, unlike cotton, could be eaten by the farmer, the family, and the hogs if all else failed. Those who could not afford to buy a sheller often brought their harvest to Tom Huston Manufacturing, and some of Huston's payment from these cash-strapped farmers came in the form of their peanut crop, which shaped and seeded some of his later ideas.

The improved hand crank peanut sheller patent speaks to many of Huston's design principles. It was, he wrote, "quite simple in its structure, readily assembled and repaired, and . . . capable of operating efficiently and with large capacity to shell peanuts of different varieties with a minimum breakage of the kernels." The sheller did so via what Huston described as a significant advantage over its rivals—it crushed the shells against each other in order to break them rather than grinding them against the harsh metal of the machine. Furthermore, the grid used to separate kernels from shells could be replaced and refitted at intervals to accommodate various sizes of peanuts, adding to its versatility.

Huston's industrial-grade machine operated on the same principle but was designed for shelling at scale, in Huston's own factory and in units sold to outside buyers. In fact, by some accounts, the first peanut-shelling plant in Georgia opened in 1916 or 1917 in Edison, a town about seventy miles south of Columbus that was named, appropriately enough, for the inventor Thomas Edison, and the plant very likely used Huston's machinery, which was advertised around the same time as "the only successful machine on the market." Huston wrote that his machines could shell peanuts at the same rate as the competition, yet by crushing the shells with friction against each other his models boasted a significantly lower percentage of damaged kernels. The separating grate was also designed so as not to clog and was made of sturdy materials, giving it an exceedingly long life. As Huston put it, "a further object of my invention relates to the very simple and convenient manner of assembling the sectional concave gate in the end walls of the shelling machine so that the latter can be easily set up and quickly repaired at a comparatively small cost." Some models of Huston's shellers have lasted more or less intact for over one hundred years.

The 1920 U.S. census lists Huston as living with a boarder family in Columbus; by this point his shellers had given him a taste of entrepreneurial achievement, but apparently not enough to purchase his own house. For a time Huston lived at the home of J. Madden Hatcher at 1516 Second Avenue, a large estate on which Hatcher, the youngest of five children, cared for his ailing parents in a house with plenty of spare bedrooms. Huston was engaged in non-peanut business as well. In 1923 he filed a patent for a

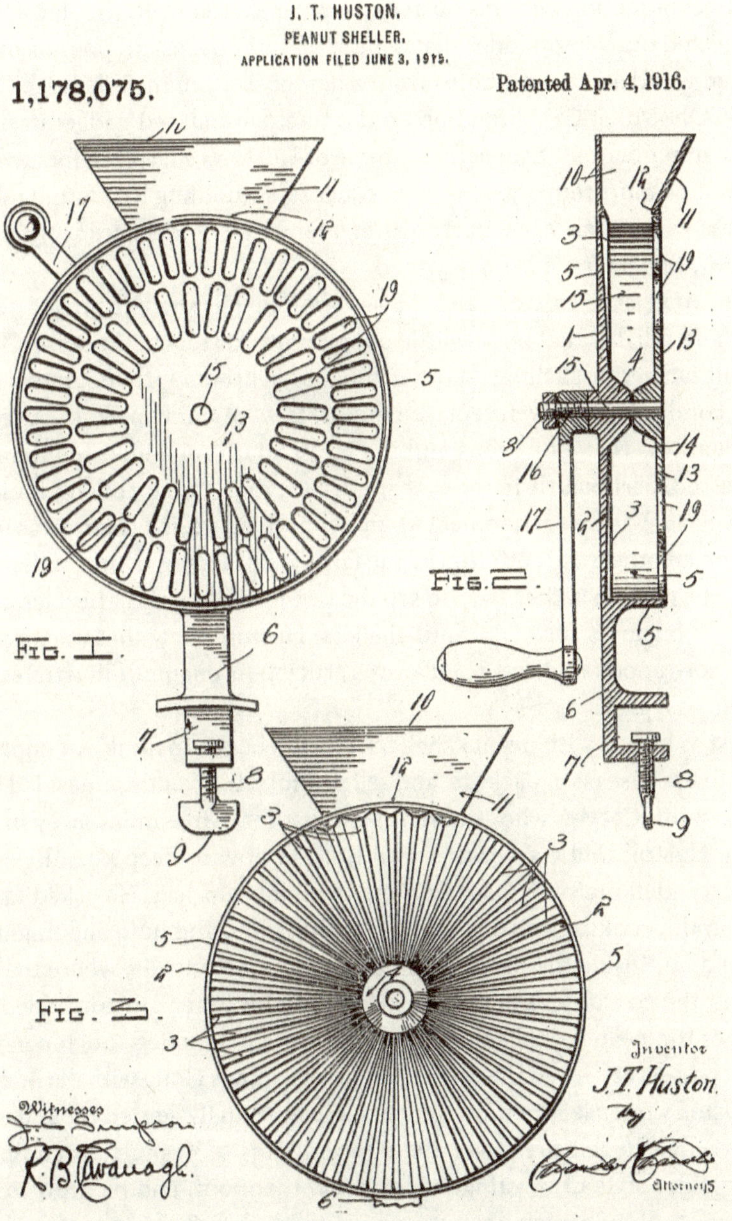

Huston's hand-operated peanut sheller was one of his first patents. The machine grew to dominate the market in the lower peanut belt.

disc-shaped tractor plow, this time under the shortened name "T. Huston" and in conjunction with his business partner, Clarence R. Medley. Huston also tested out a log skidder that could pull forty thousand pounds of condensed wood at a time. Photos from a demonstration include large "TOM HUSTON MFG. CO." branding on the tractor-mounted gadget itself and on a banner behind it, an early example of Huston's sharp eye for advertising. But peanuts remained his main squeeze, something he'd found relative success with by his early thirties after spending two decades working out that raw fingers issue from boyhood.

The next issue Huston ran into was twofold. His shellers proved so efficient and reliable that he saw little opportunity for repeat business. Once a peanut farmer or shelling concern bought his product, there tended to be no second sale, and even replacement parts were rarely needed. A related problem was that Columbus and the Deep South remained economically depressed, particularly in the 1920s, a decade that was so difficult for farmers even as Wall Street boomed. Many peanutters, raising the crop as insurance on an otherwise cotton-growing farm, paid Huston in nuts rather than cash. His next task, then, was to sell the peanuts piling up at his factory. To increase business for his peanut shellers, Huston knew that making peanuts more appetizing and popular was crucial. As chapter 1 illustrates, this was no easy task.

Just as he had with peanut shellers, Huston began to think out improved ways to toast, season, package, and sell peanuts. In 1924 this quest led Huston to write Carver, who was stationed just forty-five miles away in Alabama. Huston told Carver that he'd learned how to keep peanuts edible "almost indefinitely" by placing them in an airtight bag. He asked for advice on the cooking and seasoning process, inquiring how one might put salt and oil "inside the peanut" rather than on the outside, where they got all over the consumer's hands. As an aside in his letter, Huston added that most of the peanut shellers in the South were his models. Such concerns about preservation and the placement of seasonings along with flavor speak to Huston's intense attention to detail. He eventually settled on a toasting process that he felt preserved the oily goodness of peanuts, as compared to the older style of roasting, which dried them out, and he grew to prefer small white Spanish peanuts, which thrived in Georgia and packed a sweeter flavor than the competition.

Huston's next steps proved to be his greatest masterstroke of inventive genius. Through exhaustive trial and error he perfected the product that would bring his name to the masses. *National Nut News* put it this way:

Under conditions by which peanuts were marketed at that time, he could not see an immediate chance for any appreciable increase in demand.

Some peanuts were being roasted and sold in first one form and another; but they were not being eaten as a food or even as a regular confection. No one had perfected a method for cooking the peanut to make it be both delicious and digestible. If there were some special process for making the peanut more palatable then the consumption would be greater. Tom thought along this line for several years before he actually did anything about it.

Then finally he perfected a special process for toasting peanuts whereby the peanuts were properly cooked and seasoned. The peanuts prepared by this process were toasted to a rich brown color, and so seasoned that the salt was in the peanut. Here were peanuts that not only made hunger a joy, but were an aid to digestion, because they were properly prepared.

Thus was born Tom's Toasted Peanuts.

Huston's exact cooking process remained something of a trade secret akin to the recipe for Coca-Cola, but it involved toasting peanuts at 350 degrees, blanching the skins, dipping them in boiling coconut oil, and then cooling them as rapidly as possible before adding salt. Huston did not appear to file any patents related to the toasting process but obviously felt the taste would speak for itself.

Yet for all of his work in the preparation of peanuts, it was arguably the bag in which they were sold that made the biggest contribution to his success. In fact, the bag may have been the single most impactful invention of Huston's entire career. He was far from the first person or even the first large company to sell peanuts in nickel bags. It was again his attention to detail that stood out.

On June 9, 1925, Huston filed a patent for his "paper bag and seal" featuring images of a tall, narrow bag of toasted peanuts that would look familiar to anyone browsing around a gas station today. There's a reason his model became so common: According to the patent, it contained no less than seven significant improvements over previous iterations.

As Huston wrote, "My invention relates to a new and improved type of paper bag and seal, which is particularly designed for the packaging and displaying of salted peanuts and the like. It has been the practice heretofore to supply salted peanuts, salted almonds and the like to the market

Tom Huston.

in bags of ordinary shape, i.e. either wide, nearly square and flat, or short flat-bottom satchel type bags, made from smooth glassine, or oiled paper, the bags, after being filled by hand from a bulk container, having their open ends folded together as the only means for closing same. Such practice is objectionable because unsanitary and because, not being sealed air tight, the contents of the bags become quickly unpalatable." He then outlined more problems with existing models: They were "short, squat and unattractive" and often burst open, spilling their contents, when pressed or shaken together, which also made them impractical for shipping. The flat, stumpy bags could not be arranged in glass display jars, which would keep them attractively in view on store counters while protecting the product from moisture. If such bags were somehow displayed in jars, one would need to reach far down into the glass apparatus to reach them, which was awkward. Having purchased one of these inferior peanut bags, the buyer would have to use their fingers to remove the nuts, which Huston considered unsanitary and inconvenient since it left the hand doused in salt and oil. And finally, the oil also tended to cloud the glassine paper, making it translucent and less desirable. Huston's narrow bag addressed each of these issues in turn.

First, by being tall and narrow, the bag could be easily grasped with one hand. Second, its shape and narrowness allowed pouring of the nuts directly into the mouth, circumventing any need for contact with the hand. Third, being narrow, the bags required a much shorter sealing point, reducing in size the most vulnerable portion of the bag and providing a more secure seal during shipping and handling. Fourth, Huston found that the bag, being constructed of ribbed glassine (a slightly cloudy forerunner to cellophane), actually became more transparent as it absorbed oil from the contents of the package and also had no tendency to collect salt. Thus the bag became more attractive over time rather than less so. Fifth, the ribs, by being arranged lengthwise of the bag, helped it stand erect during shipping and while in the display jars, "preserving and presenting the merchandise in a most effective and attractive manner." Sixth, the seal itself represented an improvement. Made immediately at the factory under sanitary conditions, it was clean in appearance and ensured a "positive tight closure" that prevented the contents from rapid deterioration. The process involved a label or seal folded upon itself and gummed on the inner part of each side of the fold, with Huston's red triangular logo reinforcing the seal even while branding the product. And seventh, the tall bags were easy to arrange in display jars and easy for buyers to grasp after removing the lid without having to reach deep down from atop the counter. The logo on the bag read "Tom's Toasted Peanuts."

The bag provided Huston with all of the practical and marketing advantages described above, and the patent itself proved invaluable. Not only did he successfully sue imitators of the bag's construction over a period of several years, Huston even won in court arguments that the bag's shape, removed of any branding or other particulars, was part of the patent and could not be used by competitors until the patent's expiration. Some early Tom's Toasted Peanuts bags carried legal warnings right on the packaging, reading "label and bag patented Oct. 12, 1926" inside the branding triangle, adding at the midpoint that "any infringement or imitation of this package will be vigorously prosecuted," and reading "U.S. Pat. Oct. 12, 1926" and "Canadian Pat. Aug. 7, 1928" on the lower third of the bag. Two other points about this patent are worth mentioning. One is that it was the first patent under which he listed his name as "Tom Huston." His first five patent applications, made between 1915 and 1919, came under the name "J. T. Huston," while his 1923 tractor plow patent was issued to "T. Huston" and signed "Tom Huston." Beginning with the 1925 bag patent, "Tom Huston" is the name he settled on and used exclusively. A similar evolution can be seen in U.S. census data. In the 1900 census, which came the year Huston turned eleven, he was listed as "John T Huston." He had switched to

The original logo designed by Tom Huston, with the blue shield and five-cent price point.

"Thomas Huston" for the 1910 census and then, mysteriously, to "Thomas C Huston" in 1920. Finally, by 1930, the year he turned forty-one, he had settled on "Tom Huston," and he used that name in the 1940 census and again in the 1950 census, the last census publicly available as of the publication of this book. Several marketing moves he made later speak to the affinity Huston developed for going simply by "Tom."

The second notable aspect of the 1925 bag patent is the absence of Clarence R. Medley's name. Medley was Huston's business partner at the Tom Huston Manufacturing Company and was listed as assignor on Huston's 1923 patent, yet he was absent from the bag patent. Medley, it turns out, was not sold on the idea that would become Tom's Toasted Peanuts. Perhaps the tractor plow idea hadn't worked out as well as the two men had hoped. Another reason may have been the volume needed to make packaged peanuts profitable. The shelling machines Medley and Huston built sold for $5,000 each (all dollar figures are given in their original values—the reader is encouraged to calculate for inflation to the present day), while Huston sold his toasted peanuts for a nickel, meaning he'd need to sell 100,000 packages to generate the same amount of revenue as a single shelling machine, all with a perishable, fragile product that needed to be shipped repeatedly to market. Moreover, peanuts at the time were at best associated with poor people and children, and at worst with slavery and literal pigs at the trough. Medley stayed in shelling machines.

Huston did secure a new business partner—V. H. Talton, a Texas man with a peanut background—to move forward with the toasted peanut venture. However, Medley wasn't completely hostile to the new business, as he allowed it to set up a two-room shack in the yard of Tom Huston Manufacturing (later renamed Medley Manufacturing). The shack could be found at 400 Thirty-Second Street and measured thirty feet long and fourteen feet wide. The Southern Peanut Company, as Huston and Talton's business was first known, began with just three employees and, reflecting the small scale of the experiment, initially tried selling the peanuts at retail stores in Columbus and nearby Bibb City as a test, a step insisted on by Talton. When those sold out in one day and the salesmen hurried back asking for more, Huston knew he had a hit. He filed the bag patent June 9, 1925; on July 1, Huston bought out Talton's interests in the business for the price of $2,325.20 and renamed it the Tom Huston Peanut Company.

"I started this business in a little shack about ten by twenty feet," Huston said later. "About all I had was youth, good health, and an idea. The idea was to give the public the best nickel's worth of food they had ever

The Tom Huston Peanut Company got its start in a two-room shack at 400 Thirty-Second Street in Columbus.

had. Something that would repeat. I thought that if I could do this, I might make some money. So I set about experimenting with peanuts until I was satisfied I had the right thing. Then I took some out and placed them with a few dealers. They sold. And the dealers called for more. I knew then I had a good thing."

Things progressed quickly from there. Huston moved out of the shack, contracting with Charlie Frank Williams to establish a location on Thirteenth Street less than a year later. That building was enlarged twice yet still proved inadequate, and in 1927 the business moved to the corner of Eighth Street and Tenth Avenue, replacing an old wagon factory, where it remained permanently. (The site had also been home to the Southland Pecan Company before that business moved elsewhere.) Salesmen struggled to keep Tom's jars filled, as the peanut venture soon reached a dozen and then two dozen states. Displays grew as well, migrating over time from the single glass jar to free-standing floor displays with six products. Huston switched seamlessly from engineering to marketing. Having devised the tall, narrow airtight bag to package his peanuts in, he carefully considered exactly where and how the peanuts would be sold inside a store.

One existing method of sale involved two-gallon cans of Virginia-style peanuts. These were stored under the counter, likely due to their large size, and handed over to the consumer in a big brown sack. And as mentioned earlier, roasted, salted peanuts were sold in smaller bags by street vendors, but with all of the accompanying problems Huston mentioned in his bag patent. He filed yet another patent for marketing purposes at the end of 1925, bringing his peanuts right up into the customer's face.

The patent, filed December 4, 1925, was for a large glass jar that would hold forty bags at a time and that became universally known as a "Tom's jar," along with a display stand and advertising. It appears that he patented not the jar itself but rather the full assembly, including a circular apparatus for fitting and placement constructed of a grippy material that prevented it from sliding around on the countertop. The grip protruded outward and down to showcase what Huston envisioned as a four-by-eight-inch display frame that could be filled with new five-color lithographed advertising cards at regular intervals. This "tiny billboard" made up for the fact that Huston had no marketing budget. Further, it meant that the entire display had to sit at the very edge of the counter, closest to the customer at the point of sale, all but ensuring they'd notice the assemblage, and the toasted peanuts themselves, at the most critical moment.

The patent described it in dry legalese: "The object of my invention is to provide a combined jar holder and advertising display stand which will not only hold the glass jar containing the merchandise securely in position on the counter but will also serve to display both permanent and changeable advertising matter relative to the merchandise so as to make the display more attractive and increase the sale of the articles displayed."

Huston put it more colorfully when speaking to reporters: "I wanted to grow big—to advertise; but I had no money to do it with. So I must think up some way to advertise without money. I was displaying the peanuts in glass jars, and the idea came to me that I could attach a tiny billboard to the jars, and change the copy weekly. I did and there you are. . . . I always try to get the most and best I can out of my dollars and 'sense.'"

A final jewel in Huston's string was his decision to let people selling his products be owners of their own businesses rather than employees, a model that would last throughout the history of Tom's. Giving "Tom's truck" drivers a stake in their own fate and a financial incentive to sell more and sell better created a symbiotic relationship between the company and its distributors.

With all of this in place, in the late 1920s Tom Huston became an "overnight" success. He'd invented his first peanut sheller in 1912 to solve a problem that dated to childhood, yet all the public knew was that suddenly these little peanut packs were everywhere and somebody was making money on them. Huston leaned into this notion by actively and aggressively courting the public's attention. He not only took out advertisements in newspapers and radio once he'd obtained sufficient funds to do so but also hired trucks to drive around blasting Tom's ads from mounted speakers. Huston commissioned Robert Bowers, musical director of the Columbia Phonograph Company, to compose a jazz tune called "The Peanut Dance," over which were read slogans such as "Tom's Sweet, Toasted Spanish Peanuts. They Melt in Your Mouth." He also commissioned a parody of the song "Dixie," recorded in New York and sung by vaudeville performer Irving Kaufman. "Now we eat Tom's Toasted Peanuts, Hooray! Hooray!" Kaufman sang in the reworked version, which can be found on YouTube. "In Dixieland they're toasted grand, the way down south in Dixie." Both songs were heard on traveling trucks and in paid radio spots, apparently without drawing much controversy at the time. Yet another performer, "Jack Rose, the Peanut Boy," scored a minor hit with a tune titled "Go Buy Yourself Some Peanuts—Some Tom's Toasted Peanuts."

Huston didn't stop there. At one point he passed around a small jukebox with a record that thanked customers for buying Tom's each time a package was sold. Huston dubbed it the "Tom's Talkie." There was also a nationwide contest to select slogans for the jars' "tiny billboards." Winners were initially awarded $25 (later increased to $50) and got their name listed in the local newspaper. They hailed from a wide range of cities, including Clarksburg, West Virginia; Key West and St. Petersburg, Florida; Troy, Marion Junction, and Jacksonville, Alabama; Seguin and Beeville, Texas; Chattanooga, Tennessee; and even Chicago, Illinois.

Among the slogans that appeared on the billboards were "Imitated but Never Duplicated," "Entertain Your Taste," "Popular Every Season—There's a Reason," "Worth Loving," "Food for Fun," "The Modern Way" (accompanied by an image of a young woman eating peanuts directly from the bag), "Be Peanut Minded," "Bleachers or Grand, They Fit Every Hand," "Society's Selection," "A National Pastime," "A Meal in a Minute," "I Wanna Be Chewed by You," and "More Smileage per Nickel." These were rotated out weekly, and Huston wrote many of them himself, in spite of the contest. Some scholars have argued there was a generalized effort around this time to "gentrify" peanuts away from their pre–Civil War association with

The packaged peanuts, glass jar, and "tiny billboard" combination became a ubiquitous sight at mom-and-pop stores by the end of the 1920s.

enslaved Black people and reposition them as suitable for "white society." If so, these images and slogans, particularly "Society's Selection" and "The Modern Way," could be seen as contributing to that effort.

The contest even generated a bit of controversy. An entity called the "contest bureau" apparently investigated it at one point, though it was later cleared, and an angry letter to the *Columbus (Ohio) Citizen* newspaper complained that "invariably not a single award comes to a Northern contestant, all being confined to the Southern states." The writer claimed that he and his friends all sent in fine slogans and were snubbed each time, concluding that "Southern people never will send a dime north of Mason and Dixon's line." The editor of *The Peanut Journal*, a trade publication, fired back that "Dixie practically spends all she makes north of Mason and Dixon's line, and that is responsible for much of her backwardness."

Huston ventured into the absurd at times. In 1928 a Rio Hondo, Texas, man named Bill Williams lost an election bet, and as punishment he pushed a peanut eleven miles along the ground—with his nose. Huston read about this bizarre story and thought he could do it one better, so he cut a contract with Williams to push a peanut twenty-six miles with his nose, this time from Colorado Springs to the top of Pikes Peak. Williams was paid $250 for the gig, a perhaps unimpressive figure for what must have been grueling work under decidedly unglamorous conditions. In any case, the stunt got the attention of newspapers across the country, including *The New York Times*, as daily updates marking Williams's progress were wired to the press. He wore specialized knee and elbow pads made from repurposed car tires to keep from scratching up his arms and legs, along with a "device" on his nose to ensnare the nut, and he supposedly ate Tom's Toasted Peanuts to refresh himself along the journey. Not everyone was impressed. The *Times* asked, "Has no one thought to get a testimonial from Mr. Williams lauding the durability of the rubber used for the gloves and kneepads, or the comfort derived from their special design?"

More seriously concerned was the author of a letter to the editor in the July 1929 issue of *The Peanut Journal*, who felt that the journey risked damaging the peanut's already lowly reputation. "It is an undignified escapade and does not add glory or prestige to the industry," the letter read. "Men in the industry have spent thousands to take [the peanut] out of the circus ring. Why, then, put it in the tumble bug arena, the biggest joke of all?"

Huston, needless to say, did not share these worries, and the Williams stunt represents the figurative and literal peak of his unorthodox, eccentric approach to marketing. Newspaper writers could argue with the tactics, but there was no arguing with the results. The Tom Huston Peanut Company's 1929 balance sheet listed more than $1 million in assets just four years after its founding. It had $2 million in net sales, spent $182,000 on advertising, and made an $800,000 profit. Huston led an eight-man board of directors, with the other officers being Tom's vice president Walter Alan Richards, sales manager Allen Reid, and secretary-treasurer Ben Z. Holmes. He was selling 2.25 million bags of Tom's Toasted Peanuts a week from 100,000 stores.

The plant was constantly expanding, and there were 400 employees in Columbus and 150 distributors in the field. The marketing charge continued as well: The program for the first Georgia Bulldogs football game at Sanford Stadium in Athens included a Tom's ad, and in late November 1929, Santa

Claus arrived on the fourth floor of Cromer-Cassel's department store in Miami, Florida, with three thousand bags of Tom's Toasted Peanuts.

Huston's unorthodox approach extended to the home office, where he enjoyed a richly upholstered office with a mahogany desk located just inside the main entrance but with no secretary, "office boy," or guard of any kind. In theory, any employee could simply walk in and have a chat with the founder. A bronze nameplate atop the desk read "TOM," which is what everyone was instructed to call him. Anyone offering a "Mr. Huston" would be gently corrected, and in fact it was company policy for all employees to call each other by their first names.

Members of the press were awed by Huston's genius and "overnight" success, but mostly they were amazed that anyone could actually make a fortune on peanuts. Among the crudest examples of the media's fascination with Huston was an Associated Press story that ran in twelve hundred newspapers in December 1929. It began, "The humble goober, once the chief food of blacks in slave trading days, has made Tom Huston a millionaire in four years." It also stated, incorrectly, that Huston was "still under 40"; he'd crossed that milestone two months prior. The shack of the company's founding featured prominently in the story, as it would in later years, held up as the physical embodiment of Huston's self-made success.

The magazine *Candy* laid out the scene in more charming prose in its October 1929 issue:

> And now we come to that part of our story which may be truly classed as romance in modern business, founded on the exploitation of a merchandising idea, new and yet so soundly right that in less than three years' time the enterprise grew into the largest industry of its kind. That concern is the Tom Huston Peanut Company. It was Tom's idea that a better salted peanut could be made—that it could be distributed more efficiently than through the existing channel of trade and brought to the consumer with dependable freshness; and that if he performed this service he would reap a suitable reward. Thus in 1925 the Tom Huston Peanut Company was organized.

What's more, Tom's was pulling all of its considerable sales out of just twenty-five states and the District of Columbia. The simple logic of geography spelled out vast growth ahead. "The prettiest picture in the world to my company is the map of the United States," Huston said. "We have a vision of all the candy, drug, cigar and grocery stores scattered over that map, each with a jar of Tom's Toasted Peanuts."

With the U.S. map showcasing a business battlefield in which an army of Tom's salesmen fought for new territory, especially in the more prosperous North, Huston's patents provided defense against would-be competitors. Huston waged those battles in a series of lawsuits, often against established firms that he felt were biting his style. The first suit, filed early in 1929, was against the Barrett Potato Chip Company of Atlanta, which used a bag similar in appearance until a court, ruling in Huston's favor, told Barrett to cut it out. A lower court actually ruled against Huston initially but was overruled by Georgia's State Supreme Court.

A larger case followed, this one against the mammoth Curtiss Candy Company of Chicago, which had launched a product called Chicos via an Atlanta-based subsidiary known as the Capital City Tobacco Company. The lawsuits brought their own round of press coverage for Huston, with one wire service noting that "peanuts have ceased to be a joke industry, since the American public has learned to pay seventy-five million dollars a year for the nickel packages," and thus the suits were no laughing matter. Huston sought damages in addition to cease and desist orders, describing his patented package as "inviolable as any trade name, trade mark, or other merchandising symbol." Several other suits emerged in the early 1930s, including one in which the Planters Peanut Company threw its considerable weight behind the defendant in hopes of voiding Huston's patent, but to no avail. When it was all over, Tom's had either settled with or placed an injunction on thirty-two would-be competitors.

Ever the marketer, Huston spun the legal saga into more advertising copy. In a print spot, he dared readers to hold a bag of Tom's Toasted Peanuts level with their head and then drop it on the ground, guaranteeing that it wouldn't break, and adding that "you would not try this with any other peanuts because you know the bag would burst all to pieces." In bracketed smaller print, the ad read, "Perhaps the greatest compliment ever paid to Tom's Toasted Peanuts is the fact that over one hundred imitating and infringing bags have been put on the market since we invented this famous little package.—Tom."

Huston remained busy on core business issues as well. The company was already expanding its product lineup, with Red Robin peanut butter and peanut butter sandwiches promoted particularly heavily. Huston patented a card display stand for these products in 1927, and some of the firm's trucks were refitted to advertise Red Robin first, calling it "Highest Quality," with "Eat Tom's Toasted Peanuts" in smaller print. Other new offerings followed, including Tom's Chocolate Peanuts, Tom's Cocoanut Bar, Tom's Peanut Plank, Tom's High Roller, Tom's Spun Gold, Tom's Gold Bar, Tom's Golden Belle peanut brittle, and Tom's Peanut Bar. In 1929 Huston filed one more peanut-related patent, this one for an improvement to the machinery that measured and filled his glassine bags. The apparatus tended to get clogged or jammed with salt over time and needed to be cleaned and scraped with brushes. The patent, filed in the name of the company, was for a new machine that blasted the bags open with a burst of air, thus removing excess salt, and included a heating element to help prevent buildup. It proved to be his last patent in the peanut business.

As the Roaring Twenties rushed to a close, the Tom Huston Peanut Company was expanding exponentially. Net earnings grew 44 percent from the first half to the second half of 1929. Tom's—and its visionary founder—brought in major media attention and major money from around the country, all of it flowing into the Deep South textile town of Columbus, a feat in and of itself in an era when capital almost invariably flowed from the South to the North. And Huston, as founder and president, got the most praise and most profits of all. The company went public on September 22, 1928, with Huston controlling 75 percent of the shares, and by the next year it had 225 common stockholders and 175 preferred stockholders. In March 1928 he married Columbus socialite Minnie Bullock, who came from a prominent family and was seventeen years his junior. The couple moved to a house in the 1400 block of Second Avenue and built a summer home on Lake Harding, located north of the city in Harris County. The lake itself was formed in 1926 with the construction of Bartlett's Ferry Dam. Huston built their lake home, which they named Halawaka Lodge after nearby Halawakee Creek, on a newly created island (located at latitude 32.68366, longitude -85.10256). He discovered the island on a boating trip, fell in love, and, in the interest of authenticity, had trees cut from the island and taken to a nearby sawmill to be turned into lumber for use in building the house, which resembled a giant log cabin. It became known as Huston's Island, though it also has other names, including Kudzu Island, Chimney Island, and Herrington Island. The home burned down decades later.

Huston dabbled in philanthropy as well, sponsoring an archaeology expedition led by Frank Schnell Sr. and Margaret Ashley to survey the Chattahoochee Valley area for Native American artifacts. The weapons, utensils, and objects of adornment they uncovered made their way into an exhibit in the Columbus Museum.

The biggest deal of all for Huston, and one he surely harbored second and third thoughts about in the years to come, was an offer he received for full control of the company from a New York syndicate. The total value of the offer stood at $4.4 million, a colossal sum at the time. "The lowly peanut seems to have attained a position of dignity," one news story read, noting the astonishing offer. The details are even more intriguing than the raw total. Not only did the Wall Street firm want to buy the Tom Huston Peanut Company, but it also sought to purchase Huston's two biggest competitors, the Planters Peanut Company of Virginia and the Curtiss Candy Company of Chicago. Tom's was actively suing the latter company and was considered by some sources to be the largest of the three at the time. The deal would have created a national peanut colossus, assuming it was approved by federal regulators. News of the offer circulated in July 1929, with Huston reportedly considering his options over that summer.

Hindsight is 20/20, no one can predict the future or revisit the past, and Huston was no doubt one of the most optimistic, forward-thinking gentlemen of his generation, especially at this point in time. Still, by all accounts he pained to the end of his days over his actions between mid-1929 and the mid-1930s. Riding a wave of good press and high profits, Huston rejected the offer that fall, saying, with tongue in cheek, "I wouldn't know what to do with all that money." Industry press approved his decision, with one magazine writing, "Why should he [accept the offer]? The business seemingly is in its infancy; and he shows figures to prove it." The Tom Huston Peanut Company had brought in $25,139 worth of sales in 1925, $407,607 in 1926, more than $1 million in 1928, and $2.5 million in 1929. At that rate of growth, Huston might soon be pulling in $4.4 million in revenue each and every year. And he had ideas for creating other fortunes in adjacent industries.

News of Huston spurning the New York offer circulated in October 1929, coinciding with a much, much larger financial story. On October 24, the stock market lost 11 percent of its value on what came to be known as Black Thursday, then lost another 23 percent the following Monday and Tuesday. Given the timeline, it's possible the deal might have fallen through even if Huston tried to accept it. The market stabilized somewhat through the first half of 1930, and Huston and his company persevered as well. In August 1930 Huston earned his biggest press feature yet, a spot in *Time* magazine. Tom Huston Peanut Company stock had been listed on the New York Curb Exchange (later rebranded the American Exchange) the week before, prompting the article. *Time* marveled that Tom's was the first ever publicly listed peanut-only company. "The peanut came to Wall Street," it said, displaying again the novelty of peanuts becoming big business. Huston was described as "youngish" and "The Farmer Boy Who Became Peanut King," who, "like Republic Steel's Tom Girdler . . . is simply, proudly Tom."

Both "Tom" and "Tom's" did not exist in 1920. Huston was still listing his name as "J. T. Huston" or "Thomas Huston" at the decade's opening, lending it to peanut shellers that could be found in a few factories or on large farms in the peanut belt. He was living with a boarder family in Columbus that year, and at thirty-one was not particularly young to be unmarried and apparently unable to buy a place of his own. The *Montgomery Advertiser* joked that "in 1920 . . . we suspect he was poor." Yet the same paper wrote that Huston finished the decade as the most celebrated businessman in Columbus. In the five years since the founding of the Tom Huston Peanut Company in 1925, it had changed locations twice due to rapid growth and was by 1930 housed in a ballooning permanent factory that stretched an eighth of a mile and employed four hundred people. Huston in 1930 was a married millionaire with a young socialite wife, massive stock holdings, and a private summer lake home. His products were sold in two dozen states by 150 distributors working as independent businesses, with another two dozen states still untouched—providing, theoretically, the potential for a doubling of 1930 earnings through geography alone.

What's more, Tom's revenue emanated from those disparate points of sale back to Columbus, Georgia, a rare feat in a region that, as the editor of *The Peanut Journal* had argued, "practically spends all she makes north of Mason and Dixon's line." And Tom's proved, in myriad ways, that peanuts were and would remain big business, providing a new means of employment for hundreds and a new cash crop for at least some of the suffering cotton croppers in the fields. Huston promised top dollar for high-quality peanuts and focused especially on farms within a sixty-mile radius of Columbus, which encompassed seven counties in Alabama and seventeen in Georgia. He actively recruited new farmers to plant peanuts and paid more than $500,000 a year for the local crop.

More difficult to guess is the state of life at the factory for those early Tom's employees. The company was not yet producing in-house magazines, and most newspaper accounts focused on the business as such rather than on Tom's as a means of employment. What is known is that four hundred people in the Columbus area gave up whatever it was they were doing previously to start working for the firm between 1925 and 1930. Just as it diversified the fields of agriculture, Tom's helped diversify the Columbus economy away from the dominant cotton mills. In fact, Tom's was the city's first major new industry since the first cotton mills set up a century earlier. Sadly, as at other Southern manufacturing concerns of the era, it appears that all of the better jobs in the factory were open only to white people, a situation that led many Black Georgians to head north seeking opportunity. The transition wasn't always easy for the factory-bound either; almost all were uneducated and unskilled and thus poorly prepared for their new life in the city. Tom's and its factory simultaneously contributed to the long, gradual urbanization of Georgia and the wider South. According to census data, Columbus added twelve thousand residents between 1920 and 1930, a ten-year growth rate of 38.6 percent, while neighboring Talbot County lost 24 percent of its population. Other nearby counties such as Clay, Early, and Stewart lost population as well, some of those residents no doubt bound for industrial cities near and far. The loss of population in those areas vexed their communities and caused both economic and social problems for decades to come, and many had smaller populations in 2020 than they had in 1920. New innovations such as Huston's peanut sheller and a host of other new machinery meant that farm yields actually increased even as fewer people did the work. According to United States Department of Agriculture statistics, peanut production in Georgia nearly tripled between 1919, when 115.6 million pounds were produced, and 1931, when production hit 311.9 million pounds.

Here we must acknowledge that not all of this was due to Tom's Toasted Peanuts, and that Huston did not operate in a vacuum. Just as the Gilded Age produced many industrial barons, and the tech sector created various empires across the late twentieth and early twenty-first centuries, agricultural innovations in the early twentieth century produced a number of new peanut products and "brands" as food-based corporations began to mature. The Curtiss Candy Company made its name with the peanut-based Baby Ruth candy bar, which was introduced in 1920. Oh Henry! was launched the same year, Butterfinger followed in 1923, Mr. Goodbar was born in 1925, an early form of Reese's Peanut Butter Cups could be found by 1928, and Snickers emerged in 1930. Closer to home, Philip Lance launched his sandwich cracker business in Charlotte, North Carolina, back in 1913 (it began when he got stuck with five hundred pounds of unwanted peanuts), though that entity wouldn't really take off until the late 1930s.

But Tom's Toasted Peanuts astonished the press and the public nonetheless. For one, it was a completely Southern venture, whereas all of the candy bars mentioned above were created by Northern firms. Moreover, chocolate candy bars had a limited usefulness in the South in the days before air-conditioning, their sales largely relegated to the winter months, when they wouldn't melt in the sweltering heat. And third, Huston's peanuts stood alone behind transparent plastic and glass, staring straight at the customer in something approaching their natural form. There was no opaque wrapper, no can, no cracker, no nougat, no chocolate for the peanut to blend with or hide behind. Tom's Toasted Peanuts were recognized in their early years as a revolutionary and even a romantic new product, hailed by the press and purchased by the public at a rate of better than two million packages a week by the end of 1929. If imitation is the sincerest form of flattery, Huston had flattery to spare, as he unleashed teams of lawyers on would-be competitors from across the country, including from the largest peanut confectioneries in the nation. Looking forward, and with a rapidly expanding product line, Huston saw nothing but growth in his company's future. Roughly half the states were still there for the taking, and much of that unexplored territory lay in the more prosperous Northern states, where spare nickels were plentiful. Huston and the Tom Huston Peanut Company were off and running, ready to discover fortunes anew in a nation that was now on alert and taking him, and his product, seriously.

CHAPTER 3

Carver's Assist; Huston's Exit

Tom Huston was formally involved in the harvesting, cleaning, shelling, seasoning, roasting, packaging, distribution, and marketing of peanuts. The only part of the process he never engaged in for business purposes was growing them. But Huston understood early on that if he was going to build a successful peanut business, he needed to have a tasty, healthy, reliable, and abundant crop to pull from. This is what led him to contact the most famous "peanut man" of his and perhaps any era, the previously mentioned George Washington Carver of the Tuskegee Institute in Alabama.

It was probably inevitable that the two men would come in contact, given their close proximity and intense interest in the peanut industry. Huston just wanted to grow a business, while Carver was driven by wider economic and humanitarian concerns about helping "my people," meaning Black farmers, though Carver understood that successful peanut-based businesses were critical to this mission. The Peanut Man and the Peanut King collaborated extensively on peanut agriculture and peanut diseases, but it took a while to get there. Once their collaboration took off, Huston and two of his employees built an astonishingly close friendship with Carver given the place and era in which they lived, dining together and meeting each other's families, and trading gifts, praise, and endearment in roughly seven hundred letters exchanged between Carver and the Huston team. The partnership, which ended only with Carver's death in 1943, is the subject of an excellent book, *More Than Peanuts: The Unlikely Partnership of Tom Huston and George Washington Carver*, by former Tuskegee University Professor Edith Powell.

As noted, it was Huston who made first contact, writing to Carver on October 18, 1924, while developing Tom's Toasted Peanuts. Carver had studied peanuts since 1903 and was now firmly established as a national figure thanks to his dazzling appearance before Congress in 1921. Huston was still in the experimental phase, describing one of his dilemmas to Carver and laying out his peanut bona fides.

"Aside from any interest coming from a machinery standpoint," Huston wrote, "I have always been greatly concerned in the consumption of peanuts. I have always felt that there should be many times the amount of peanuts consumed by human beings as is the case at the present time." He noted that while peanut butter consumption was on a multiyear upswing, the same thing could not be said for whole or salted peanuts. He identified two reasons for this. The first was that someone buying a five-cent bag from a confectioner's stand couldn't know if the peanuts would be stale or not, and the second was that the buyer was guaranteed of needing to wash their hands afterward to remove all the salt and oil.

"I have learned how to keep peanuts from becoming stale almost indefinitely simply by displaying them and keeping the stock in moisture proof containers," he added. "Moisture is to a salted peanut as poison gas is to a man." His next task was to put the salty flavor "inside the peanut" without having to use oil in an effort to stick salt on the outside. For this he sought Carver's counsel, saying that Carver was an expert in both chemistry and peanuts and that he'd be glad to pay for Carver's services. Along with the letter, he sent a small amount of "exceedingly delicious" salted peanuts. "There is no way to make them more delicious," Huston wrote. "The only possible improvement I believe would be to put the salty flavor on the inside of the peanuts instead of sticking the salt on the outside with oil." As a postscript, Huston mentioned that the machinery used in practically every peanut-shelling plant in the Southeast was made by his company using his designs.

In another letter sent the same day, Huston shared how the peanuts he sent Carver were prepared: They were roasted to loosen the skins for blanching, then dipped in boiling coconut oil to finish the cooking process. After being removed from the oil, the peanuts were cooled as quickly as possible and then salted. Carver was hooked. He wrote back five days later to say that he read Huston's words "with a great deal of interest . . . in fact with much more interest than usual," and he confirmed that he'd like to set up a meeting. He continued:

> I am very much interested in what you propose and you have certainly made a great contribution to the industry as this has been one of the greatest. I have received the package of roasted nuts also. The mice had gotten through the package and destroyed one box. I must say they seem to me the most delicious that I have eaten. If you could succeed in getting the oil into the nut, it would be a wonderful addition. I really believe it can be done but will require a great deal of experimental work. I shall be glad to give some attention to this when I can get to it as I am very much interested.

Huston and his associates worked closely with "peanut wizard" George Washington Carver, who lived just forty-five miles away in Tuskegee, Alabama.

Huston followed up just two days afterward, proposing that the two meet at the Montgomery Fair, which was scheduled for November. All indications are that they did meet at the fair and became fast friends, with Carver providing advice on new products and visiting Huston's summer home on Lake Harding as well as the company's office in downtown Columbus. Huston eagerly shared his products with Carver, and Carver eagerly shared them with folks in his circle. In April 1926, Carver gave Tom's peanut samples to the Tuskegee Board of Trustees and to a group he referred to as the "Enter-racial Commission." "It was equally as interesting to hear their comments, which were exactly the same as mine, the best they had ever eaten," Carver wrote.

The relationship evolved, and by 1928 Carver was communicating more with Huston's employees than with Huston himself. The mission shifted as well. Huston's quest to put the salt and oil "inside the peanut" was never fully realized, as evidenced by his heavy emphasis on eating peanuts directly from the bag. However, Carver and the Tom Huston Peanut Company did collaborate with great success on another initiative, one arguably more difficult and certainly more sprawling in scope. This was the challenge of fighting peanut diseases and getting the United States Department of Agriculture and powerful land grant universities to focus on and fund research into the emerging cash crop. It was a long journey.

In July 1928, Carver wrote to Huston's research department director Fred A. Woleben to acknowledge a question about what part of the peanut causes rancidity. Carver did not know but promised "much work is being done in this direction." Huston fell ill with food poisoning later that year, and Carver wrote in October to wish him well and to discuss an idea Huston had for crystallized nuts. Carver crystallized some himself and added a mint flavor, which he said was "delicious," and even suggested that the nuts could be sold in different colors, displaying some of the wide-ranging if not always practical ideas Carver was known for.

Powell notes in *More Than Peanuts* that the pace of letters between Carver and Huston dropped off between 1924 and 1928, likely because they spoke on the phone and met in person rather than writing letters. Carver wrote on October 16, 1928, that "I still consider my week-end visit with you one of the most pleasant and profitable to me that I have had, as my vision has been so enlarged." But their letter writing picked back up in late 1928 as Tom's faced growing pains. One problem was that so many peanuts were now moving through the factory that blanched skins piled up and were discarded as waste. Carver suggested mixing the skins with sugar waste to create a stock food for hogs that could be sold at $25 per ton. Peanut shells added to the waste issue, and Carver and the Tom's team experimented with turning the shells into paper or a cardboard-like substance for boxes. (Neither of those ideas worked out, but for a while the company did use cotton letterhead with a message at the bottom reading, "By the use of cotton stationery we are helping the Southern farmer. Why don't you?")

The larger issue, and the one for which Carver worked most closely with the company, was that of increasing the yield of peanuts from the fields and fighting off emerging peanut diseases that threatened the budding industry. Domestic peanut production rose almost 40 percent between 1925 and 1930, and consumption totals broke records, while imports fell by more than half. Aiming to preserve this growth, Carver wrote extensively to Tom's field manager Grady Porter and especially to shelling department manager Bob Barry. The USDA at the time studied cotton and soybeans yet was doing little if any peanut work, leaving Tom's to fill the void by conducting its own research and even preparing its own brochures and public relations campaigns to teach farmers the best way to maximize their peanut crop. Porter visited growers to talk about their successes and problems and report back about diseases, becoming a kind of informal cooperative extension agent. Carver and the team knew federal funding would be required to properly identify and control diseases in the long run, and they knew it would be an uphill battle to get Washington interested in doing this type of work with peanuts. As Powell wrote in her book, "Both challenges would require funds, leadership, and manpower, which Tom Huston Peanut Company was willing to provide until the federal funds could be secured." A trade magazine called it the "greatest single effort ever made by Tom to promote the sale of his products."

Though Tom's never grew peanuts, only purchased them, it was so dedicated to business growth that it sold its own branded seeds and conducted peanut crop research on company-owned acreage to increase the size and quality of yields. By September 1929, Carver was predicting big results. "'The Empty Dinner Pail' is one of our greatest national problems," he wrote on September 23. "Your great commercial and educational institution will make a great contribution to this and by giving and demonstrating to the world how easy it is to get a cheap, wholesome, nutritious, appetizing, well balanced food stuff from the peanut." The work began in earnest in 1930, with the team of two white men and one Black man working together despite the limitations of the segregated South.

"We feel that you are more competent to work this out than anybody we know," Barry wrote to Carver on August 16, 1930. "Our Mr. Porter . . .

should be able to take you to one of these fields, without any expense to you at all, and bring you back the same day." Carver wrote a lengthy letter to Porter on September 1 in which he discussed peanut diseases, adding, "I shall consider it a great privilege to cooperate with you and Mr. Barry in any way I can in your efforts to suppress these diseases which threaten one of the South's great money crops." Barry and Porter traveled to Tuskegee and Carver made a return trip to Columbus within the same month.

That's not to say that race was never an issue, or that the men weren't sensitive to it. Barry once wrote to Carver saying he'd received a request from a man named Charles J. Brockway asking for help with items for a peanut exhibit. Barry told the man to see him in Columbus, but after doing so he realized "Mr. Brockway might be a colored man and feel a hesitancy in accepting my invitation." He asked Carver to tell the man that "I do not care what color his skin is as long as he is doing something constructive along peanut lines. My office is open to anybody who is doing that." Brockway, it turned out, was a white man and a graduate of Alabama Polytechnic Institute (now Auburn University), but Barry's hesitation showcases the general sensitivity to the issue on both sides.

Barry was less sensitive when it came to sharing his opinions on Washington, D.C. His letters reveal a distrust of government officials generally and of the USDA in particular. On September 16, 1930, he wrote to Carver that his mind was going around in circles over how to combat peanut diseases and sell the idea to government agriculture officials. "Possibly some high official in the Department of Agriculture in Washington could be startled into an appreciation of the seriousness of the situation," Barry wrote. "He could call a meeting of the agricultural powers of the Southeastern States and learn all the details of your discoveries. It might be the rest of them would boo at the situation because somebody else found it out. Then too people in political jobs are not looking for hard work as a rule." And even if the feds did take an interest, Barry feared their efforts to help would "scare the farmer to death and cause him to reduce his peanut acreage unreasonably. . . . It would be like running a bear out in front of him without giving him anything to shoot with."

Barry nonetheless acknowledged that securing USDA and land grant university funding was key—*the* key—to their mission; he just wanted to go about it gradually, as the letter mentioned above indicates. He was similarly unimpressed in his correspondence with government types concerning peanut diseases, finding them usually less than interested, and less than knowledgeable when they were interested. In another letter, he shared the story of a man who spoke up at a called meeting of the Southeastern Peanut Association to explain that he had noticed a disease on his crop and sent specimens to Washington. In response, he'd received a full report diagnosing that the problem was due to a fungus but offering no information on how to fight it.

Carver often felt the same as Barry about D.C. One day prior to Barry's letter, Carver wrote to his long-time friend Dr. M. L. Ross: "All last week I was called upon to inspect farms of peanuts in Ga. Ala. and Fla. A very serious disease has appeared among them. They have had it before the leading experts in Washington D.C. and many Exp. Stations, they knew nothing about it. I happened to know what it was from experience."

Barry did, however, trust Carver. He once wrote him three letters in a single day and often complimented Carver in their correspondence. Barry praised Carver as "so much more competent to do this than we are," saying he wished Carver were "either twins or triplets" because his work was so valued and making it clear that Carver had decision-making power.

Tom's tried to fill the educational void at the USDA by sending out its own publications on peanut cultivation. By the end of 1930, the company had already published two books, one on the culture and marketing of peanuts and one on peanut grading. The team also discovered new problems during its research. One was an apparent stigma on peanut-fed hogs—a perception that they were inferior to corn-fed hogs—that Carver took charge of combatting. Another was that hundreds of pounds worth of peanuts were being left in the ground, which was yet more evidence that better education could lead to vastly increased yields. Barry even took his work international, sharing letters with extension programs in Australia, India, and South Africa.

In early 1931 Tom's and Carver began in earnest their public relations/education blitz by sending out a bulletin on the cultivation of the small Spanish peanut along with a report from Carver on peanut diseases. The report included sections on both the problem—peanut diseases and how to identify them—and the solution, a set of recommendations that Carver wrote with advice on where and how to plant the crop. The report went out to five thousand peanut growers, shelling plants, and county extension agents of both races in Georgia, Alabama, and Florida, as well as to newspapers and banks and to Washington, D.C. Sharing his excitement at the bulletin, Barry wrote Carver, "The further we go the bigger it gets and the more interesting. I don't know what we would have done without you."

By the end of February Barry had received mostly positive or neutral feedback on the bulletin, and Tom's was running off another dispatch on

Virginia peanuts that would go out to only about two hundred people who could "do some work to further the cause," such as university researchers. There was one scathing reaction, however, from a Georgia experiment station botanist named B. B. Higgins, who attacked the bulletin and Carver's qualifications to write it. He appears to be among the first of many people who questioned Carver's skills, knowledge, and participation in the Tom's project. "You have been misinformed somewhere," Higgins wrote to Barry. "Dr. Carver is not a 'mycologist of international fame,' neither is he a mycologist of any kind. He is supposed to be a chemist. At any rate he knows nothing about fungi. That is shown by a cursory glance at this report in which every single discussion is wrong." Higgins recommended checking out Alabama Bulletin No. 108, written by Dr. F. A. Wolf, and promised that after Barry had read it, "it will not be necessary for me to point out Carver's errors."

The issue appears to have been Carver's use of common or informal names for peanut diseases rather than scientific names. Barry alerted Carver of the criticisms and gently explained what he thought the cause was, then wrote back to Higgins with a defense of Carver (using the correct number for the bulletin, 180, rather than 108):

> At your recent kind suggestion I have sent for bulletin No. 180, put out by Auburn in 1914, on peanut diseases. I have gone thru this bulletin and made an effort to understand it, which is hard for a man like me to do of course.
>
> Dr. Carver's recent bulletin was not intended as an exhaustive scientific treatise on peanut diseases. The object was to give the peanut farmer, in language that he could fairly well understand, enough information to make him realize that it is necessary for him to make a study of peanut disease control.

The rest of the letter spelled out Carver's contributions and recognitions, which included identifying various fungi and even discovering new ones that bore his name, and invited Higgins to visit Tuskegee, meet Carver in person, and join the project. Barry took on a lot of risk by defending a Black person in such a way, both personally and professionally, yet he and Carver had built a level of trust by this point that was not going to be broken. Carver continued writing to farmers explicitly in language they could understand, and hundreds of his bulletins were reprinted over the years for the same reason.

Clearly moved by Barry's letter, Carver described it as "a masterpiece." He went on to write, "Your letter to Mr. Higgins is the most convincing, sympathetic, high class letter that I have ever read. Only persons possessed with great hearts and souls could write a letter like that."

The Carver/Huston team soldiered on undaunted or perhaps emboldened by the letter from Higgins, and soon saw that its plan was working. In March 1931, Barry received news that the University of Georgia was to conduct a multiyear survey of peanut diseases over the southern part of the state. He called it "the best news I have had in a long time," though Tom's continued publishing its own peanut magazines and brochures for farmers in the meantime and later added a focus on the wives of peanut farmers. The UGA study was important in and of itself, and it provided a direct link to the federal government, which was the big prize. Tom's continued sowing seeds in its quest, mailing out peanut seed packages to government experiment stations as a kind of research bait.

In May 1931 the personal relationship between Carver and the Huston team reached its apex. Tom Huston commissioned a bas-relief plaque of Carver by the Baltimore-based artist Isabelle Schultz, which was cast in Italy at a cost of $2,500. "You have contributed much to an industry that is close to our hearts, thereby endearing yourself to us all," Huston wrote. "This bronze is a small token of our appreciation. To look at it is to receive inspiration. Surely it must inspire workers of the future just as you have inspired those who have been fortunate enough to work with you."

Carver received the bust at Tuskegee's graduation ceremonies. Huston was unable to attend, so Barry and Porter presented it on his behalf, explaining that Huston did not like publicity and was busy with a new frozen foods venture. Robert R. Moton, who took over as president of Tuskegee from Booker T. Washington, said that the plaque was deeper than it appeared on the surface, and he was moved that a "Southern gentleman" would spend his time and money to so honor a "black man." Barry wrote Carver a moving letter afterward, showering the scientist with compliments as he often did, and sharing a bit of his personal background:

> It will be even more significant when I tell you that I am the grandson of a Confederate Major who went through the whole War, but afterwards started off the great colored Missionary, to Africa, Dr. Shepard, on the right track when he was only a boy. My other grandfather was killed in the War. Sherman's army came to Savannah and destroyed everything on this grandfather's plantation, leaving his wife

> with 5 young children to raise alone. She had to make everything for them, even their shoes. I am from this seed and you know the rest. To your people this should prove that the man within is greater than his skin. Many of my race also have that lesson to learn.

The Huston company got its own copy of the bronze plaque, which it displayed in a small museum inside the lobby of the home office. Meanwhile, the project spun on. The same day as his letter about the plaque, Barry wrote Carver that twelve experiment stations were showing interest, and that "the senior mycologist at Washington has sent for one of the peanut bulletins.... Almost any kind of an egg will hatch if you set on it long enough."

More of those eggs hatched in the coming months. Another Washington figure, this one a senior pathologist at the USDA, mailed out envelopes to be filled with diseased plants for study, and when those came back full, he asked for more. Tom's kept on the front foot by sending, at company expense, three separate peanut magazines to interested county extension agents, following an idea Carver had hatched more than a decade earlier. Eventually, Higgins, the Carver critic, joined in the effort, as did dozens of other industry stakeholders in positions of influence.

"It is indeed great to know that people are really getting to work on peanut diseases," Barry wrote to Carver on July 8. "To me one of the most gratifying developments is that the other pathologists around the country are now taking you seriously and reporting on the specimens which you send in. The fact that they find the same thing that you do makes you stand out that much more."

By August 1931, the USDA was paying for a UGA professor to make three trips into the peanut belt studying diseases. Tom's was involved and encouraged growers to assist with the professor's work, but sufficient momentum was now building that the company could downshift toward a lesser role, leaving the work to the agriculture professionals in Washington and the land grant colleges. Barry predicted an "explosion" when another USDA researcher got down to the peanut belt and was "dumbfounded" by the disease situation he found. The word was out.

The Great Depression sank in during the early 1930s, slowing progress. "It is hard to make anybody spend these days," Barry lamented in November 1931. Yet even the sinking stock market and the severe crunch it placed on the economy could not stop the momentum of the Huston/Carver team. The next month, the USDA's *Plant Disease Reporter* dedicated a full eleven-page issue entirely to peanut diseases. Barry hurriedly wrote to Carver that he "had to shake hands with myself in the mirror and feel that you . . . will want to do the same thing." He arranged a trip to Tuskegee to celebrate the "crowning point of all the work we have done for the last two years." Barry directly credited Carver's bulletin, even with the blowback it received, for ultimately attracting the interest and funding of the USDA.

In February 1932 Barry and Porter authored a fifteen-page report, "Disease Control Experiments with Peanuts," which included a summary statement declaring the research project successful and complete: "We have spent a great deal of time and money making a study of peanut diseases and interesting others in it. It seems that everybody is now convinced that it is a serious proposition and that much work needs to be done on it quickly. Hence we have accomplished our purpose and now feel that we should be allowed to discontinue any further work in the field along this line. It is the job of men who are much more highly trained to it than we are and who have the U.S. Dept. of Agriculture behind them." Left unsaid, however, was that financial issues at Tom's almost certainly played a role in their declaring the work finished.

Even so, the project left the company with a healthier and more stable and consistent crop of peanuts to purchase in future years, and for Carver, it aided the Black farmers he always had in mind with better seeds and better crops they could sell to make a living. The scientist had identified peanut diseases as far back as 1903 and had long tried to interest Washington in tackling the issue. He accomplished that task thirty years later via the partnership with Tom's.

Less important materially than on a human level, Carver, Barry, Porter, and to some extent Huston and Walter Richards built a very close personal friendship in which skin color was certainly seen but otherwise not considered. The team had been working closely for months, traveling together, visiting each other's work and home spaces, meeting family members and sharing meals, and building a shared respect that saw the project completed successfully. As Powell wrote, "They were colorblind."

The pace of letters between Carver and the Huston team trailed off considerably in 1933 as the USDA took over the work studying peanut diseases, and by 1934 Barry was reassigned as a Tom's sales manager in Greensboro, North Carolina. Carver did make occasional trips to Columbus throughout the 1930s, and he stayed involved with the research, consulting frequently with Dr. Paul Miller of the USDA Bureau of Plant Industry until his death.

Just as Tom's never profited directly from the project, Carver was not paid for his consulting work with the company, other than receiving gifts.

(Aside from the bas-relief plaque, Huston bought Carver a gold peanut, an Underwood typewriter, a sealskin blanket that Carver mothballed in a closet, and a diamond ring, which Carver placed in his "geological specimen case.") It wasn't because Tom's didn't try. In July 1929 the firm offered Carver a job in its research department, which he declined. In a letter, Carver spelled out eight reasons he could not take the position, most of them related to his obligations to do research on other plants and to his employer, Tuskegee. "I, with others, am clannish enough to want my people to receive credit for my work," he wrote. "I do not want my work to be swallowed up and lost [to] the race to which I belong. Even though I, personally, may not receive a dollar of it for myself, that will come to somebody by and by." Yet he added, "The Tom Huston Peanut Company's plan interests me more than anything that I have come in contact with, as it is of real service to the people in general and to Southern Agriculture in particular."

Tom's was in good company—a decade earlier, Carver gave a similar response in turning down a job offer from Thomas Edison. But Carver was proud of his association with the company. After Tom's Toasted Peanuts took off, Carver kept a glass jar full of them on his office desk at all times and doled them out freely to visitors.

The Carver/Huston partnership represents a fascinating study in cross-racial collaboration in the segregated South during the rapid rise of peanuts as a money crop in the late 1920 and early 1930s, and it is an uplifting story about overcoming societal obstacles to achieve a common goal. "Thank God I love humanity; complexion doesn't interest me one single bit," Carver once wrote.

On a more granular, insular level, it also showcases across time the growing distance between Tom Huston and the peanut company he founded. Huston was the first person to write Carver, doing so even before he founded the firm, but he was increasingly absent from the conversation beginning in 1929. In fact, when Tom's offered Carver a job that year, it was Walter Richards, the company's vice president, who met with the scientist and made the offer over the summer.

As the correspondence and closeness among Carver, Barry, and Porter developed over the next few years, the absence of Huston became more apparent. He'd assigned the team to consult Carver in order to focus his own time on a frozen peach venture, and he did not look back. After Carver visited Tom's in September 1930, Richards wrote to thank him, and Barry and Carver regularly mentioned ideas and suggestions Richards made regarding their research, indicating the vice president was effectively in charge.

Carver and Richards exchanged pleasant letters again in early 1931, after Richards received a copy of a Carver bulletin on Virginia peanuts. Regarding the bulletin, Barry later wrote to Carver that "Mr. Richards read the whole thing over and was of the opinion that it would be effective." The letter makes no mention of Huston, who had also received a copy.

Huston did write to Carver when the bas-relief plaque was presented at Tuskegee's spring 1931 commencement, saying at the end of his letter, "It is disappointing that I was not able to present it to you in person. I have looked forward to it. But I thought it best to send rather than delay longer."

Barry explained to Carver that Huston did not like public appearances and was busy with the new frozen peach venture. "Busy" was an understatement, as Huston was spending almost all of his time on peaches at this juncture. The peach project did impact the peanut company, however, and not for the better. Beginning in 1930, Tom's worked with another famous consultant, the agricultural chemist Charles Herty, who, across a distinguished and varied career, revolutionized the turpentine industry, saved the southern longleaf pine, and organized the first varsity football team at the University of Georgia, among other accomplishments. It was again Walter Richards who established contact with Herty, seeking help with a range of issues that included rancidity and musty smells emanating from peanuts in transit. Herty decided the glassine bags were at fault and suggested switching to cellophane, a then-new DuPont product he'd noticed on Camel cigarette packages, as a way to better preserve and present Tom's peanuts. The change was made, and Herty was given other tasks to study, but the partnership ended in January 1932 due to financial issues at Tom's, which were related partially but not fully to the Depression.

Huston wrote to Carver again in November 1932, this time on personal rather than company stationery:

> While a little slow in saying so I must congratulate you on your very wonderful and interesting write-up which recently appeared in the American Magazine. You certainly deserve a place on America's front page. The American Magazine is just that for those who have accomplished things.
>
> You have my sincere good wishes for continued good health that will enable you to continue your good work.
>
> Sincerely,
> Tom Huston

Not stated, though it's obvious enough reading between the lines, was that Huston had lost control of his company and had been replaced as president by Richards.

The same restless drive to innovate that launched Huston to prominence washed him out in turn. While retaining the title of president and majority shareholder, he effectively left Tom's in the hands of management around 1930, deputizing Richards to run day-to-day operations. Huston had noticed that Georgia's peach fields, often situated alongside peanuts, were woefully inefficient. Peaches were overproduced and underconsumed, as he saw it, and moreover, they were edible for only a few weeks each year. For Huston, whose crowning achievement involved keeping an agricultural commodity fresh for months at a time, the connection was natural. He aimed at performing a similar miracle with peaches.

Yet there are vast and important differences between the two crops. Peaches could not be kept fresh just by wrapping them in glassine or cellophane, for example. Huston thus developed an elaborate "quick-freezing" process, which meant icing the fruit at thirty degrees below zero. One account holds that he even traveled to Boston to meet with Clarence Birdseye, widely considered the father of the frozen foods industry, for research and consultation. Huston set up his new enterprise in Montezuma, Georgia, roughly sixty miles east of Columbus in the heart of the peach belt, and planned to market his year-round peaches under the brand name Frosty Morning. This was not a simple operation to set up or execute, requiring large amounts of subzero storage and transportation, which was uncommon in the early 1930s.

Any cursory look at a modern grocery store stands testament to the soundness of Huston's idea. Frozen foods had a big future, and he was generally on the right track. But several complications sunk not only this business but also his standing in the other one. According to Huston's own account of events, he never formally launched Frosty Morning peaches, deciding, as the Depression put a squeeze on finances, to cut his losses rather than risk adding to them. But the red ink was considerable nonetheless. Huston invested lots of money to build a packing plant with specially designed machinery for freezing and storage, and to finance the debt he was later forced to take out a loan from First National Bank in Atlanta (via a holding and subsidiary firm called the Trust Company of Georgia, later renamed SunTrust and then Truist). The Tom Huston Peanut Company remained profitable but was less so than it had been a year prior thanks to the cratering economy. As collateral on the loan, the bank demanded,

Tom Huston's Frosty Morning peaches were far ahead of their time.

and Huston agreed to, his controlling interest in Tom's. The loan had only a one-year maturation date, and according to Huston, the bank granted no extensions when he failed to meet it. He lost his controlling stock and was promptly removed as head of the company and replaced by Richards. "To this they had a perfect legal right. And they got it," he wrote.

Hubris almost certainly played a role in the unfolding of events during this portion of Huston's life. When Huston first set up Tom's Toasted Peanuts, it was with a business partner and fellow peanut toasting expert named V. H. Talton, who insisted on small-scale trials in local stores before distributing the product widely. Huston bought out Talton once those trials proved that the product was a hit. However, he had no such collaborator to restrain him in the Frosty Morning venture, as he racked up enormous debts prior to launch. The other contributing factor, of course, was that Huston was widely celebrated as a business genius by this point, praised by everyone from *The Columbus Ledger-Enquirer* to *Time* magazine. Even his wife wondered if he'd started believing the things he read about himself.

Soon after losing control of Tom's, Huston wrote his version of events in a four-page pamphlet called *What Happened to Tom Huston? The Whole Story in a Peanut Shell*, the purpose of which was to quickly clear the air with the public as he launched another pair of new ventures. He explained that losing control of the Tom Huston Peanut Company meant that he found himself "in the predicament of thousands of other people—out of a job and broke" and lamented that he was "shrewd enough to build a worthwhile business; then fool enough to lose it. I had nobody to blame but myself." But he vowed to get back to work, quoting his father as saying, "Son, never cry over spilt milk. Just get busy and drive up another cow."

And so he did—or at least he tried. Within a year he'd launched two products, Sport Pack Peanuts and Julep Gum by Tom Huston (the latter offered in a mint flavor, as in the drink, and a fruit flavor), each sold under an umbrella company he named Tom Huston System. The idea was that he had engineered faster and better distribution systems that would make both products a success thanks to their freshness. "Julep Chewing Gum is today's greatest 5¢ value," Huston wrote in the pamphlet. "Smart as the new fall fashions. Introduced early in 1933, it is already on sale throughout the entire South and Middle West. Also, it is now being successfully introduced in New York, Chicago and other of our largest cities. It is gratifying to know that Julep Gum sells as readily on Times Square and Broadway as in our own home town."

As for Sport Pack, Huston wrote, "Sport Pack Peanuts represent the best 'PEANUT' job that I have ever done. When placed on sale beside older brands, the public readily shows a preference for Sport Pack."

It does not take much stretch of the imagination to guess which "older brand" he had in mind, though apart from the supposedly superior distribution system, it is unclear exactly what separated Sport Pack from Tom's Toasted Peanuts. The new brand was sold in the same types of glass jars bearing a blue Sport Pack logo with a horse and jockey or a running greyhound and with script that indicated the company was based in Atlanta. Huston sold stock in Tom Huston System in 1933. "Now that you are a partner in our business, I know you will help us to boost Sport Pack Peanuts and Julep Gum more than ever," he wrote to a new stockholder on July 17 of that year. He continued:

> I want to tell you a little about ourselves. The TOM HUSTON SYSTEM is a system of modern merchandising and controlled distribution. We do not sell through the medium of wholesalers or jobbers. Our own distributors make weekly deliveries to each store that we serve. They sell our products for cash-across-the-counter. I feel that we are fortunate to have you as a stockholder. And we shall strive to make you feel that you were fortunate when you decided to invest in our stock.

The stockholders were not fortunate. Huston's peanut patents remained with the Tom Huston Peanut Company, as did most if not all of the company's employees and distributors, and Huston resorted to increasingly aggressive and possibly desperate measures to compete. Animosity flared up at both firms. Over time, these issues found their way into lawsuits and then a pair of dueling open letters between Huston and Richards that were mailed to hundreds of people in February 1934. Huston's letter of February 21 has been lost to time, but the one Richards sent in response two days later remains. Written in terse language yet spanning four pages and more than fifteen hundred words, Richards's letter pleads for Huston to leave his old company's affairs alone.

"Back in 1929 you decided to go into the frozen peach business," Richards wrote. "Because you were not willing to sell a sufficient amount of your common stock in the Tom Huston Peanut Company at the then prevailing price of $32.00 per share, you elected to finance your new venture on borrowed money, using your Tom Huston Peanut Company stock as collateral. You took this step of your own free will and against the advice of your associates." Huston, Richards said, would agree this decision was a purely personal one that had no bearing on his relationship with the Tom Huston Peanut Company. Huston later became seriously involved in the side venture and drew heavily on the peanut company's resources to prevent personal insolvency. Here Richards included details that Huston surely wanted kept private. "I think you will agree with me that you insisted upon voting common dividends in 1930, 1931 and 1932 and charged large amounts to your personal account with the Company by virtue of your stock control," Richards wrote. "The Company records show that the Directors repeatedly protested against this policy but went along with you in the hope that you could work out of your personal difficulties." Huston was reminded that he'd borrowed a very large amount against his peanut company stock, and when the bank began pressing him for payment, his associates in the company assisted in helping refinance the loan (Richards did not mention it in this letter, but he himself was one of those associates). But when the due date came, Huston was still unable to pay, and he then transferred stock representing the common stock control of the company to the bank. "They, generously I felt, accepted your stock in full settlement of your loan and interest and gave you an option to repurchase your stock over a long period upon payment of the amount of the loan," Richards continued. "While these facts are all known to you, I recite them here to call to your mind that these were purely personal transactions of your own and had nothing to do with the affairs of the Tom Huston Peanut Company except as your personal difficulties affected your actions as the majority stockholder and chief official of the Company."

The letter continued with its history lesson, recounting that Huston was then named chairman of the board of the Tom Huston Peanut Company upon transferring his stock interest, with a salary of $12,000 a year, on the condition that he devote his full attention to the company. He failed to do that, however, developing new products he was not willing to put in the company's name and otherwise acting against the board's wishes, and the board unanimously removed him from the chairmanship on September 1, 1932. Richards then reminded Huston just how many people were counting on him and devoting their lives to the Tom Huston Peanut Company, the one in which Tom Huston himself no longer seemed interested:

> Some three hundred stock holders had invested nearly $1,000,000 in preferred and Common Stock in this Company because of its record. Some six hundred employees were dependent upon it for employment in Columbus and over one hundred and fifty distributors in twenty-two states had invested their capital and time in building up businesses dependent upon the sale of its products. A little empire of over one thousand people had been built around "TOM'S TOASTED PEANUTS" and other products of this Company. Therefore, this Company had created an obligation, both legal and moral, which it could not and cannot side step. It must carry on.

While Tom Huston was within his legal rights to dispose of his stockholdings and to leave the company, Richards felt that his former boss retained a moral obligation to those stockholders, distributors, and employees. "In building this company and creating its goodwill thru advertising, you chose to tie the name Tom and Tom Huston in with it in such a way that the public looked upon these names as synonymous with peanuts and confections," Richards continued. "You spent over $1,000,000 of this Company's money to make them popular. Having assigned all of your goodwill, copyrights, patents and merchandising methods to the Tom Huston Peanut Company, you as an individual had no further claim on them." That, of course, led to Richards's complaints over Huston launching a business with the intent of sinking Tom's, which Richards said was done in violation of multiple contracts and caused confusion in the minds of the public. "By direct attack upon our Company and its distribution system you have sought to tear it down and damage it," Richards said, alleging this was done because Huston felt he'd lost control of his old company unfairly but was nonetheless "most unethical."

"Can you honestly face the stockholders whom you induced into this business and your former employees who slaved for you and say you are giving them a square deal?" the letter continued. "You cannot, and the best proof is that when we were forced to bring suit against you in the courts to protect our rights, you voluntarily came and offered to cease these practices of which we had repeatedly complained." When the lawsuit was threatened, Huston agreed in writing not to use the names "Tom's," "Tom," "Tom Huston," or "Tom Huston System" as a trademark, not to letter his trucks in a similar manner to those of his old firm, not to put Sport Pack Peanuts in Tom's peanut jars, not to make disparaging remarks about the company, and not to sell his products to Tom's distributors, and to respect the validity of the patented peanut bag, which now belonged to Tom Huston the company and not Tom Huston the man. Richards and the Tom's board then dropped the suit in January 1934. Yet even that didn't stop the conflict, and Richards was forced to consider suing Huston again on February 17. The two men met in Atlanta that day, with Huston agreeing to send out a letter outlining the "affirmative acts" he would take to clear up the matter.

Four days later, Huston mailed a letter to hundreds of distributors. But according to Richards, it did not conform to what the two had agreed on and included entirely new material that Richards was not consulted on and did not agree with. Richards wrote that this mass mailing of misinformation was "contrary to ethical practices" and "so foreign to your expressed views that we cannot believe that they are intended as an honest effort on your part to reach an amicable settlement of our difficulties." He concluded,

> You know that we have never done anything to injure you or your Company. We have never hired or attempted to hire any of your

employees or distributors. We have never imitated or attempted to imitate your merchandise or trademarks.

It is our sincere desire to operate on our own merit in our own way and we simply ask that you respect our legal rights. That is not unreasonable, is it?

Because of the uncalled for and willful misrepresentations that have been given widespread circulation, I am sending a copy of this letter to each of our stockholders, distributors, and employees, together with a copy of our agreement with you so we may all understand the situation clearly.

I think you will agree that I have not made any untrue or exaggerated statements in this letter and because it is an exact statement of facts, I can see no reason for offense on the part of anyone.

Sport Pack Peanuts, and Tom Huston, were gone from Columbus within a year.

Julep Gum showed a little more promise but ran into its own headwinds. An unopened pack, labeled "Mint Julep Gum by Tom Huston," can be found in the Texas state archives, in a box of bill files from the Forty-Third Texas Legislature of 1933. Given his eye for marketing, Huston likely distributed free samples of the gum to legislators to try and hook influential Texans. If that's the case, at least one legislator didn't bother to chew it, leaving the pack to history in the artifacts collection.

When Tom Huston was featured for a second time in *Time* magazine, the story was about his struggles with Julep Gum. In a piece in the March 19, 1934, issue, Huston complained that his gum was crippled by legal code sections favoring major players like Beech-Nut and Wrigley. The story caught readers up on the recent past, noting that "Tom Huston's market for quick-frozen peaches froze almost as quickly as Tom Huston's peaches," but also that his gum was now available in forty thousand retail outlets. Huston was busy lobbying the National Recovery Administration (NRA)—an entity President Franklin Delano Roosevelt had launched in 1933 to help the "little fellow" compete in business—to change laws that Huston felt favored big gum manufacturers. Writing to General Hugh S. Johnson, the head of the NRA and a member of FDR's "brain trust," Huston said a law preventing gum manufacturers from making money-back guarantees was hampering his salesmen. Not only did he want the code section gone, but he accused Big Gum of effectively writing it through their own lobbying: "My hopes of making Julep Chewing Gum a nationally known product from coast to coast are hopes that have been blasted by the NRA. . . . General Johnson, this is a matter of life and death with us." Along with his complaint, Huston sent Johnson a carton of gum to sample. "The General," the article concluded, "is no gum-chewer."

Huston was certainly calling up the wrong general. *Time* had named Johnson its "Man of the Year" in 1933 for his leadership in fighting the Depression, but his leadership of the NRA was a major mess, as the agency upset both big business and big labor with contradictory policies. Johnson was fired in August 1934 amid reports of drinking on the job, and the entire agency was scrapped the following year. However, in truth the NRA was almost certainly not the reason for Julep Gum's failure, just as the Great Depression and peaches ultimately weren't the reasons Huston lost control of the Tom Huston Peanut Company. Inventing was a deep-set part of Huston's makeup and psychology, leading him both to vast success and to spectacular failure. As a friend of Huston's put it, "Once a thing got to be routine, Tom lost interest in it." Huston could have realistically kept the peanut company long-term only in an absentee capacity, which is effectively what he tried to do before the failure of Frosty Morning peaches put him on the outs.

All indications are that the failure of Sport Pack and Julep Gum, coming on the heels of Frosty Morning's deep thaw, crushed Huston in body and spirit and left him severely embittered toward Columbus. Richards's letter to hundreds of employees, stockholders, and distributors meant practically everyone in town knew the ugly details. Huston left the city as a shell-shocked soldier, never to return in his living years, and wandered in the Western states for a time seeking a way forward—"a part of my life that I'd just as soon forget," Huston recalled later. Slowly, he began the process of rebuilding his life elsewhere. According to U.S. census records, by 1935 he was living in Hartford, Connecticut, and by 1940 he had relocated to Miami, Florida, where he remained. Miami attracted Huston first because of its warm weather, which helped him recover from a mysterious illness. He moved there permanently in 1939 with wife, Minnie, and their only child, Tom Huston Jr. Huston by this point was around fifty years old. He'd developed a photography habit and was able to land a *Miami Daily News* feature of his work later that year. Huston's photos were dark and silhouetted, gloomy in a style that would continue in the coming decades.

Otherwise, Huston kept such a low profile that many Columbusites assumed he'd died. But behind the scenes he kept up the same furious pattern of tinkering, patenting, and launching as before. Among his later inventions were new kinds of fruit, a rose-scented facial tissue, a brand of orange juice, insect traps, fertilizer, a device that dispensed and applied shoe polish, and a batting practice game for children called Rick Rack. None of them took off. But Huston did hit another home run with a pet products business he named Pal Pet Shop. One day in the early 1940s, he went out to buy flea powder for his dog and found the process surprisingly difficult, with only three or four stores in the entire Miami area carrying the product. He also noticed during that time that grocery stores were starting to move beyond selling just food and were fanning out into other types of products. He thus presented to local supermarkets the idea of an in-store miniature pet shop. The wares were given Huston-esque names like Kitty Care flea powder, Sunday Shower dog cleaner, Finer Dinner bird seed, Itch Witch, Ear Cheer, and Beauty Bath. Pal Pet Shop was a hit, operating on a Tom's-like model in which truck-driving distributor/salesmen refilled the displays each week. Huston claimed that the shops could be found in every major supermarket chain in America by the 1950s. In 1958, an offer for the venture came from Sterling Drug Company, a major firm that held the license to Bayer Aspirin, and this time Huston sold.

He was paid in Sterling stock shares worth more than $2 million, allowing him to officially retire on a five-acre Miami spread filled with roses, pine trees, and subtropical plants. At sixty-nine, Huston had reached an age when truly retiring was a reasonable expectation. He did no such thing. Huston kept up frequent correspondence with patent offices and research firms, looking for his next great success and nursing his unquenchable creative urges. He formed two businesses dedicated to his patent work, House of Huston and Huston Research Corporation, and continued looking for that next big thing during the 1960s.

Interestingly, he continued to dabble in peaches and peanuts during his elderly years. Huston looked into a brand of dry roasted "big peanuts" and spent considerable time on a brand of peanut butter, both named Bow & Arrow. The peanut butter came in stackable glass jars that he envisioned as reusable collector's items. Most of the branding and nutritional information was written on the lid, on the premise that an opened, unblemished jar could be placed directly on the table for serving even in the presence of high-class company. Huston developed two different forms of peaches that were adapted to south Florida's near-tropical climate and that he named Early Amber and Rio Grande. He tested fourteen hundred peach hybrids to create Early Amber, so named because it ripened earlier than other breeds, which he thought would bring a market advantage. It wasn't the success Huston hoped for, but that variety is still grown in central Florida.

While his reputation as a semi-recluse continued, Huston dabbled in newspaper interviews during the mid-to-late 1960s. In 1965 he agreed to a series of stories written by Tom Sellers, a Pulitzer Prize–winning journalist for *The Columbus Ledger-Enquirer* who made his name covering corruption in Phenix City, Alabama. Sellers marveled at the "genius in exile," writing that "his legend still thrives wherever peanut products are sold, which is almost everywhere," and that Tom's Toasted Peanuts were as famous in the South "as the ubiquitous 'Coke' and the famed combination of 'RC Cola and Moon Pie.' . . . One is transfixed by the bounding intelligence" of the "wealthy Florida wizard" and "Columbus peanut prince." Huston still held more than forty patents as of the Sellers interviews, which were conducted when he was seventy-five years old.

Sellers also mentioned Huston's interpretive photography habit, of which the inventor would only say, "I paint with a lens instead of a brush." He gave the same line to other reporters as well and said little else about his methods or approach to the craft. Huston's photography was dark and abstract, typically such that it was unclear exactly what was being pictured. He preferred it that way, viewing his photos as modernized paintings left to the eye of the beholder, a Machine Age take on art in the same way that his peanut shellers and standardized cellophane bags remade agriculture. The abstract photos went on tour to universities and museums, with a traveling show called *Escape from Reality* visiting Columbus on the heels of the Sellers series. Minnie Huston typically played host, with her husband, the mysterious semi-recluse, staying home in Miami. Huston separately funded a scholarship for budding photography students at Florida Southern College.

He dabbled in poetry too, sometimes writing verse to accompany his photographs. A typical example is a poem Huston named "Brute Time":

Time, Time tyrant Time
The most unkind of all
Ere I begin the rugged climb
Brute Time has clocked my fall.

Now, over me and you, O hear,
With branding iron he stands
To turn the imprint of each year
On all. On seas. On lands.

CHAPTER 3

Stone castles bow in sad disgust,
Time slowly grinds them down.
Ye marble tombs are doomed to dust—
Brute Time defies renown.

Huston's correspondence with patent offices and research firms continued into the early 1970s, as he sought out new and profitable innovations in his eighties. But he also began arranging his affairs due to escalating health problems. Huston made several alterations to existing documents and even a few of his poems during his last years. Finally, on July 20, 1972, Huston passed away due to complications from a chronic illness, the details of which were never publicly disclosed. He was eighty-two years old.

Even though more than forty years had passed since he left Tom's—and despite the photography and the poetry, despite Pal Pet Shop and Early Amber peaches and the scholarships, despite the five-acre Miami spread and the presence of his socialite wife—Huston's obituaries focused almost entirely on the fact that he had founded Tom's Toasted Peanuts. Returning to Columbus at last, he was buried at Linwood Cemetery beneath a simple, humble headstone. "Tom Huston," it read, listing his dates of birth and death, followed by "Founder of Tom Huston Peanut Company."

In 1978, Minnie Huston was asked to contribute to a series of stories celebrating the Columbus sesquicentennial. She wrote about her late husband's considerable contributions to the city, the state, and the peanut industry in a moving tribute that not only detailed the particulars of Tom Huston's life but also gave insight into his state of mind.

"Tom was a seeker but not a finder," she wrote. "He was forever reaching for a nebulous goal that constantly eluded him. He was a sower of seeds who never stayed around for the harvest. His restless mind, the tool of his talents, never found a resting place. It was his glory and his defeat. But, the seeds he planted in Columbus have flourished into a business that is a benefactor and a blessing to the entire community."

CHAPTER 4

The Stabilizer, Walter Alan Richards

When Tom Huston left the company he founded in 1932, it fell firmly and fully into the hands of the Columbus business and social establishment, where it would remain for the next two generations. New president Walter Alan Richards was a different man, with a different approach from Huston in matters both large and small.

Richards was a Washington, D.C., native who might never have even heard of Columbus save for a stroke of chance. His college roommate at the Virginia Military Institute, Ben Hardaway Jr., was the son of Hardaway Construction owner Ben Hardaway Sr. Hardaway Construction was a major firm in Columbus, building, among other structures, the first concrete bridge across the Chattahoochee River and some of the city's most important hydroelectric dams. Richards majored in civil engineering at VMI, so between connection and experience he was a natural fit to work at Hardaway after graduating from college in 1913. Richards helped with hydroelectric projects in his early career, and he liked Columbus, thanks to the big river and the good fishing it afforded.

Walter Alan Richards.

Knowing Hardaway Construction's owner through friendship with his son gave Richards a quick in with the city's other power brokers. Among them was Frederick B. Gordon, another local kingpin who had founded the Columbus Manufacturing Company mill in 1899. Gordon was born in Massachusetts, and, like much of the textile industry during his lifetime, he moved south for new opportunities and cheaper labor. He was also quite a character, unafraid to loudly and publicly share his opinions on business and political matters. Gordon supported child labor because he felt some children were "better employed in some industry than learning the first lessons of a vagrant's life." He backed public schools because, as he put it, they kept the "less bright, slower, more plodding" Black children from becoming "idlers and young criminals." Unions came in for particular scorn. Following a battle with would-be union organizers at his mill, Gordon told the Southern Textile Association that the South "will never . . . allow itself to be bound hand and foot . . . by that THING that seeks to stab in the heart that inherent right of selective employment. . . . That unholy, foreign-born, un-American, socialistic, despotic THING known as LABOR UNIONISM." But it wasn't Frederick Gordon's politics that interested Richards so much as Gordon's daughter, Margaret, whom Richards began dating during the middle of the 1910s. The Gordon family lived in a 7,500-square-foot mansion at 1420 Wynnton Road that they called "Gordonido," Spanish for "Gordon's nest" or "residence." Margaret inherited the house when her father died in 1933.

Richards joined the army in April 1917 as the United States was entering World War I, and he married Margaret Gordon that December. He then went to Europe to serve in the war and won a Purple Heart and the Distinguished Service Cross while fighting in France. "Leading his platoon in attack," the War Department book of medals reads, "Lieutenant Richards was subjected to fierce and devastating fire of enemy artillery and machine guns. Although he himself was wounded and 90 percent of his platoon made casualties, he continued to press forward until he was felled by machine gun fire after reaching the foremost position of the entire action." Richards returned to Columbus in 1919. After a few more years of engineering work, including a stint as assistant superintendent at his father-in-law's mill, Richards was named one of Columbus's first city managers in 1922, at just thirty-one years old. He excelled in the position, turning the city's $45,000 debt into a surplus within one year. In 1926 Richards was named city manager of fast-growing vacation spot Daytona Beach, Florida, but that endeavor lasted just two years before he returned to Columbus. His new position upon moving back: vice president of the Tom Huston Peanut Company. He started on March 1, 1928.

It's unclear exactly what connected Richards with Tom's initially, but within a year of joining he was effectively running the show for its four hundred employees, as Tom Huston, even in 1929, was already turning his attention to frozen peaches. By all accounts, Richards was an effective and attentive manager. The company superintendents who consulted with George Washington Carver repeatedly praised Richards for his recommendations and careful study of materials. Richards's engineering background made him a natural fit for Tom's, which was a manufacturing business using then-new technology. Not only was Richards the de facto leader of Tom's by 1929, he was soon leading it through a financial crunch due to two challenges. One was the Great Depression, and the other was Huston draining the company coffers to fund Frosty Morning. A 1930 estimate held that Huston planned to spend $75,000 opening the venture, all of which fell on Tom's one way or another. Huston also redirected some of Tom's top employees, including research department director Fred A. Woleben, to join him in promoting frozen peaches.

The situation went sideways, as detailed in the previous chapter, leading to an ugly and rather public battle between Richards and Huston. Richards formally became president of Tom's in January 1932, replacing his old boss. After that, Huston served for a short period as chairman of the board and then launched a competing peanut firm to try and knock out his old company. By the time the dust settled with Richards's final, mass-produced letter to Huston in 1934, the company's finances were severely compromised. Tom's ran red ink in the early 1930s.

Cost cutting was the first order of business once Richards solidified control. The company made no effort to expand its geographic footprint between 1931 and 1936. Its consulting partnership with the well-known agricultural chemist Charles Herty was cut short. Employees working on projects with long-range research and development goals were reassigned to sales and operations positions. Outreach to farmers, the main thrust of the Carver connection, was left to the federal government and state universities. Even then, the accounting department was delaying payments and asking for extensions. "Gentlemen: Received your letter of September 23rd requesting check which to date we have been unable to send, due to the very poor collections in this section," Tom's secretary-treasurer Frank R. Burn wrote to Brooklyn-based copper kettle maker Thomas Burkhard, Inc., on September 26, 1933. "We will have your account set up in the next few days, so please bear with us a few days longer, until we can forward check."

Huston's quirky marketing, with mountain-climbing peanut pushers and truck-mounted loudspeakers, was gone too. Richards operated much more traditionally, with a top-down emphasis on community, loyalty, and family at the home office. Tom's launched an in-house company magazine, the *Toaster*, on November 25, 1933. Purchasing agent Al Lewis came up with the name, vice president Jack Williams was the first editor, and assistant purchasing agent Raleigh Strickland did the drawings. Richards often wrote letters himself, signing as "Rich."

"We believe our company is the best company to work for in these United States," announced the first page of the first issue. "WHY? Because we are one great big happy family that has been built on humanitarian principles." The piece announced that Tom's had lost money for two and a half years but was in the black as of October 1933, which may have occasioned the magazine's launch. Richards was certainly tuned in to the company's finances, keeping a chart on his office wall to track financial progress throughout the 1930s. It was a hard time, regardless of the new magazine's rosy optimism. All office staff, including executives, took a pay cut in 1933, the first full year of Richards's presidency, and everyone was asked to work one full week without pay. The factory labor, true to its time, was often grueling. There was no air-conditioning, and there were no minimum wage or overtime laws. Shifts often lasted twelve hours, or they simply kept going until the final order shipped. General superintendent John Usher took pride in his ability to guess a prospective employee's age. If he thought an applicant looked old enough, they were hired. The women in the factory, invariably referred to as "girls" in contemporary publications, worked on a per-piece basis filling peanut bags or wrapping crackers, so most of them eschewed breaks even if they were offered. Women typically earned at least twelve dollars a week, more if they kept a quick pace.

By the late 1930s, things had improved, and the company was again looking to expand by adding new "franchises" to extend its reach. The product line expanded too, especially in the high-margin candy line. Candy

Teams of women worked at Tom's from its earliest days, filling peanut bags or wrapping crackers on a per-piece pay scale.

department foreman L. I. "Ickey" Marshall took advantage of the era's lax regulations to roll out confections as the mood struck him. A colorful figure and "big-hearted man" who had the word ICKEY stitched on the front of his shirt, Marshall would cook up a new candy item and hand out samples around the office, and if it was a hit, the new "product" could be shipped to market within two or three weeks using labels that read "1 oz. or over." This led to a rapidly expanding line that topped seventy offerings by 1938. Not everything worked out after it left the factory, however. A Marshall creation named "Big Chief" that was heavy on nulomoline, gelatin, and marshmallow was launched in the dead of winter. In the summer months, when the inside of a delivery truck could top one hundred degrees, Big Chief soured and swelled under the heat, rupturing and ruining anything within bubbling distance. It was soon discontinued, and the candy department added the word "blivet" (meaning "overfull") to its vocabulary.

Tom's briefly sold potato chips when a New England man named Roland King started frying them in the back of the peanut department. They were soon discontinued due to poor sales, and King became a district sales manager. Along with its own brand, the company also pushed "affiliated" products made by other firms, including Chasers, a foul-tasting tablet designed to neutralize alcohol and onion breath, and Tom's Chex, a corn chip product that tried, and failed, to compete with Fritos in Texas. Some products were moderate sellers—for example, Divinity, consisting of cane sugar, corn syrup, egg whip, roasted milk powder, coconut oil, pecan meats, and vanilla flavor, and the Tom's Goody Roll, made of sugar, corn syrup, whole milk, coconut oil, fondant cream, vanilla flavor, and salt.

There were some big successes as well. Opposite from Big Chief and Tom's Chex were the Peanut Plank and the Peanut Butter Log, the latter of which featured honeycombed cane sugar, corn syrup, and peanut butter, providing a creamy flavor and a pleasantly flaky texture. The Peanut Butter Log quickly established itself as a core product, outselling Tom's Toasted Peanuts in some locations upon its 1937 introduction. However, Tom's Toasted Peanuts remained solidly number one overall. Richards dubbed it the "papa product" from which all others descended, and Tom's letterhead in the 1930s featured a glass jar and a bag of peanuts at top left. Columbus called itself the peanut capital of the Southeast, with peanuts being an ingredient in almost everything Tom's made. Most of the crop was sourced from within one hundred miles of Columbus, and farmers selling their wares usually shopped in town before heading home, injecting even more money into the city's economy.

The Tom's product lineup expanded rapidly in the 1930s thanks to the efforts of candy department foreman L. I. "Ickey" Marshall. Under the lax regulations of the day, new items could be rolled out in a matter of weeks.

One non-peanut product in the "affiliated" lineup was a silent link to Tom Huston. The official 1937–38 Tom's product lineup included Julep Gum, offered in fruit and mint flavors. Gum orders could be sent directly to Tom's, and the sales catalog said Julep was "made exclusively for the Tom Huston Peanut Company by a chewing gum manufacturer" that remained unnamed. Huston either was still selling the gum or had sold distribution rights to his old company.

Tom's under Richards was conservative financially, though not always rigid in approach. In contrast to Huston's free-spending ways, there was little money budgeted toward advertising once Richards took over. In fact, the February 18, 1939, issue of the *Toaster* ran an article titled "Why Don't We Do More Advertising?" responding to a question frequently posed to company leadership. The main explanation put forth in the article was that Tom's enjoyed a profit margin of only around 5 percent, whereas Coca-Cola carried a 25 percent margin, allowing more marketing. The story said that ads would come one day ("It is not a question of what we *want* to do. Rather, it is a matter of what we can *afford* to do."), and Tom's did spend on occasion. Later in 1939, it ran a modest ad campaign featuring the Lone Ranger, in which five bags of Tom's Toasted Peanuts could be exchanged for a Ranger-themed "bat-o-ball" game. Another celebrity spot, this one in conjunction with the YMCA, featured Bob Hope and children grasping tins of Tom's Toasted Peanuts. An unofficial regional custom also developed that involved pouring a bag of Tom's Toasted Peanuts into an open bottle of Coca-Cola or RC, mixing two Southern favorites at once.

The *Toaster* wasn't strictly a business magazine. Along with sales and factory updates, it mixed in stories of loyalty, faithfulness, and accountability designed to inspire the sales team, along with results from the company bowling and baseball games, family news such as weddings and workplace anniversaries, and a few off-key jokes. From a 1936 issue:

> Judge: "You had to live on fifteen cents a day? Your husband must be impecunious."
>
> Mrs. Chloe: "Jedge, I'd believe anything 'bout dat man."
>
> —
>
> A frantic man rushed into a police station and handing the desk officer a woman's picture said: "My wife is missing, I want to find her."
>
> Officer (after looking at picture): "Why."

All of these features would remain staples of the publication for years.

The chart in Richards's office climbed steadily through the late 1930s, and the company grew into a six-hundred-person outfit. A major milestone came in 1940 when the Trust Company of Georgia turned Tom's back over to management, making it a stock-issuing local firm once again. Total sales tipped back above $2 million for the first time in eleven years.

George Washington Carver made his last appearance in Columbus in 1939, speaking before a standing-room-only crowd at Spencer High School, which at the time was located just across Tenth Avenue from Tom's. Aged seventy-five and frail, Carver remained a major international celebrity. The event generated a huge buzz in the city and a huge crowd the night of the speech. Tom's was heavily involved, as Richards spoke briefly and presented Carver with a large bronze plaque valued at $750 as a gift from the company. This was in fact the same bust Tom's commissioned for Carver at the beginning of the decade. The piece sat in a Carver-focused museum at Tom's headquarters between 1931 and 1939 and remained at Spencer High following the speech. The company may have been involved in the event in other ways as well. One account, written later, holds that Carver was pressed into action to cool race and labor relations at the company, with Black male employees threatening to strike on behalf of Black female employees. If that's so, it was not mentioned in any newspaper stories about the speech at the time. Carver spoke before a mixed-race group, though attendees sat in segregated seating sections. He delighted the crowd, speaking pleasantly and displaying various peanut specimens such as peanut milk, peanut cream, and peanut buttermilk.

"More and more as we study the peanut, we learn of its potentialities," Carver told the audience. "By putting various of its chemical constituents together in differing proportions, you can make from it almost anything you want."

The crowd marveled as Carver pontificated on "the mysteries all around us," mentioning the simple fact that rubber will stretch when pressed or pulled. Just why that is, he said, "nobody knows, except the freshman in college, who can usually give a reason for everything." He'd asked God to tell him what a peanut is, Carver recalled, and was told to "seek and you will find." So he went to the laboratory and sought. Carver passed away less than four years after the speech; Carver High School and the Carver Heights neighborhood in Columbus were later named for him in tribute.

Like the rest of the economy, Tom's got a significant boost when the United States entered World War II. Both its manpower and its products were shipped overseas. Richards led the charge by joining the army again, this time as a colonel. President Roosevelt appointed Richards director of field service for the Fourth Service Command, a unit headquartered in Atlanta. This of course required an indefinite leave of absence from Tom's, which the board of directors quickly granted. The post added to a growing list of positions Richards held over the years, including president of the Columbus Chamber of Commerce, head of the Columbus Defense Service Council, and deacon at First Presbyterian Church.

Luckily for Tom's, when Richards rejoined the army, he took the peanuts with him. Sales jumped as peanuts and candy were included in army and navy rations, sent overseas by the ton during the war years, and were aided further by the widespread rationing of sugar. Tom's delivery trucks started advertising war bonds along with peanuts, and the *Toaster* shared stories and letters from the front lines. From September 1944 to August 1945, the company made over $1.5 million on government shipments alone. Total sales topped $10 million in 1945, tripling the number seen just a few years earlier. Some 350 Tom's employees volunteered or were drafted into the service and were honored with a plaque at headquarters. Of those employees, eleven made the ultimate sacrifice in the war.

World War II and Roosevelt's aggressive New Deal programs lifted not just Tom's but the entire economy in the early 1940s. Georgia remained 65 percent rural in 1940, and many people in the state's hinterlands still lived as their grandparents had—in unpainted shacks lacking indoor plumbing or window screens. It was still one of the nation's poorest states per capita. Yet by this time the state led the nation in peanut production, farm tenancy was in decline, and cotton dropped from representing 66 percent of Georgia's crop value in 1920 to 40 percent in 1940. Peaches and tobacco aided in the diversification. Agriculture was slowly entering a healthier era across the South, and the march of industrialization continued, as seen in the rapidly expanding workforce and distribution system of the Tom Huston Peanut Company.

After the war, the company worked to expand its benefits program. Tom's was now one of the country's largest manufacturers of peanut snacks and one of Columbus's biggest employers, with the smell of roasting peanuts drifting daily through the neighborhoods surrounding the factory. Like other larger Southern companies of the era, Tom's was aggressive about perks—always with an eye toward warding off unions. Tom's opened a company health clinic in 1944 and a pension program, for which it paid all costs, in 1946. Two years after that, Tom's bought fifty-five acres bordering what is now Victory Drive, then exchanged that parcel along with cash for six hundred acres in rural Harris County. Developer Charlie Frank Williams owned the rural property and had named it *Uxahatchee*, supposedly the Native American word for "head of the spring." The acreage did include a spring, along with a lake, a swimming pool, two houses, and a few other buildings. Film star Bette Davis had stayed at the "Big House" for a few months during World War II, causing a stir locally. Williams was a longtime partner of Tom's dating back to its earliest days and had joined its board of directors by the 1940s. He used the in-town acreage to build the Camellia Apartments (which were probably named after Camille, one of his four daughters), along with the Traffic Circle Shopping Center, located on what was then the edge of town at the corner of Victory Drive and Fort Benning Road. The Harris County property was renamed Lake Huston and later Lake Richards, though some people just called it "Tom's lake." In any case, the company built bathhouses and barbecue pits as it transformed the land into a retreat for employees. The big house was typically reserved for officers, while special events like Family Day brought in children and other relatives who, if they dared, could try their luck in the icy spring-fed pool. The children of employees could also attend summer camps on the property, continuing the family theme. While the lake plan worked out well, Tom's still needed land in town to expand beyond the single city block it occupied in the late 1940s. To achieve this expansion, it made an arrangement with the Seaboard Air Line Railroad Company for acreage that would eventually become plant space and a warehouse.

A few of the company's distributors were out building little empires of their own. Roughly 347 Tom's distributors operated a total of 1,094 routes, and while many were single-truck operations, others grew into sizable enterprises with more than a dozen trucks and their own office staff. Over the years, these top operators included John Edenfield, who started as a route man in 1946 and eventually ran fifty trucks in middle Georgia. Edenfield later became mayor of his hometown of Thomaston. Other examples included the Barber Sales Company of Talladega, Alabama, which lasted through three generations of Barbers; Graham Snack Foods of Tennessee, another three-generation enterprise that at one point had twenty routes; and Ernest West's Houston operation, which reached seventeen trucks even in the depths of the Great Depression. Knowing how utterly dependent Tom's was on this field army, Richards referred to distributors as "the life blood of our company." Given the times and the working conditions, sales routes were almost exclusively the domain of men, though a few enterprising women such

Lake Huston (later renamed Lake Richards) was a getaway for generations of Tom's families beginning in the late 1940s. Children tested their luck in the frigid waters of the property's spring-fed pool.

as Helen Gardner Alden and I. B. Hubler served on the force as well. The trucks as a collective were called the Silver Fleet owing to the paint scheme.

Richards moved on to new horizons himself after the war. Always an exceptionally busy man, in 1945 he was "drafted" into running for the Columbus City Commission by a group calling itself the Friends of Walter Richards. He ran in the Democratic white primary (which in that era served as the de facto election), looking to add elected government office to his list of duties. "We persuaded Walter Richards to make this race, and WE HAD TO DO A LOT OF PERSUADING," read a full-page ad for Richards's campaign in the September 30, 1945, edition of *The Sunday Ledger-Enquirer*. "He agreed to become a candidate only upon the condition that he would not make a personal campaign. He imposed this condition because he knows that any politician who owes his office to hand-shaking, baby-kissing, and whispered promises CANNOT POSSIBLY BE UN-SHACKLED after his election. Walter Richards will be an UN-SHACKLED COMMISSIONER—he would rather be beaten than go into office with hands tied!"

According to the ad, Richards agreed to run only after a petition asking him to do so was circulated and signed by hundreds of "registered and qualified voters." When primary day arrived, the other candidates nervously paced about the courthouse, whereas Richards was largely absent from the scene. He won a two-year term anyway, coming in second out of four candidates in the Democratic white primary to fill one of two open slots on the commission, and then was "formally elected" in the December 2 general election that included non-white and non-Democratic voters. In early 1947, just a year after joining the commission, Richards was elected mayor by his fellow commissioners, adding that title to others he held over the years, including Chamber of Commerce president, chairman of the Columbus Planning Association, member of the Columbus Housing Authority, president of the National Peanut Council, director of the Associated Industries of Georgia, and president of the Ninth Street USO. Richards's wife, the former Margaret Gordon, was frequently in the newspapers as well thanks to her involvement in the Society of Colonial Dames and the United Garden Club. Following the custom of the day, she was referred to always as "Mrs. Walter Richards."

Mr. Walter Richards managed to fill numerous posts simultaneously by utilizing an engineer's eye for efficiency. As mayor he became known for his short speeches. When a new Davison's department store debuted in Columbus, Richards spoke at the grand opening. His speech: "We are glad to have Davison's in Columbus." He won a second two-year stint on the city commission in 1948, remaining as mayor for the duration, but declined to seek a third term, explaining that he thought commissioners should be limited to a single term lasting five years. For him, four was close enough. "I feel that I have served my time and I am not going to be a candidate for re-election this year," Richards said in his typically direct manner. However, the day after his mayoral term ended, he was named chairman of the Muscogee Board of Education, a position he held for the next decade.

In some respects, the almost unbelievable number of board, director, and volunteer positions that Richards held in addition to leading Tom's put him in the same orbit as Huston, who flitted between a wide array of seemingly unrelated interests throughout his life. Yet Richards kept the Tom Huston

Peanut Company first and foremost in his professional affairs, the center of gravity around which those other positions rotated. Some of his outside responsibilities, such as leading the Columbus Chamber of Commerce and the National Peanut Council, almost certainly helped him accrue benefits back to the company. And there is no evidence that any of these side gigs involved risking or leveraging large amounts of company funds.

The word to describe Tom's in this period is "stable." Its 1949 annual report listed net sales of just under $9 million, with a nearly $2 million earned surplus, and with shareholders paid a $1 dividend per share. Net sales had been $2 million a decade earlier. There were no big grand slams leading from $2 million to $9 million, no surprises—just a slow, steady climb year over year. The product line changed only modestly and by increments, but on the other hand Richards didn't risk the firm's bottom line or its reputation on a speculative venture, and certainly not on one based in a completely separate line of business. It was a similar story across Georgia and the South, as the number of people employed in manufacturing in the state surpassed the number employed in agriculture for the first time at the end of the decade, with factory work tending to pay much better than farmwork. The population of Muscogee County grew by 56.3 percent between 1940 and 1950, climbing from 75,494 to 118,028. As before, many of the city's new families hailed from nearby rural counties like Schley, Chattahoochee, and Taylor, all of which suffered population losses of 15 percent or more during the 1940s.

Tom's prepared a larger-than-usual publication in 1950 to mark its twenty-fifth anniversary. Richards had been involved with the company for all but three of those twenty-five years, and he gave credit for its success to the country and culture in which he was born. "Like many other American Corporations, our existence and future progress is dependent upon the American way of life and our system of free enterprise," he wrote in the pamphlet. Tom's still worked directly with what it called "progressive and able farmers," buying 21 million pounds of peanuts from them and selling peanut hay back for cattle feed. "We are Peanut Folks," declared one subhead, above images of peanut fields, peanut stacks, and men inspecting the harvest. The history of the peanut was depicted too, with its origins traced from South America across the world. The little shack Tom's started in, which had been converted into a company cafeteria, featured heavily, and Tom's Toasted Peanuts, "the leader and all-time favorite," was the first product mentioned in the thirty-page pamphlet, with everything else referred to as a cousin. But those cousins were growing in their own right, with four hundred people employed in the sandwich cracker division and three hundred working in the candy department. Tom's bought 4 million pounds of sugar and 2 million pounds of corn syrup annually.

The company's sandwich crackers, all bearing the slogan "Tom's Sandwiches Make a Good Drink Better," included Red Robin Butter Toast, Eat-a-Snax, Vanilla Joys, Cheese Crisp, Afternoon Teas (to go with tea, that is), and Cheezers. A limited candy line, made according to "carefully guarded recipes," included the aforementioned Peanut Plank and Peanut Butter Log, along with Tom's Divinity, Coconut Krisp, Dixie Crisp, and Milk-Whip. Through a 1946 partnership with the Virginia and North Carolina–based Tom Black Potato Chip Company, Tom's was again offering chips, along with other "rack goods" like toffee, mints, and hard candy. Its products were sold in 230,000 stores across thirty-five states. The distributors and route salesmen of the day were all listed by name and state in the twenty-fifth-anniversary publication, offering a window into the company's decidedly regional reach. Ninety-nine routes operated in Georgia, and seventy-one traversed Alabama. Texas had the largest list of all, with thirty-eight people serving Houston alone. Michigan? Only two salesmen. There were just four in New York State, even though it had more than four times the population of Georgia in 1950. Five people served the Washington, D.C., area, five served Utah, sixteen operated in Minnesota, and thirty worked in California. All of the Southeastern states were heavily saturated. Only thirteen states had no Tom's presence whatsoever. Of note, Puerto Rico had a distributor, F. C. Pujals, with A. Pujals and H. Pujals, presumably his sons, listed as salesmen.

Elsewhere in the 1950 pamphlet, various displays were showcased, as Tom's continued moving beyond its glass jars to the use of baskets, cabinets, glass shelving, and elevated platters designed to save counter space. These displays were provided to the retailer at no cost. The Harris County lake featured prominently, complete with drawings of picnickers and fishermen—all of them white—as did the company cafeteria, the World War II plaque, and trophies won by the Tom's bowling, basketball, softball, and baseball teams. A few Black employees were pictured, though based on photos of Tom's headquarters from that time, the work appeared to be segregated by both race and sex. An impressive fifty-one people were listed as having worked at Tom's for at least twenty years, meaning they dated to Huston's era as president. The pamphlet's back page listed the Creed of the Tom's Salesman ("To be loyal to my Company, considerate towards my associates, and thereby keep true to myself").

Sadly, the twenty-fifth-anniversary pamphlet is probably most noteworthy for marking two tragedies that struck the Tom's workforce. Texas-based vice president J. Fred Cleveland died unexpectedly on August 24, 1949, at the age of fifty-four and was honored with a picture and a short paragraph of acknowledgement on the pamphlet's back page. He was replaced as vice president by Thomas Clarence "T. C." Kendrick Jr., who lived in Columbus and had been with Tom's since its founding days in the 1920s. Among Kendrick's duties was compiling the anniversary publication. However, his promotion would be short-lived, as he died of a heart attack two days before Christmas in 1950. At forty-three, Kendrick died at an even younger age than Cleveland, and he left behind a wife and two sons aged eight and six. He was honored with a rushed insert on page two of the anniversary pamphlet. "It is with a feeling of sadness that this book is dedicated to our very close friend and fellow worker, T. C. Kendrick, Jr." the page read. "He gave untiringly of his efforts and interest through the past six months to compile a picture of the company that he spent twenty-five years to help build." The insert was added so late that Kendrick was still listed as vice president in other parts of the document. He was buried at Riverdale Cemetery on Christmas Eve, with all of the pallbearers being Tom's employees. One of them, James Wilbur Feighner, would take Kendrick's place as vice president, becoming the third man to hold the post in fewer than eighteen months.

The pamphlet made no mention of Tom Huston at all, a fact that eventually reached him down in Miami, leading to another tense exchange of letters between Huston and Richards. As with their dustup of 1934, only Richards's letter remains, but this time he took a much more conciliatory, somber, even regretful tone. Huston's letter was dated March 26, 1954, and Richards struggled with how to respond to it for more than two months. Finally, on June 4 he replied, beginning his letter "Dear Tom" and writing that he'd "started to answer [your letter] a number of times but, frankly, it is not an easy task." T. C. Kendrick had prepared the twenty-fifth-anniversary booklet, he explained, and as far as anyone remembered, "the question you raised," presumably whether or not to include Huston, never came up. But general company policy since Huston left had been to refrain from using his name in any published literature. Why? Because that's what Richards thought Huston wanted. "In fact, I have a distinct recollection that you made this request shortly after you started the Tom Huston System and we have never been advised that you had changed your mind," Richards wrote. "Now with your House of Huston well launched on a national scale, it would seem to me that such references on our part might prove objectionable to you." He continued:

> I have always held you in the highest regard, Tom, and I have never failed to give you full credit for the great part you played in establishing this business. Whenever I tell the story of the Tom Huston Peanut Company I begin with the hand peanut sheller and go right on through to the circumstances that led up to your leaving the Company.
>
> I try, sincerely, to be completely fair to you and I do not believe you will ever find a person who will say otherwise.
>
> You laid the foundation of this business and it was your creative efforts that made it possible. You needed help on production and financial matters and I feel that I contributed substantially along this line.
>
> I am sure you remember that I did everything in my power to get you to stay with the Company and even after you went into a competitive business I urged you to come back with the organization. I believe this would have been accomplished if your serious illness had not intervened.
>
> I told you at that time that I felt sure we could pay off the bank and get back your equity in the Company in less than five years.

Recounting the battles of the 1930s, Richards said he didn't agree with Huston's bitterness toward the Trust Company of Georgia. Richards himself had helped Huston secure the loan from the bank, and thus "I had no alternative but to help them work out of their problem, even at the risk of your friendship." Yet even with this admission made, Richards said he told the bank at the time that if a settlement could be made, he'd like to see Huston return to the company he founded. Richards still believed that it could have happened "had it not been for your protracted illness."

"Of course, this is all water over the dam," Richards wrote. "My great regret is that you are not here with us now to enjoy the fruits of this fine company which you founded and started on its road to success." To answer Huston's question specifically, Richards said it would be his pleasure to give Huston full credit in any future historical brochures as the founder of the company and the originator of Tom's Toasted Peanuts—if Huston would provide written permission to do so.

Even after two decades, animosity between the two had not quite subsided. As Richards noted, Huston was building a second great fortune by this time, which Richards hoped might lessen any hard feelings toward the first. At the same time, Huston was the "Tom" in Tom's, and it must have been jarring to read an entire book about the company he founded without seeing his name mentioned. Richards's delay in replying, and the exasperated tone in which Richards wrote, belies the difficulty with which he still struggled to interact with his onetime boss.

Their strained relationship wasn't the only thing that hadn't changed much in twenty years. The letterhead on which Richards wrote still bore the peanut bag, glass jar, triangular logo, and "tiny billboard" Huston had created in the mid-1920s. They remained the company's calling card and the core of its identity. Richards, as a stabilizer, was not an innovator in the same manner or to the same degree as the polymath Huston. His expansion of the business was strongly focused on the old-school fundamentals of sales and operations, watching the chart on his office wall climb month by month. He did make a few unorthodox moves over the years, however. In 1939 Richards traveled to Cuba, and for a time Tom's products were sold there from trucks reading *Mani Tostado Tom's. Nutritivo, Siempre, Fresco,* which roughly translates as "Tom's Toasted Peanuts. Nutritious, Always, Fresh." And in 1952 Richards made a trip to Europe, visiting candy plants in England, France, and Norway to get new ideas for the high-margin Tom's candy division. Candy sales reportedly jumped 50 percent over the next three years, with new offerings like the peanut butter and chocolate Full Dinner bar, which was introduced in 1955, and a bigger focus on sweet staples. Tom's was selling more than 1 million Peanut Butter Logs a day in the 1950s. Individually wrapped, bite-sized versions of the Peanut Butter Log, Peanut Plank, and Peanut Krisp were also heavily promoted as a "wholesome" Halloween candy, meaning an entire generation of children grew up eating them after a night of trick-or-treating.

Even if the growth was incremental, one could not argue with the results. Total annual sales had slumped well below $2 million around the time Richards took over as president; they topped $20 million in 1956, near the end of his tenure. The total number of distributors climbed above four hundred that year, with 1,252 trucks in operation, while the workforce in Columbus stood at more than one thousand strong. A new round of innovation was beginning to form in this period as well, one that would give Tom's a major market advantage and propel it to even bigger things in the next two decades.

CHAPTER 5

Innovation Again

Toward the end of Richards's tenure, Tom's began a second journey of innovation and discovery that arguably marked its biggest step forward of the entire post-Huston era. This was the crucial, paradigm-altering, and decidedly less sexy advent of the glass-front snack vending machine. As with cellophane-wrapped packs of peanuts, no one stops and looks twice at a snack vending machine today unless they happen to be really hungry, but in the 1950s and 1960s the Tom Huston Peanut Company revolutionized the industry with new concepts in the vending arena, this time with the help of some outside partners.

As with salted peanuts, the history of the vending machine dates surprisingly far back into history. The first known automated vending device was invented in Roman Egypt by Hero of Alexandria all the way back in the first century AD. The product? Holy water. Hero's system involved placing a coin in a slot atop an otherwise closed box. The coin would fall on a metal lever, a kind of balance beam, and its weight would tilt the apparatus, which at the other end was tied to a plug stopping a container of water. The tilt temporarily removed the plug, allowing water to flow until the weight of the coin tilted the beam so much that the coin fell off and the beam returned to level, re-engaging the plug until the next customer arrived. These machines were devised to distribute holy water within the temples of Egypt because, prior to their implementation, some worshippers took more water than they'd paid for.

Roughly nineteen hundred years later, the Tom Huston Peanut Company faced a similar problem. The company had experimented with rudimentary vending machines since its earliest days, using a gumball-style design that distributed a handful of peanuts in exchange for a penny. Such machines were a common sight in American cities before Tom's was founded and thus offered little in the way of branding opportunity; they also failed Tom Huston's sanitation test, as the peanuts simply spilled out into the customer's hand, along with salt and oil. Another early example was Huston's "Tom's Talkie," a unique jukebox-type contraption that thanked customers for buying the product. But the greater desire was always to sell a variety of Tom's-branded, factory-wrapped products in more elaborate machines, and at five cents per sale rather than a penny. Vending carried a host of potential revenue streams, allowing sales outside of normal business hours, such as at night, on holidays, or on Sundays during the "blue law" era when stores closed on the seventh day of the week. Vending also created new points of sale, including the outdoors and places where people congregated, such as in public buildings and workplace break rooms that generated steady traffic flow and demand but not enough to justify a full retail store. Many of these places, such as offices or factories, also brought a captive audience with few other food options during the workday. Last, as a form of automation, vending machines cut out a step in the sales process and some of the labor. Instead of acting as an intermediary between manufacturer and retailer, Tom's distributors could sell directly to the customer through the machine, increasing their profit margin and thus making the distributor job itself more appealing.

Tom's was so eager to realize these advantages that it even tried vending without the benefit of a functional machine. For a time, it set up glass jars filled with products in an unsecured location and attached a small metal box, painted red, with "Tom's HONOR SYSTEM" in white letters across the front and a coin slot on top—basically a piggy bank. The coin box itself was somewhat ironically kept under lock and key, but the peanuts and crackers were not. This practice lasted into the 1950s, but the drawbacks are obvious. Like the Egyptians in first-century Alexandria, not everyone was honorable, and some patrons took more than they paid for, if they paid at all.

But in the early 1950s, an outsider named William F. Shepherd approached Tom's to gauge interest in his concepts for a fully secured mechanical vending machine to replace the honor system. Born in 1898 in Carrollton, Alabama, Shepherd later moved to Jackson, Tennessee, where he became vice president of Long-Johnson Printing Company, and then to Memphis to serve as president of Shepherd Printing & Lithographing Company. At the age of fifty, when he might have eased off his business responsibilities or handed things over to a manager, Shepherd instead created an entirely new snack vending enterprise. He set up William F. Shepherd Inc., this time in Cincinnati, and began splitting his time between Ohio and Tennessee.

This was no simple venture. Vending machines were gaining in popularity, especially "gravity-fed" designs in which products were stacked one atop another and chucked to the customer from the bottom. Chewing gum and cigarettes were widely sold this way, but stacking crackers, candy bars, and especially packs of peanuts proved much more difficult because they were not quite uniform in size and shape. Shepherd figured out a way to vend all of them and presented his concept for a gravity-fed machine to Tom's management in 1950. Company leadership was interested enough to pull the lever, but as a test run they ordered only five hundred "P" model Shepherd vending machines to start. These proved to be a hit, and while Tom's ordered more machines, Shepherd got to work patenting his invention.

He filed two patents, one on March 27, 1951, and another a few weeks later on April 25. "The problem of dispensing non-uniform packages is one which has troubled vending machine designers for a number of years," Shepherd wrote in the first patent application, which never mentions the Tom Huston Peanut Company but seems to be written with it in mind. "With merchandise such as packages of peanuts and certain types of candy bars, it is impossible for the packages or manufacturers to make each and every article exactly the same size. For the most part, non-uniform types of packages have been dispensed by vending machines having a series of individual compartments, one for each article, and in these machines it was necessary to provide an indexing mechanism to bring each compartment in turn to a discharge point. Such constructions have been expensive to manufacture, difficult to service, and necessarily quite large."

Stacking the products on top of each other was easy enough, but how to dispense exactly one product per nickel—never two or zero, and never any that weren't paid for—prevent the machine from jamming, *and* make it easy to service, and tamper-proof to boot, presented major challenges.

As Shepherd put it, the "vending machine delivery mechanism in general must be absolutely fool-proof, discharging one package, but only one, each time that a coin is inserted in the machine and the appropriate lever operated. This is of considerable practical importance, not only to protect the customer from wasting his coin, but to protect the machine from the spontaneous wrath of the customer who has pulled at the lever fruitlessly."

Whereas the honor system could appeal to a customer's character and morals, attaching a trace of guilt to any stolen goods, vending machines seemed to have the opposite effect. As Shepherd acknowledged, "A shortcoming of a machine in this respect is instantly taken advantage of, if for no other reason than the sport involved in 'beating' the machine." His design used spacers to account for products of different sizes, and he described as "perhaps the most important feature of the invention" a thin, metal, barbed plate upon which the bottom package of the stack would rest. The plate was formed of stainless steel as little as 0.005 inches thick and used the barbs, which were angled toward the front edge of the machine, to grab and pull the product forward at the crucial moment of purchase.

It worked.

"The dispensing mechanism is not dependent upon a package being rigid nor upon its being of a particular size or outline," Shepherd wrote. "It is primarily intended for such hard-to-handle packages as loosely packaged nuts or candy, however, it can be utilized just as efficiently for uniform packages if desired."

Shepherd's second patent involved the guts of the machine, or what he called the "cabinet structure," which was designed to be both secure and easy to service by a humble Tom's distributor. "Children and even certain adults are often inclined to regard unguarded vending machines as fair game for ravishment by means of any tools at hand short of the kit of the professional burglar," he wrote. "Yet, as a matter of cost, it is not feasible to employ design or material for the machine which is orthodox for establishing boundaries between private property and the criminal world." His machine was thus guarded by a nonbreakable plastic window that was "immune to entry by means of ordinary hand tools such as pocketknives, screw drivers, wires, and the like." The machine was also lightweight enough to be moved with simple tools such as a hand truck, if not so light as to invite being taken for pleasure by a mischievous teen.

As to the second issue, that of service, Shepherd added that "the operators of vending machines are continuously confronted with the problem of the ineptness of the labor force which is engaged in the occupation of servicing vending machines," and while an operator must be financially trustworthy to handle the money taken from them, "high mechanical skill is by no means the inevitable concomitant of common honesty." Shepherd's machines could thus be used "by a man of very little mechanical skill," being operated with a single key that locked a number of movable parts in place.

The Shepherd machines worked as advertised, and they were a smash. Tom's eventually ordered 66,000 of them. Along with a red paint job, the familiar Tom's triangle, and the five-cent price, Shepherd's devices were imprinted with the message "SERVE YOURSELF." The models were given letters, starting with "P" and then "C." A larger, seven-column machine was named "L," and a smaller one with only five columns was named "J." Later models got slightly more complex designations such as "LC," "D-60," "306," "308," and "GF-77." The various iterations grew to offer as many as eight selections, and some later models offered larger columns for chips, but all operated on the same basic principle of levers operating a gravity-fed selection of merchandise. The machines enabled Tom's products to be put in places they had never been before, sold directly to the customer and without ever taking a day off.

As with its peanuts and crackers, Tom's sold the machines to distributors, but since they were pricey, most salesmen opted to finance them. To facilitate credit, the company established a wholly owned subsidiary called Muscogee Sales Corporation, which was officially incorporated by order of Muscogee County Superior Court Judge T. Hicks Fort on March 24, 1951, three days before Shepherd filed his first patent. The subsidiary's role was simply to buy and sell vending machines, usually to distributors, and usually with a loan. Muscogee Sales Corporation provided yet another source of vending-related revenue for the home office.

Just as Tom Huston invented his toasted peanuts amid a wave of new confectionary products, Shepherd's vending machines came about as the wider industry grew. As the technology improved, allowing cold sodas, candy bars, cigarettes, and other items to be sold directly and discreetly, a kind of moral panic arose in the newspapers. For example, the headline of a 1947 Newspaper Enterprise Association story warned, "Coin Vending Machines Called Lure to 'Buying on Impulse.'" "Are you the 'impulse buyer' type?" it asked in the lede. "If not, watch out. There's a move on foot to turn you into one. And it's all going to be done with automatic coin vending machines." The story quoted experts from the U.S. Department of Commerce cautioning that the machines inspired impulse buying by making the purchase so seamless. "Just a coin in the slot, and you've had it," it read.

William F. Shepherd's "gravity-fed" vending machines
were a revelation for Tom's in the early 1950s.

Some $300 million worth of cigarettes were already being sold each year through vending, with the article predicting that books, frozen foods, ice, wood, beer, and sunglasses were or would soon be sold in this new manner. Those forecasts did not work out, but snack foods certainly had a future in vending machines, one that Tom's capitalized on in a major way.

The company's home office was growing as well during the early 1950s. Fueled by rising revenue and profits, Tom's opened a ten-thousand-square-foot infill office complex at headquarters on April 17, 1953, with an address of 900 Eighth Street. The two-story office space provided new room for management, with the old office converted to factory use. A grand opening ceremony for the office space doubled as the celebration of Richards's twenty-fifth anniversary with Tom's, with district sales managers coming in from thirty-two states. As another way to mark the occasion, Tom's commissioned a portrait of Richards by the painter Robert Brackman, whom Richards had posed for on January 18. This was no small gesture, as Brackman was among the top portrait artists of his day. A Russian immigrant who lived in New York City and Connecticut, Brackman painted portraits of John D. Rockefeller Jr., Charles Lindbergh, and U.S. Secretary of State John Foster Dulles during a lengthy career. His work hung in the Metropolitan Museum of Art in New York, the Brooklyn Museum, and the High Museum of Art in Atlanta, among other places. He claimed to paint just four portraits a year.

Richards wore a brown-on-brown suede vest to his sitting and was reported to look "a little sheepish but all in all a bit pleased" as Brackman brushed and talked away on a Sunday afternoon. "Bob Brackman is a dynamic man with a head jammed with ideas that he expresses as easily in words as he does on canvas," the *Columbus Ledger*'s Latimer Watson gushed, "a stimulating man who has you doing mental gymnastics to keep up with him." Brackman talked almost as much as he painted during the session, speaking on everything from President-elect Dwight D. Eisenhower to the celebrities he'd painted to the craft itself. "An artist's forte is to discover beauty in ordinary things," Brackman said. "An artist sees beauty in things around him, beauty that 100 percent of passersby would never notice. He sees lights and shadows and translates them to the canvas." Hands were the most difficult part of the body to portray, he mused, requiring extra attention and an eye for lighting and shadows. After the office space opened, the portrait, designed to inspire awe at Richards's business acumen and leadership, hung on a wall in the company directors' room. While in town, Brackman also created a portrait of Tom's board member Charlie

Frank Williams for Williams's home, one that, given the location, aimed to show a softer side of the man for his family, in contrast to the business-oriented Richards painting.

Tom's had reason to celebrate. It worked out an exclusive deal for the Shepherd machines, ensuring their benefits would accrue directly to its bottom line. On this point history repeated itself again. Just as Tom Huston faced imitators in the 1920s, William F. Shepherd found himself defending his work against illicit encroachment. In October 1953, Shepherd sued the Brunhoff Manufacturing Company and Herschel Condon Enterprises, Inc., both of Cincinnati, claiming they broke a contractual agreement to manufacture the machines only for him, and thus only for Tom's. Though the "contract" was only a word-of-mouth agreement, Shepherd sought $1 million in damages, saying the firms sold machines elsewhere against his wishes. The breach of exclusivity caused Tom's to cancel a contract with Shepherd, according to the suit, leading to the bulk of his damages.

Tragically, Shepherd died of a heart attack the following July at the age of fifty-five. He was buried in Memphis's Memorial Park cemetery and eulogized as a "genial, kindly man" whose friends called him "Shepp." The whirlwind turn of events between the lawsuit and Shepherd's untimely death did not seem to have much impact on his firm's relationship with Tom's. The Shepherd machines remained part of the Tom's lineup for two more decades, a partnership that worked out extraordinarily well for both parties. Total annual sales at Tom's doubled from 1950 to 1955, and the company continued growing at an annual rate of 14 percent afterward.

Owing to this quick growth, just three years after the infill office space opened, management took on another big construction project, contracting once again with Williams Construction for a dramatic factory upgrade—emphasis on the "up." A set of fourteen peanut silos were commissioned in 1956, with each silo 30 feet in diameter, and with the project reaching a total height of 135 feet, making it one of the tallest structures in Columbus. The $300,000 project freed up the former, floor-heavy peanut storage area for other use while creating room for thirty million vertically stacked pounds of peanuts. Billed as the largest plant expansion in the company's history, the silos were built in just one week between July 6 and July 12, 1956, by a team of 240 sweating workers pouring concrete twenty-four hours a day. The concrete was laid into a "slip-form" mold that stood four feet tall and was gradually raised upward as the material hardened, with the walls growing about ten inches in height every hour. In total, eleven thousand tons of concrete, along with five hundred tons of steel rods, were used to build the

Vending made Tom's a national player in the snack food scene. Here, Georgia Senator Herman Talmadge (D-GA), a member of the Senate Agriculture Committee, accepts a bag of peanuts from Tom's representative J. L. Bumpas Jr. on February 8, 1957, as part of National Peanut Week. With them is Delta Air Lines stewardess Mary Adelia Morley. Photo taken at Atlanta Municipal Airport.

seven-inch-thick walls. Peanuts arriving from country farms were hauled up via conveyor belt, loaded into the silos from the top, and then shipped elsewhere in the factory by a second conveyor belt system located at ground level. It was a big deal in Columbus, with a local newspaper headline blaring "Presto! Goober Silos Change City's Skyline," and a symbolic triumph for the lowly Georgia peanut, which would soon surpass the state's cotton crop in market value. By the late 1950s, the Tom's plant covered three city blocks, with more than 1,600 employees on-site—and mercifully for them, most of the factory was now air-conditioned. The silos project marked another collaboration between Tom's and Charlie Frank Williams, who remained a member of the company's board, raising more than one conflict-of-interest question. Internally, the silo build was managed by a thirty-two-year-old Auburn graduate and World War II veteran named Lee Grose, who would join the board himself in 1965.

The fourteen-story peanut silos went up in just one week in July 1956, becoming one of the tallest structures in Columbus.

The Shepherd vending machines no doubt helped make the giant silos possible, and they proved a godsend long after their creator's death by placing Tom's products in places where they would not otherwise be and making them available at times no one wanted to work, and at the same five-cent price point as a retail store, providing higher profit margins to the distributor. The Shepherd company continued rolling out new models, and Tom's came up with a few innovations of its own—creating, for example, a series of cardboard placards in 1958 that shaded the glass front of the machines from damaging sunlight. But even bigger things were on the horizon. For snack food firms like Tom's, the Shepherd machines and, soon enough, a litany of imitators represented a sea change of improvement from the old honor system. They could reliably secure the product from theft without a human keeping watch, dispense exactly one irregularly shaped peanut bag, candy bar, or cracker stack upon receipt of a nickel, and be serviced easily enough for the average route salesman to stop by perhaps once a week to refill them. Still, they also had limitations. Depending on the model, a Shepherd machine held at most eight products at a time and as few as five—not much of a selection for a company that already boasted about one hundred different items in its catalog. The other issue was that, because the candy and crackers were stacked one atop the other, most items sat facing downward toward the ground, leaving the customer staring at the side of a peanut bag or candy wrapper in a less-than-appealing fashion. Going back to the days of Tom Huston, the company had focused on attractively displaying whatever it was selling, making these sideways stacks less than ideal.

After fifteen years of exclusively using Shepherd machines, Tom's began working with a second partner in 1965: the Conway, Arkansas–based Metal Stamping Company and its owner, James Patrick "Pat" Stoltz. Stoltz was a Pittsburgh native who moved to central Arkansas to set up the regional branch of a firm called Customade Products Corp. Once there, he also established a mannequin manufacturing operation known as American Mannequin. But as president of Metal Stamping, so named because it initially made things like highway signs and license plates, Stoltz developed a new concept for snack vending machines. Like the Shepherd machines, these featured a glass front, but most other aspects of its operation were entirely different. Stoltz utilized a tall, boxy design, with products facing forward toward the customer on a series of metal spirals, known in the industry as spindles, which upon purchase rotated using an electric motor to release one bag of chips, peanuts, and the like into a receptacle that could be accessed by the customer. The Stoltz machines were somewhat more complicated than the Shepherd machines, requiring electricity and everything that entails, and were certainly larger, but they provided two key upgrades. One was that merchandise was presented more attractively to customers, staring them straight in the face from behind glass, just as Huston had envisioned forty years earlier. The second was that the machines provided a much wider selection of products. The first Stoltz design was known as the H-17—"H" for "Huston," and "17" because it offered seventeen selections, or more than twice as many as the largest Shepherd models. The H-17 was also much better for selling potato chips, a product Tom's started giving more attention to in the 1960s. In fact, it was chip division manager Tom Q. Black whom Stoltz first contacted. As it did with Shepherd fifteen years prior, Tom's ordered five hundred machines from Stoltz as a test run, displaying a few at the World's Fair in New York. The machines worked out so well that the company ordered fifteen thousand more H-17s within the next twelve months.

The deal was a success for Stoltz too. He renamed his company "Polyvend" to reflect the expanded vision of his firm and its new moneymaker. Just one year after introducing the H-17, Stoltz created the bellwether H-22, which, as the name suggests, was similar to the H-17 but offered five more selections. The spindles were arranged with four rows of three in the center of the machine for chip, pretzel, and popcorn items, flanked on either side by two columns of five for smaller products like peanuts, sandwich crackers, and candy bars. Everything had to be hole punched to hang from the spindles, and everything sold for the same price. The Stoltz machines took up more space than the Shepherd, though the trade-off in selection was worth the hassle. A Shepherd D-60, for example, stood 67 inches tall, 28 inches wide, and 14 inches deep while offering six selections. The H-22 was 33.75 inches wide and 25 inches deep, stood 1 inch taller, and offered nearly four times as many choices to the customer.

For better or worse, the revolution in vending machines did not capture the imagination of the press for Stoltz/Polyvend or for Tom's. Few newspaper articles document the emergence of these machines in America's rest stops, public parks, and storefronts or detail their romantic origins and the visions that inspired their creators. Yet short of the advent of Tom's Toasted Peanuts, the expansion into vending was the single most important event in the company's entire history. The Stoltz machines in particular developed into an industry standard, a design still used with relatively few modifications some sixty years later. Pat Stoltz and J. W. Feighner, who by the 1960s was president of Tom's, reportedly operated on an exclusive basis

The H-22 vending machine became an industry standard following its introduction in 1965 and was stocked exclusively with Tom's products.

but without ever signing a contract, as the company ordered more than 150,000 Stoltz machines over a twenty-five-year period. "Tom's pioneered the glass-front vending machine," the company later boasted about this innovation. "Thus the entire vending industry is indebted to the Company, for today this concept is copied around the world."

In one more important way, vending changed things at Tom's. The glass "Tom's jar" Huston devised began to fade in light of the new technology. The jars went through a few different iterations in the very early years, but by the 1930s management handed them out to distributors in unlimited amounts at no charge, and they spread accordingly. Any little mom-and-pop store might have between six to ten of the jars, and any decent Tom's route had three-hundred-plus stores. This state of affairs remained until the 1950s, when the number of tiny stores dwindled thanks to the automobile, and the number of glass-front vendors rose thanks to Shepherd. During the 1950s, Tom's management began a new policy of handing out just twelve jars to distributors for free and charging twenty-five cents for each additional jar over that figure. Shipments dropped accordingly, which marked the beginning of the jar's slow march to the antique circuit.

Pioneering the automated snack vending business provided one more big boost for Tom's in addition to the many previously mentioned, which is that the machines were completely proprietary. Company logos marked not just the snacks but the machine itself, and inside each machine Tom's enjoyed a complete monopoly on the merchandise. If an office break room, a motel lobby, an auto shop, or anywhere else featured only one snack machine, as many did, the customer had no choice but to snag a Tom's-branded product.

As annual revenue hit $50 million a year and kept climbing, Feighner saw no end to the potential that vending held for the future. "In the food business, as in all types of business and industry, mechanization-automation will continue to play an increasingly important part," he wrote in *The Columbus Ledger-Enquirer* in January 1969. "A good example of how this will affect the consumer is the vending machine industry which, in many ways, is still in its infancy. While vending machines for candy, peanuts, cigarettes and certain other products are rather common now, the application of the vending idea is practically limitless. In certain parts of Europe, machine vending of many types of food products is becoming quite common. This is a trend we will see more and more of in the United States. Complete machine vending grocery stores are very much a possibility within the next decade."

It's unclear if Feighner really saw Tom's getting involved in a vending machine grocery store, but the column speaks to the promise, even the awe, that the automated machines inspired at the time. The first glass-front, electronic H-17 was still less than four years old. If these devices could make such an impact so quickly, the future possibilities must have seemed limitless. Though Feighner mostly wrote with an optimistic tone, he also saw the potential for change as a warning and made that concern known to the public:

> Probably the most important point is the rapidity with which these new ideas will be coming in the future. Competition in business and industry is such that new ideas and new approaches are an absolute must. A fine machine or piece of equipment which is highly satisfactory today may be obsolete five—or even less—years from now. A food product which is highly acceptable to the consuming public today may well be "off the shelf" a year or two from now. The problem of obsolescence has been difficult in the past, but all indications are that this will be a much more serious problem in the future.

CHAPTER 6

J. W. Feighner and General Mills

When Walter Richards began searching for a successor after leading Tom's for thirty years, he didn't have to look far to find one—he didn't even have to leave his own house. Ready to take over the reins was Richards's son-in-law, James Wilbur "Bill" Feighner, who had been prepping for the gig since the early 1940s. Like Richards and Tom Huston before him, Feighner was not a Columbus native. He was born in Marion, Indiana, on September 17, 1916, and was raised in the Hoosier State as one of four children in a reasonably prominent family (one of his brothers, John R. Feighner, would become majority leader in the Indiana House of Representatives). J. W. Feighner graduated from Purdue University in 1939 with a mechanical engineering degree and worked in Indianapolis for a theater supply company and then for Westinghouse Electric Company. Whereas Richards learned of Columbus through his college roommate, Feighner did so because he met Margaret Richards, daughter of the Tom's president, at the James Whitcomb Riley Hospital for Children in Indianapolis, where she was studying occupational therapy after graduating from Stephens College in Columbia, Missouri.

It's unclear what brought Feighner to the hospital, but meeting Margaret Richards there profoundly impacted his life. The two coupled up quickly and married in Columbus in August 1941, remaining in town afterward. As happened with Walter Richards, war interrupted Feighner's early marriage, as the bombing of Pearl Harbor in December 1941 led him to enlist as a cadet in the Army Air Corps. Feighner served in the Calcutta, India, area and rose to the rank of captain before being discharged from the army in January 1946. After returning to Columbus, he joined the sales department of the Tom Huston Peanut Company, where his father-in-law was president. Feighner began as a salesman, rose to sales manager, and, following the sudden deaths of J. Fred Cleveland and T. C. Kendrick Jr., became a company vice president and board member on January 10, 1951.

The bald and bespectacled Feighner had a lot in common with Walter Richards, especially during his early years in Columbus. Both men enjoyed bass and bream fishing at Lake Huston, both were deacons at First Presbyterian Church, and both enjoyed a stint as Columbus Chamber of Commerce president and lengthy service on the Muscogee County School Board. Feighner ran through several other volunteer gigs as well, again in a similar manner to his father-in-law—leading the Muscogee Red Cross, becoming vice president of the Georgia-Alabama Boy Scout Council, and serving as a director of the local Kiwanis Club, among other roles. Feighner and his family lived at 1803 Park Drive in the prestigious Overlook neighborhood.

Feighner was in many ways a natural successor to Richards, though being married to his daughter certainly raised questions about nepotism and favorable treatment from inside the walls of Gordonido. Either way, when Richards finally gave up the Tom's presidency in October 1958, it was his son-in-law who got the nod as his replacement. Richards turned sixty-seven that year; Feighner had just turned forty-two. It was a big shakeup; Tom's had its first new president in almost thirty years, and six other men were named vice presidents at the same time—John Usher, J. Robert Chambless, Robert L. Edmond, J. W. Stewart, Rupert A. Triplitt, and Sherwood Baxley. Richards, always in motion, was not ready to walk away completely from the Tom Huston Peanut Company, however. He was named chairman of the board and maintained a measure of influence over the company in his retirement years.

While Feighner undoubtedly had much in common with his father-in-law and predecessor, he brought a different, more expansive, broader, and perhaps more ambitious vision to the president's office at 900 Eighth Street.

J. W. "Bill" Feighner.

Feighner himself wrote in 1960 that "it has often been said that a company is the lengthened shadow of a man." The lengthening of Feighner's shadow began slowly at first and then accelerated with a series of big moves that would transform the company within a few short years. The first of those moves came in December 1960, when Tom's bought the assets of Tom Black, Inc., a potato chip company with plants in Knoxville, Tennessee, and Salem, Virginia. Tom Q. Black built a chip empire in the Mid-South beginning in 1938 and had partnered with the Tom Huston Peanut Company since 1946, but the merger formally brought both operations under a single umbrella. Black was also the originator of the "Big Tom's" semitrailer delivery system. Tom Q. Black joined the board of directors, his son Tom B. Black was also given a prominent position, and the conveniently named Tom's chips began to receive greater emphasis in the product line. Black's plant at 1340 West Main Street in Salem spanned 45,000 square feet and employed a hundred people, and the larger Knoxville plant at 2300 Sutherland Avenue boasted 125,000 square feet and two hundred employees. Knoxville was thereafter the Tom's chip division headquarters, while the combined company remained based in Columbus. While Black had manufactured chips exclusively for Tom's since the 1940s, the formal merger still represented a big change in the size and direction of the company.

A second new wrinkle was that Tom's temporarily ventured back into major advertising under Feighner, signing up Cincinnati Reds pitcher Joey Jay for a sponsorship deal hawking Tom's Toasted Peanuts. Jay started and ended his career with the Braves—beginning with the Milwaukee Braves in 1953 and ending with the Atlanta Braves in 1966—but teamed up with Tom's during his time in Ohio, which ran from 1961 to the middle of the 1966 season. "Tom's Toasted Peanuts hit the spot for a quick energy pickup before and after the game," he was quoted as saying in the ads, which featured Jay in a post-pitch stance in his Reds uniform, along with his signature. Whatever the ad's merits, it was not repeated, and Tom's doesn't appear to have sponsored any other players going forward.

The other major event of 1961 was a sad one, as Richards fell into ill health during the year; he was eventually flown to the Mayo Clinic in Rochester, Minnesota, for treatment, and then to the Ochsner Clinic in New Orleans, where he passed away at the age of seventy on July 31. The news was a front-page, above-the-fold story in *The Columbus Enquirer*, which described Richards as "a first citizen and one of the most prominent and beloved men in Columbus." Though he had certainly been wealthy enough to retire, Richards remained active as ever in his last years. At his death he was chairman of the board at Tom's, chairman of the Muscogee County School Board, and a director of the First National Bank and the Gas Light Company of Columbus. Along with Richards's wife and three daughters, Feighner was at Richards's bedside when he died, the only person present who was not a blood relative. Richards was buried at Parkhill Cemetery. A middle school and the administration building at Columbus College/Columbus State University were named for him within the next few years. At some point after his death, Feighner, his wife, and their three children moved in at Gordonido, with Richards's widow Margaret taking over the Feighners' old house at 1803 Park Drive. Feighner was named board chairman and chief executive officer after Richards died, and in the ensuing years he began more aggressively implementing his vision for Tom's.

He had plenty of firepower to do it in the early 1960s. Tom's grew at an annual rate of 14 percent between 1956 and 1962, with a 57 percent surge in profits during the last of those years. As of 1962 the company had more than $3.8 million in cash on hand exceeding all liabilities and $7 million in working capital, and its stock was selling at $200 per share. Though its 1962 revenue of $26 million was well behind Frito-Lay's $97 million, Tom's had actually grown much faster than Frito-Lay within the previous twelve months. Standard business practice held that Feighner should invest some of those big cash holdings to try and grow the company. He wasted little time in doing so. In the summer of 1962 Tom's bought another company, the Macon-based McAfee Candy Company, which was founded in downtown Macon by Charlie McAfee in 1932. By the early 1960s McAfee was located on Riggins Mill Road and had 150 employees making things like toffee, hard candy, and chocolate. Tom's bought the main manufacturing plant; seven warehouses, including one that was refrigerated; and everything else McAfee owned, other than the land under the buildings, in an effort to bolster its own candy line. Three years later Tom's bought the land as well. "We are pleased to have the McAfee plant as part of our Tom's family," Feighner said, with Richards-like brevity. "We look forward to a pleasant relationship with the good folks of Macon." The factory would soon become the largest consumer of sugar in middle Georgia, churning out 500,000 pounds of candy a week.

Tom's executed a ten-for-one stock split in December 1962 to make its sky-high stock price more affordable for would-be investors of modest means and then proceeded to open another new plant in 1963. This one was a little further afield, in Corsicana, Texas, an agribusiness center fifty-five miles south of Dallas. The plant was announced in 1962 and opened toward the end of 1963, serving the company's strong Southwestern contingent and, like the Tennessee and Virginia plants, focusing mainly on chips and popcorn. Located on East Highway 31, the Corsicana facility opened with two days of fanfare, as Tom's executives and local business types dined inside the Navarro Hotel's Cactus Room and took guided tours of the plant. Feighner missed the early festivities when the Tom's company plane blew off the runway before takeoff and got stuck in a muddy ditch, though he made it for the second day of events. In his stead, chip division vice president Tom B. Black spoke, along with plant manager Don Marett. Tom's vice president of sales Rupert Triplitt estimated that chips represented 25 percent of the company's business at the time. The $750,000 plant spanned 45,000 square feet on twenty acres at its opening, making it similar in size to the Salem plant, and began with a workforce of fifty, while expecting to grow quickly to one hundred employees. Big Tom's driver Bobby Robinson hauled the first load out of the factory on day one of operations. Within a few years, the Corsicana plant was processing 350,000 pounds of potatoes a week, good for $115,000 in weekly sales.

With the debut of the Corsicana plant, the company had gone from owning a single factory in 1960 to operating five factories in 1963. The plant's opening also hinted at changes in the product line, or at least changes in which products would be most emphasized, as the Tom Huston Peanut Company now owned three factories dedicated to potato chips and related products against just two focused on peanuts, crackers, and candy, its original lineup. Chips were starting to take the upper hand. In fact, when Tom's began work on its innovative H-17 vending machine in 1964, the explicit goal was to create a device that would accommodate chips, which were not a good fit for the gravity-fed Shepherd designs. When the H-22 premiered, peanuts, crackers, and candy bars were relegated to the outer two columns of its glass front, giving chips, popcorn, and pretzels the prime real estate. The company described it as a "potato chip vending machine." Nonetheless, Feighner saw only positives ahead, saying that vending held "unlimited possibilities for the future." Since Tom's manufactured each and every item in the machines, the firm also broadened its offerings, introducing thirty-two new products in 1965 alone. Tom's was growing like a weed largely on the strength of vending and was starting to get attention far beyond Columbus and the South. By 1963, sales topped $35 million, with 1,385 employees, 424 distributors operating 1,604 routes, and sixty-three "Big Tom's" semitrailers ambling down America's highways. Total sales grew from $23.5 million in 1960 to $43.2 million in 1965, another near doubling in just five years. Earnings per share more than doubled during that time frame as well, likely due to the higher profit margin offered in the vending space. The company slogan in this period was "Goodness is made into Tom's," and the amount of "goodness" seemed to be increasing all the time.

Major firms began to notice what Tom's was up to, especially as its industry-leading vending technology opened up new markets and revenue streams. That meant its days as a locally owned firm were numbered. In February 1966, after a few months of behind-the-scenes talks, Minneapolis-based General Mills announced it was acquiring Tom's through a stock exchange. "Our combined strengths will enable us to move ahead faster than either might do alone," Feighner said of the deal. "Tom Huston has unique skills and capabilities in distribution systems and areas not covered by General Mills. General Mills has one of the largest and most intensive research and product development programs in the food industry and can obviously help to expand our family of Tom's products."

General Mills had tried, mostly without success, to develop its own line of snack products and had already bought the Dallas-based Morton's Potato Chip Company in an effort to crack the market. Tom's was its next attempt.

Tom's stockholders received one share of General Mills stock for each share of Tom's stock they'd held before the sale in a deal valued at $78 million. General Mills president E. W. Rawlings described the Tom's distributor network as a "substantial asset" that would allow his company to reach new markets. "Although Tom Huston products are sold through food stores," said Rawlings, "their greatest volume is through nonfood retail outlets and vending machines. These are new channels of distribution for General Mills." Rawlings and Feighner held a "snack swap" photo in Columbus to celebrate the deal, with Feighner holding a large bag of Tom's chips and Rawlings holding Whistles, a product General Mills had introduced earlier in the decade along with other "shaped snacks" such as Buttons, Bows, Daisies, and Bugles. Four of those five snacks were discontinued shortly thereafter, with only Bugles sticking around. With Tom's, General Mills aimed to fill the void in its product lineup. Snacks aside, vending and distribution were undeniably one of the biggest (if not *the* biggest) factors in attracting General Mills' attention to Tom's. On the back cover of General Mills' 1967 annual report was a full-sized photo of a Tom's distributor refilling an H-17. In Columbus, the news generated huge buzz and more than a little controversy, with locals less than thrilled about having their Southern snack giant swallowed up by a Northern firm. The Tom's board approved the deal by a vote of nine to one; it's unknown who cast the dissenting vote. In Minneapolis the board's vote was unanimous.

Feighner was named a director and executive vice president at General Mills, and Rawlings, a retired four-star Air Force general, became chairman of the Tom's board. Tom's continued to operate with a high degree of autonomy after the acquisition, making most of its decisions locally in Columbus, though there was no denying it gave up a lot in the deal. It became a wholly owned subsidiary of General Mills and one part of a giant portfolio for the conglomerate, which boasted revenue of over $550 million a year. Tom's was now playing in the big leagues of American business, with everything that entailed. But initial results were positive, and in December 1966 Tom's announced it was building a 600-foot-long, 95,000-square-foot cracker production facility on the east side of Tenth Avenue in Columbus, with an opening scheduled for the fall of 1967. Expansion remained the order of the day.

One interesting aspect of the sale is that it triggered a Federal Trade Commission (FTC) investigation over antitrust concerns. General Mills, already a corporate giant, was expanding through acquisitions in the 1960s, and the FTC at the time was an aggressive enforcer of Gilded Age monopoly-busting legislation like the Sherman Antitrust Act of 1890 and the Clayton Antitrust Act of 1914. In 1969, General Mills agreed to a consent order restricting, for a period of ten years, its ability to buy other businesses in certain product lines, mostly in the grocery field, without prior approval of the FTC. Such agreements were common in the era, as the FTC focused on the structure of businesses to ensure they could not exert too much influence over any given market segment. For another example, when Frito-Lay merged with Pepsi-Cola to form PepsiCo in 1965, the FTC came down hard with an investigation, followed by a series of restrictions on the combined company. Pepsi/Frito was told it could not advertise its snack and drink products together, and that it could not acquire any other snack or soft drink maker for ten years. Frito was even ordered to sell ten of its twenty-eight plants—representing 31 percent of the company's total sales production—over a four-year transition period. Most of these suddenly independent chip plants simply went out of business at the end of the term. Compared to that, General Mills and Tom's got off easy.

Back in Columbus, change was afoot, and Tom's began to lose any resemblance to the company Huston founded in 1925. Certainly, being acquired by a conglomerate from the Upper Midwest was different from being locally owned or controlled by the Trust Company of Georgia. But the mid-sixties also saw, after a period of forty years, the end of the five-cent price point for most Tom's products. Tom's Toasted Peanuts had kept that same sticker price for four decades—even keeping the price embedded in its logo—before finally succumbing to the realities of inflation and transitioning to a ten-cent price point in 1965. In some cases, Tom's switched to a similar branding reading "10 cents," but it gradually moved away from the blue "shield" portion of its logo, leaving only a sharp red triangle with "Tom's" in diagonal white script. On the personnel side, the last year-one Tom's employee, candy department superintendent Clarence Murphy, retired in 1969 after a forty-five-year tenure. His replacement, Doyle Mauldin, had been with the company "only" thirty-nine years. In 1970 Walter Richards's widow, the former Margaret Gordon, died at the age of seventy-four. Two years after that, Huston himself passed away at age eighty-two, and his longtime friend, company attorney J. Madden Hatcher, died in 1975, leaving only Huston's widow, Minnie Huston, as a living link to the company's founding.

For most employees, these high-level events were noteworthy but hardly defining moments in their lives. They knew the company was growing and that raises were a regular feature of life at the factory. Tom's was a corporate citizen of Columbus, and pretty much everyone in town knew someone who worked there. It was a coveted employer too, known for paying relatively high wages despite its nonunion status and for its "family" atmosphere, often in the literal sense. If someone had a family member already working there, a job could sometimes be had without even filling out an application, though the process was much harder for people without such a connection. Often, several relatives and even generations of the same family wound up working at Tom's, to the point that the company took care to place relatives in different departments. Some of this may have been done to avert accusations of nepotism and similar workplace conflicts, but another consideration was preventing a family reunion, marriage, vacation, or funeral from placing too great a strain on any single department.

Tom's actively cultivated the "family" atmosphere, for better or worse, through a series of after-hours and weekend events that brought people together in informal settings. The biggest and most noteworthy event was Family Day, held every year at the Harris County lake property. More than three thousand people attended in any given year, downing perhaps 1,700 pounds of Boston butts, eight hundred chickens, 150 gallons of Brunswick stew, and 80 gallons of baked beans. They'd square dance to live music, play bingo, take their children on pony rides, and swim in the property's icy spring-fed pool. Family Day always got a write-up in the company's

This Tom's "transitional" logo was used from the early 1960s until 1975.

in-house publications. Less noteworthy but more frequent were the city-wide, region-wide, and sometimes even national-level tournaments in which the company's softball, basketball, bowling, and golf teams competed. Led by paint shop manager Roy Gresham, the Tom's softball team was one of the best in the Southeast, traveling to regional tournaments and sometimes playing teams from as far away as New York. Twice the Tom's softball team won the Southeastern regional tournament and competed in the world championships in Parma, Ohio. The company organized and hosted the first-ever Chattahoochee Valley slow pitch softball tournament in Columbus in 1970. Tom's also sent teams to the Women's International Bowling Congress Queens Tournament in Memphis, a massive contest that included teams from forty-six states and Canada. Goldie Darby, one of Georgia's best-known female bowlers at the time, led the Tom's team during that era.

Tom's launched a second in-house publication in 1961 called the *Family Weekly* that, as the name suggests, was dedicated to covering the "family" side of the company and was edited for years by an employee named Lillian Cox, whose husband and father also worked at Tom's. The *Toaster* continued with a more straightforward focus on business affairs and sales techniques, with *Family Weekly* taking over most of the jokes, birth and death announcements, vacations, and other doings of the employees, along with publishing old photos and other lighthearted fare. Whether or not a company can or should truly approximate a family will always be up for debate, but during this period the average length of service in any given department was often seventeen years or more, long enough for folks to feel like they really were stuck together in the way of relatives. People would often start working at Tom's while in or right after high school and receive a twenty-year service pin before their fortieth birthday. The children of employees got to know the plant and each other at various summer camps, with buses taking them from the factory up to the Harris County lake and back each day.

Entering the 1970s, Tom's reached what would prove to be its peak in terms of sales, size, and influence, fueled by an ever-expanding number of H-22s in America's break rooms, public parks, hotels, schools, tire shops, fire stations, and pretty much everywhere else somebody might want a snack. The company brought in $72 million in the first year of the decade, nearly triple its 1962 revenues, and over the same time frame it grew from 1,500 to 2,200 sales routes. Feighner played an active and sometimes even controversial role in expanding the territory. He was a member of the Muscogee County School Board in the early 1970s, and he leaned on that background to lobby for vending machines in schools on behalf of the National Confectioners Association and the National Candy Wholesalers Association. Debates about whether the machines should be allowed in schools, with their captive audience of thousands of children and adolescents, emerged soon after the advent of vending machines and have never really stopped. Related arguments revolve around what sorts of products should be allowed, what hours the machines can be turned on, how much should be charged, and, of course, who gets the profits.

Feighner testified before Congress in September 1972 as President Richard Nixon prepared to sign a bill that would allow snack and drink machines in the nation's public schools. Feighner argued for allowing the machines to be operational during the lunch hour. Among his points was that such decisions are "a state and local matter" rather than a federal one, and that snacks were among the least of the sins in which a child could indulge. "Of the various temptations offered today to children, what offers more joy and is less harmful than candy?" he told the Senate Agriculture Committee. "Must the children leave school to acquire harmless confections as they must do to obtain other items readily recognized as being harmful? When confections are sold in the school, then the school retains control. Banning candy sales in schools solves nothing; it merely throws the matter out on the street." The street, it went without saying, offered vices much more dangerous than a Tom's Full Dinner bar.

Virginia H. Ball, a school food service program director from St. Paul, Minnesota, countered by telling the senators that "three candy bars for lunch will not provide one-third to one-half of the nutrients required by the growing child," while also warning against "improper choices." Feighner won the day, and the bill was amended to permit the sale of "competitive foods" in high schools so long as the proceeds went to a local school food service program. For what it's worth, labor unions joined with big business in this case, as the International Brotherhood of Teamsters said school vending machines would create new jobs for its workers. Supposedly the machines also helped keep kids on campus, though, as Feighner argued, state and local governments could still ban vending machines from schools, despite his success in Washington.

Tom's opened one more plant during this period, this one in Fresno, California. There were roughly thirty California distributors driving the Golden State roads, along with a handful in other Western states like Nevada, Oregon, and Washington, but Tom's wanted more. Beginning in 1970, the company leased a twenty-thousand-square-foot plant at 1636 South Second

Street in Fresno, later opening an entirely new plant spanning fifty thousand square feet at 2839 South Cherry Avenue in March 1974. The Fresno facility was a relatively small plant that doubled as a distribution center for products shipped across the country from Columbus and Macon. The Fresno operation started with just twenty employees led by Arthur F. Knight, a Columbus native who moved to California after leading the Salem, Virginia, operation for a few years. Within twelve months of the first Fresno plant opening, Tom's Far West sales had grown by 25 percent, and the plant was up to thirty-five employees and was looking to add a night shift. Knight saw only good things ahead, describing the future of Tom's as "a stairwell going up into infinity." Having a foothold, even a relatively small one, in the Pacific time zone was a big deal to a company from Columbus, Georgia, and Tom's began painting a map of the United States on the doors of its delivery trucks, along with the words "Coast to Coast." The company eventually had a presence in all fifty states, including Hawaii and Alaska, as well as in some overseas territories like Puerto Rico and Guam.

With the opening of the Fresno plant in 1970, Tom's had grown to six plants in three time zones, after having just one facility under its ownership in 1960. What's more, four of the six plants manufactured potato chips, popcorn, and "extruded" corn-based products, with only the Columbus and Macon plants handling the balance of production of peanuts, candy, and sandwich crackers, the old staples Tom's had been known for during its first three decades. Part of the reason was that bags of chips, consisting mostly of air, are more difficult to ship long distances and thus require closer distribution points than peanuts and candy, which can traverse the country in train cars and truck trailers; however, the reality was that Tom's was actively marketing itself as a much broader type of snack food company by the 1970s. Reflecting this shift in strategy, in August 1970 the board voted to change the firm's name from the Tom Huston Peanut Company to Tom's Foods, putting a formal stamp on the broader-is-better theme.

Breadth of operations became the calling card of Tom's marketing department. Tom's Toasted Peanuts, lightning in a bottle for Tom Huston and the gravitational "papa product" under Walter Richards, was now an important but by no means central part of the lineup. For example, a 1973 distributor's manual described the Tom's product lineup as one of the industry's "best and most complete" and said the Columbus plant "produces a line of candy items, pastry items, sandwiches, and a line of packaged nuts." A mid-seventies sales brochure boasted that Tom's offered "the greatest variety of snacks" from one source and "the broadest selection in the country."

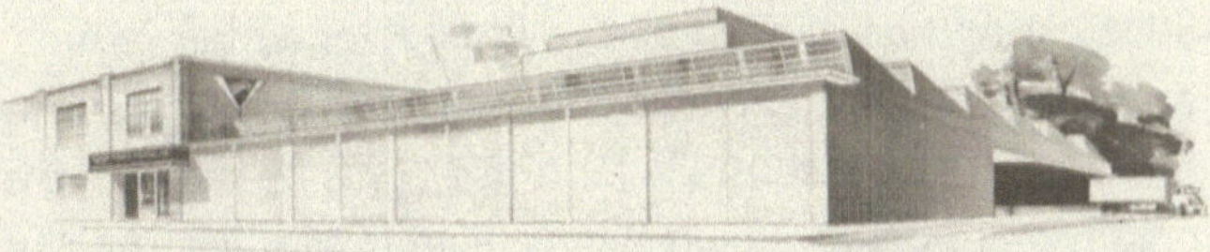

KNOXVILLE, TENNESSEE

The Knoxville, Tennessee Tom's plant is the headquarter plant of the Chip Division. This plant produces a line of potato chips, both plain and seasoned, corn chips, popcorn, corn cheese, Bugles, and other snack items.

CORSICANA, TEXAS

The Corsicana, Texas plant produces potato chips, both plain and seasoned, corn chips, popcorn, corn cheese, and other snack items.

FRESNO, CALIFORNIA

The Fresno, California plant produces potato chips, both plain and seasoned, corn chips, popcorn, corn cheese, and other snack items.

SALEM, VIRGINIA

The Salem, Virginia plant produces potato chips, both plain and seasoned, corn chips, popcorn, corn cheese, and other snack items.

MACON, GEORGIA

The Macon, Georgia Tom's plant produces chocolate products, coconut and hard candies, nut rolls, jellies, and panned items. These products are supplied to all Tom's Distributors.

Tom's grew from one manufacturing plant to six between 1960 and 1970 under Feighner's expansionist leadership. The non-Columbus factories are shown in this image from a 1973 distributor's manual.

By 1976 the product lineup included the red, white, and yellow Coconut Slice candy bar, as well as the Park Avenue bar, which consisted of peanuts, caramel, nougat, and chocolate and bore a striking resemblance to a Snickers. Tom's also made Lemon Drops; fig bars; an oval-shaped oatmeal cream pie; Boston Baked Beans peanut candies; the My Buddy bar, which resembled a Baby Ruth; the Peanut Roll, which looked like a Payday; Super Bubble gum; Slim Jim beef snacks; Penrose sausages; a hard sour candy line known as Pucker Pellets; a pair of suckers called Ding Bat and Sweet Thing; a cracker line with names like Eat-A-Snax, Chok Snax, and Sweeties; and vanilla wafers, animal cookies, and more than two hundred other items churned out by the hundreds of thousands each week. New products were tested out weekly. However, Tom's Toasted Peanuts remained the company's top-selling product despite all the internal competition.

Old-timers might have resented the shift in emphasis away from South Georgia peanuts, but it was hard to quarrel with success. By 1973 total sales, fueled in part by the move to a ten-cent price point, had topped $100 million a year, up from $2 million in 1940, $10 million in 1950, and $23.5 million in 1960. The Columbus plant alone spanned seven and a half city blocks, with three shifts of workers keeping it running at all hours. Supervisors rode bicycles inside and between the buildings, such was the size of the plant. Columbus- and Macon-based manufacturing remained effectively separate from the Knoxville-headquartered chip division, with internal documents differentiating between "Columbus-Macon merchandise" and "chip division" products. Vending machines from across the country were shipped to Columbus for repair, painting, and refurbishing. Outside of the factory, there were more than five hundred distributors operating 2,200 truck routes, all of them pushing Tom's products almost exclusively.

Feighner and other company leaders knew that success wasn't guaranteed tomorrow just because a series of factories or big trucks ran today. The 1973 distributor's manual included warnings about the future: "Everything good starts at the top . . . and everything bad starts at the top." The customer was "the Supreme Court" of business, passing the ultimate judgment. "None of us like change," it read. "Change will continue because our system, the corporate system, is built on change." "You cannot use yesterday's methods in today's business . . . and be in business tomorrow." And finally: "When you quit growing . . . you start slipping."

Tom's was definitely growing, and Feighner was a rather aggressive agent of change right through the mid-1970s. In 1975 Tom's switched up its logo again, replacing the sharp-edged "transitional" triangle with a rounded

The Columbus plant spanned seven and a half city blocks by the early 1970s.

version that had a softer edge both in the outer shape and in the script, which was regraded from a diagonal to a horizontal stance. In a nod to the past, the original product, Tom's Toasted Peanuts, retained the older logo for a few more years while the rest of the lineup got the newer one, though it too followed suit eventually. Elsewhere, Tom's faced many of the same pains as other large corporations of the era, often of the political variety. The five-cent price point lasted from 1925 until 1965, but the ten-cent price point that replaced it stood for less than a decade. By 1974 the company was already looking to go from ten cents to fifteen cents while fighting inflation headaches. President Nixon's price controls were imposed on Tom's but not on the companies that supplied it with raw materials, meaning its internal costs rose even while it was forbidden in some cases from recouping them. Only two products, stick candy and suckers, were still sold for a penny by the mid-seventies, and they were very much an endangered species. One way Tom's responded was by reducing the size of products, sometimes by as much as 20 percent. But even that change wasn't easy. Tom's had to ask the President's Price Commission for approval to remove three peanuts from each bag of Tom's Toasted Peanuts. The panel said yes, but that didn't necessarily mean Tom's could alter the size of any other product. In 1978, with both Nixon and price controls gone, the price of most items was bumped up again, from fifteen cents to twenty cents, as inflation and the oil crisis raged in tandem.

During the 1976 presidential election, peanuts got quite a popularity boost from the candidacy of "peanut farmer" Jimmy Carter, who hailed from Plains, Georgia, just fifty miles southeast of Columbus. Some even called it "peanut-hysteria." Was Carter involved with the peanut empire next door? In a word: no. Carter was more of a peanut broker than a farmer, dealing in peanut seeds and shelling peanuts grown by others for a number of large food firms. Tom's, as the brainchild of peanut sheller inventor Tom Huston, was the only major snack food company to shell its own peanuts and thus did not contract with Carter. Tom's did interact with him in a few smaller ways, however. The size of peanut crop yields exploded in the 1970s thanks to the introduction of a high-yield breed of peanuts called Florunner, which was developed by the University of Florida's Allen Norden. Florunner quickly replaced the Spanish peanut as the main crop from which Tom's made its foods, and as such the company reworked its peanut operations with an all-new "computerized" peanut plant in 1976. During the transition process, Tom's peanut purchasing and shelling manager Ben Smith borrowed some peanut-shelling grates from Billy Carter, Jimmy's famously troubled younger brother. Once things got up and running, Smith returned the grates. Tom's also held the contract for peanuts that Georgia congressmen gave to visitors in Washington on behalf of the Georgia Peanut Commission, though the peanuts did not carry Tom's branding. Somewhat more noteworthy is that during Jimmy Carter's presidency, Tom's had the vending contract for the White House. There were two H-22 machines in the White House basement, another one in the executive wing, and several H-22s serving the executive police. Tom's Baltimore-Washington distributor Ron Erickson serviced the White House three times a week. What's more, two over-the-counter locations sold Tom's products inside the U.S. Capitol building. Jimmy Carter does not appear to have been involved with

Tom's logo from 1975 through 2005.

putting Tom's in the White House; its presence there during his administration stands testament to the company's wide reach in that era rather than to any special relationship it enjoyed with the thirty-ninth president.

Carter did have a close relationship with another Columbus company. He unofficially launched his presidential campaign at the home of John B. Amos, founder of the Aflac insurance company. Amos began his rise by selling stock door to door in Columbus in 1956, and by the 1970s he had built a major firm operating both in the United States and all the way across the Pacific Ocean in Japan. Yet another Columbus man of a speculating disposition, Amos helped diversify the local economy, moving it further away from its reliance on textiles and Fort Benning, and in 1975 Aflac completed an eighteen-story tower on Wynnton Road that easily eclipsed the peanut silos in height. Elsewhere, the City of Columbus formally merged with Muscogee County in 1971 and built its own downtown tower in 1973, which, at 235 feet in height, also outshot the silos in the city's airspace. A new era of service-based industry was beginning to take hold in Columbus as well as across the United States, making its mark on the city's economy and its architecture.

Tom's in the late 1970s tried to address the sticky issue of race relations in a more open, nominally equal, and outward-facing manner than it had during its first fifty years. The company employed Black workers in its early days, but prior to the civil rights era, jobs were usually segregated by both race and sex, with African Americans and women typically given less prominent positions. In the 1970s, Tom's began showering much more attention on Black and women employees in its in-house publications—for example, by celebrating the retirements of both Black and white women in front-page features in *Family Weekly*. After Phil Badcock, a native of Seaton, England, who once taught at Baker High School in Columbus, was named vice president of personnel in January 1978, equality seemed to get a greater focus. The very next week following his promotion, *Family Weekly* featured the retirement of Mary Booth, a Black woman who had worked in the Tom's shelling department for twenty-four years. The March 10 issue was led by news of the promotion of Jimmy Fudge, a Black man who had been named supervisor in the shipping department. Badcock wrote the announcement. A November issue about Family Day included lots of photos of Black attendees enjoying themselves among the clowns, pony rides, and barbecue grills and competing in the dance contest set to the KC and the Sunshine Band hit "(Shake, Shake, Shake) Shake Your Booty."

The July 27, 1979, issue of *Family Weekly* made the company's new focus on equality explicit. The cover read "EQUAL OPPORTUNITY EMPLOYER" and featured drawings of men and women of various races. Below was a prominent note explaining that Tom's would hire and assign employees only on the basis of their qualifications and without considering their race, creed, color, age, sex, religion, or national origin. The company, it also said, would work to employ and advance military veterans and the physically handicapped. "We do have an Affirmative Action Program in effect," the note concluded, "Equal Opportunity is, of course, the responsibility of all employees, and I know I can count on you to do your part."

It's unclear to what extent this policy made a difference in the home office, though the fact that the company was now making public overtures toward equality and equal opportunity is notable. Tom's made advances on the distribution side as well. Earlier in the 1970s, it made national news by signing up Reuben J. Patton as a distributor in the Harlem neighborhood of Manhattan. Patton, according to wire service stories, was "New York City's first black distributor of a national brand product," and he headed a sizable operation, with 8 trucks serving 450 stores in all 5 New York City boroughs and in 3 suburban counties. The Woolworth store on Fifth Avenue in Manhattan even announced in 1970 that it was adding Tom's products specifically because it had a Black distributor, with Feighner and Patton posing for a ribbon-cutting photo. "Meaningful and viable black entrepreneur endeavors will provide the sound economic base so necessary for blacks today—and such economic foundations come only from ownership," Patton said. Tom's, in turn, vowed to "make available distributorships for qualified blacks across the country." In practice, there was a limit to how far these notions of equality traveled, as the overwhelming majority of Tom's distributors remained white, and the company board consisted entirely of white men. Still, in a society that had only recently ended the scourge of segregation, such overtures and efforts toward progress were noteworthy.

As the 1970s drew to a close, Tom's had indisputably attained status as a major firm, with a presence in America's largest cities and in the literal halls of power in Washington, among several hundred thousand other places. It owned and operated plants in three time zones and continued to grow through its dominating presence in the vending machine industry while remaining a subsidiary of the General Mills conglomerate, returning $20 million a year in profit to its parent company. Having led the transformation of Tom's from a one-plant operation into a six-plant, nationwide brand, Feighner decided it was time to step down. He left the Tom's presidency in 1979 and retired from the company in 1980. In 1982 Feighner followed in his father-in-law's footsteps once again by running in and winning the election for mayor of Columbus. Interestingly enough, Feighner chose to run as an independent and defeated the Republican and Democratic candidates, both of whom he vastly outraised and outspent. He promised to bring new industry to ease the high local unemployment rate, which reached 9.7 percent in the summer of 1982, and to create an affirmative action program for the city, because Columbus needed "more blacks in positions of authority and responsibility." Leading Tom's, he said, gave him experience on both fronts, as he had chosen plant sites himself and could use nationwide contacts to sell big businesses on Columbus.

Feighner was well known for his work with Tom's and for his volunteer roles, including serving fourteen years on the local school board, and he was boosted on the campaign trail by a knack for remembering names. He could meet someone a single time, even briefly, and then call them by name months or even years later, which is never a bad quality for a politician. He won the mayor's seat in a runoff against Democratic city councilman Charles Rector by just 139 votes, was sworn in with a simple ceremony on the government center plaza, and promised to run a "no frills" administration. Upon taking office, Feighner implemented an affirmative action program that set a goal of sending 5 percent of the Columbus government's federally funded contracts to minority-owned businesses. In 1982 the figure had been less than 1 percent. Despite those good intentions, Feighner was later criticized by the city's personnel officer and by *The Columbus Enquirer*, which said that the affirmative action program was "all but nonexistent" in practice because there was no enforcement mechanism for reaching the 5 percent goal. In any case, Feighner again followed the lead of Richards by stepping down after four years, leaving the mayor's office voluntarily at the beginning of 1987.

By that point Feighner had been away from the Tom's presidency for almost a full decade, having stepped down in 1979, the year he turned sixty-three. Replacing Feighner as president was Mike Tracy, a man who led an incredible journey, from sweeping the floors at a General Mills factory early in his career all the way to leading a major corporation pulling in more than $200 million a year. Soon after taking office, Tracy initiated what he hoped would be a similar transformation for Tom's Foods, which began with the dreams and experiments of Tom Huston, continued through the stable successes of Walter Richards, exploded into the vending machine–based empire of Bill Feighner, and as a final triumph would become a truly national brand conquering the final frontier of America's snack food scene: the grocery aisle.

CHAPTER 7

Sales and Struggles

Top leadership at Tom's stayed in the same family from 1932 until 1979, as first Walter Richards and then his son-in-law, J. W. Feighner, each enjoyed a long stretch as president and board chairman. That five-decade chain was broken in June 1979, as Feighner announced his retirement and Michael Loray "Mike" Tracy ascended to the presidency, though Feighner remained as board chairman for a little longer. It was a paradigm shift at multiple levels that altered the course of the company's future, even if it didn't quite seem so at the time. Feighner explained that General Mills had a mandatory retirement age of sixty-five, and though he was just sixty-three when he relinquished the presidency, he'd reach the magic number by spending two years as chairman of the board before leaving for good.

Tracy was not a member of Feighner's family or, for that matter, the Tom's family, though he did have a few things in common with his predecessors. Like Richards and Feighner, Tracy held an engineering degree and was not originally from Columbus. But his journey to the top job was much more varied and circuitous, reflecting his status as a true outsider to the city and its snack food giant. Tracy was born March 12, 1927, in Ogden, Utah, the sixth of eight children, and was the star of his family from a young age. He left home early, joining the navy at age seventeen and serving as a radioman in the South Pacific toward the end of World War II. After coming back home, he married Eva Barnett, started a family, and began working at a General Mills plant in Ogden. Still a teenager, Tracy unloaded boxcars and swept the floor in a flour mill, then moved to California to work at another General Mills facility in Los Angeles. He spent eight years working a graveyard shift in order to study engineering at Long Beach State College. After graduation he rose quickly through the ranks at the mill, becoming the plant engineer, the milling superintendent, and finally the plant manager. In 1967 Tracy was "kicked upstairs" to General Mills' Minnesota headquarters, where he was named a corporate vice president. His next move, in 1969, was to Raleigh, North Carolina, to serve as president and CEO of GoodMark Foods, a General Mills subsidiary he founded that was best known for its Slim Jim meat snacks. Tom's distributors sold Slim Jims as part of the same corporate structure, and Tracy technically reported to Feighner through the latter's position on the General Mills board, but Tracy was otherwise an unfamiliar face to Tom's when he moved to Columbus and succeeded Feighner on June 1, 1979.

Tracy never forgot his floor-sweeping background, even as the president of a $200 million company. He sipped coffee with maintenance crews in the company cafeteria at nine thirty each morning, chatting or sharing stories about his days in the navy, and was known to stroll the factory and ask after the families of frontline workers, many of whom he knew on a first-name basis. He was a family man at home (the father of six daughters), a musician who played five instruments, a cattle raiser who lived on a Harris County ranch, and a hell-raiser when he needed to be. But from a cold corporate governance standpoint, he represented quite a departure from his predecessors. Richards and Feighner weren't Columbus natives, but they married into prominent local families before joining the company, and both worked for Tom's in lesser roles before becoming president. Neither was the case with Tracy. And though Tom's had been a General Mills subsidiary since 1966, Feighner predated that arrangement by two decades, negotiated the sale himself, and earned a seat on the General Mills board in the process. Thus, "Tom Huston's," as many Columbusites still called it, felt like a locally owned and operated company through the end of the 1970s under Feighner's leadership. In fact, as president of Tom's and executive vice president of specialty foods at General Mills, Feighner answered to himself within the corporate hierarchy. Tracy, on the other hand, was a thirty-two-year General Mills man who had been with the firm his entire career. He moved to Columbus only after being named president of Tom's.

Michael Loray "Mike" Tracy.

Did the maintenance men and factory workers Tracy shared coffee with care about all of this? Maybe. But they had little reason to worry, at least at first. The good times at Tom's rolled right into the 1980s, and as far as anyone knew they would last forever. The company had grown for fifty straight years, with new ideas promising to make it even bigger in the future. People who worked there conducted their lives with the security of employment at a large and stable corporation, and management worked to foster a sense of community.

The in-house *Family Weekly* served as a kind of community bulletin of nonwork things done by people who worked together, speaking to the important life events occurring outside the factory walls. Among them were Easter egg hunts at Lake Richards (with a special notice reading "there will be enough eggs so that all the adults desiring to do so may also participate"), an employee's adoption of a dog named Barney, surgeries at Cobb Memorial Hospital, a steak dinner for the Tom's basketball team at shipping supervisor George Gafford's cabin, a forty-eight-hour seesaw marathon for kids, the sale of a 1976 Buick Electra 225, vice president Lee Grose hitting a hole-in-one at the Columbus Country Club, and lots of births, deaths, and vacations. In 1980, sandwich department employee Larry Shores ran a ten-mile race and came in third, earning a bronze medal; sacking department supervisor Audrey Carter sent Valentine's Day carnations to each of the "ladies" under her watch; and the peanut department got a new nurse named Wynnette Preston. Sometimes even former employees made it into *Family Weekly* in times of need, such as when one-time accounting department worker Darlene Richardson Walker was consoled on the loss of her father. Under Mike Tracy, Tom's created a "Quarter-Century Club" for employees who had been around twenty-five years or longer. Not just an informal group represented by a plaque on the wall or a series of lapel pins, the Quarter-Century Club was a true membership organization with officers and regular meetings, a sort of Kiwanis or Rotary Club for peanutters of a certain vintage. Tracy also established the Golden Goobers program, whereby retired women led more than two thousand schoolchildren on factory tours every year, educating the young visitors while enjoying their company.

In an era well acquainted with electricity but not the internet, much of the communication inside the factory occurred by landline telephone, and employees got occasional phone etiquette reminders in *Family Weekly*. ("Nothing is more disconcerting—and annoying—to a busy worker than the 'guess-who' caller or the idle conversationalist.") The publication also took over for the *Toaster* when it came to jokes, which got plenty of space inside its pages. For instance, "The Memo Interpreter" was a long list of official-sounding phrases followed by less heady translations. "It's in the process," for example, actually meant "It's so wrapped up in red tape that the situation is almost hopeless." "Conference room" was defined as "a place where conversation is substituted for the dreariness of labor and the loneliness of thought," while "See me" or "Let's discuss" really meant "Come down to my office—I'm lonesome." Another humorous feature titled "Grandma's Recipe for Doin' the Family Wash" included directions such as "bild fire in back yard to heet kettle of rain water" and "take white things out of kettle with broom stick then wrench, blew, an' starch," before finishing with "Go put on clean dress, smooth hair with side combs, brew a cup a tee, set an' rest a spell an' count yore blessins.'"

Outside the factory walls, everyone knew it meant something to say you worked at Tom's. Jack Warden learned it firsthand as a young engineering graduate who moved from Tennessee to Columbus in 1980 for his first job out of college. Trying to get settled in, he went to Sears to buy a microwave on credit. Being so young meant he didn't have much credit

"Golden Goobers" led more than two thousand children on tours of the Tom's factory each year during Tracy's presidency. Here, the South Columbus Boys Club preps for a tour on March 3, 1980.

history, and he had to get approval for a higher limit. The woman he spoke to over the phone, who may or may not have been a local, started asking about his circumstances. When she asked where he worked and Warden responded, "Tom's Foods," the questions ended, she raised his credit limit on the spot, and he got his microwave. "If you could get a job at Tom's, that was kind of a badge," Warden recalled years later. "You stuck your chest out when you told people you worked there." The lure of Tom's and its relatively healthy wages drew people in from a fifty-mile radius in rural Georgia and Alabama. Just across the Chattahoochee River in Russell County, Alabama, unemployment topped 20 percent in the early 1980s. Rural folks not only lacked local job opportunities but also often lacked cars, so early each morning as many as ten people would pile into a truck bed, under a camper shell if they were lucky, for a long ride into Columbus to labor at a textile mill or at Tom's. After work, they walked to "Kin-Folk Corner"—Tenth Street and Front Avenue—to get picked up, often by a close neighbor or relative, giving the intersection its name. The alternative to a Columbus commute was usually working on a farm, the type of employment Tom's replaced, and as Pittsview, Alabama, native Raymond Davis put it, "They weren't paying anything for farm work, so a lot of them had to find other jobs." Davis drove to Tom's every day with eight people in his pickup truck. Nettie Battle, another Tom's employee, drove in from Hurtsboro, Alabama, with ten people. Her husband had done it before her, and she took over when he died.

On June 26, 1980, the Tom's workforce gathered in a parking lot next to the peanut silos to celebrate Feighner's retirement, which came a year earlier than expected. He spent only one year as chairman of the board rather than two after Tracy took over as president and was given a retirement ceremony inside the factory grounds. "Bill is retiring after 38 years of service to Tom's," Tracy wrote in a memo to employees. "His leadership over these years has helped shape this company into the successful business we know today and honoring him in this way will be a memorable occasion." After it was over and Feighner headed into politics, Tracy and the corporate powers that be got to work remaking Tom's in the image of General Mills. What would that mean? How would Tom's look different than it had under Feighner?

First off, it would not mean a renewed focus on Tom's Toasted Peanuts. Even at retirement, Feighner said General Mills didn't "know a durn thing about peanuts." Why would it? General Mills was a Northern firm located more than one thousand miles from the peanut belt. The new vision for Tom's also would not mean a greater focus on vending, another area in which General Mills had little experience outside of Tom's itself.

Rather, the natural place for General Mills to look to expand its snack food subsidiary was grocery stores, the company's main stomping grounds since it introduced Gold Medal flour in 1880. In the century that followed, General Mills successfully launched Wheaties cereal, Hamburger Helper packaged meals, Nature Valley granola bars, and Betty Crocker cake mixes, all of them marketed toward women shopping for their families in supermarkets. The future of Tom's, as Tracy envisioned it, was to finally bring the company's snacks into grocery store aisles. The next question was which products to choose. Not all of the two-hundred-plus items Tom's sold in vending machines or gas stations would succeed in supermarkets, nor was it realistic to try and push all of them at once into the fiercely competitive grocery sector. While Tom's Toasted Peanuts were still its best-selling product, peanuts as a whole represented only about 10 percent of the company's business by the 1980s. Sandwich crackers and candy represented another 20 percent, while potato chips, along with their popcorn and pretzel cousins, made up more than 50 percent of its product line. Chips were the big dog, and the chip aisle was where General Mills saw Tom's hunting down Kroger, Winn-Dixie, Piggly Wiggly, and Publix.

In 1981, with considerable fanfare and the investment of a lot of research, development, and marketing dollars, General Mills launched the "Tom's Great American Snacks" line. "For over 55 years, TOM'S has been a big name in snacks," trumpeted newspaper ads. "And now we've put all of our experience into making the freshest, crispiest, lightest potato chips we've ever made. Otherwise we wouldn't call them 'Great American.'" Developed in secret using the code name "P-81" or "Project 1981," the brand launched with tens of thousands of free bag coupons and a money-back guarantee. General Mills aimed to improve the flavor of Tom's chips as well and, according to one former employee, tried to imitate the taste of the Ohio-based Mikesell's brand through trial and error. Once developed, the chips got their own logo resembling a blue-ribbon prize, with "Great American" spelled out in cursive underneath the red Tom's triangle. For a premium look, they were wrapped in "foil type packages" dazzled with stars. "Great Americans don't come along very often," General Mills said in its ads. To sell grocery store owners and managers on the product line, Tom's created a thick, glossy, textured twenty-page brochure listing out General Mills' history with Betty Crocker, Hamburger Helper, and Wheaties and bragging that Tom's Great American potato chips would be bigger than any of them. "The General Mills Family Of Fine Foods Invites Your Family Of Fine Food Stores To Join In THE GREATEST FOOD INTRODUCTION In General Mills' History," the brochure read on page one. A centerfold described it as "the largest, most beautifully-packaged chip and snack line in America." If Tom Huston created Tom's, Walter Richards grew it, and Bill Feighner made it a force in vending machines, the Great American line would be Mike Tracy's brick in the wall. The flavors and packaging were paired as expected, with plain chips in a yellow bag rippled in blue, barbecue in burgundy, sour cream and onion in green, plain tortilla chips in white, Bugles in red, pork rinds in a clear bag, popcorn in silver, and puffed "corn cheese" in orange. Other products in the Great American line included hot fries, cheddar fries, corn chips, caramel corn, and twist pretzels.

None of these products would be made in Columbus, but the reality was that Tom's had arguably been chip-first since the 1960 merger with Tom Black, Inc., and certainly since the 1964 introduction of the H-17 "potato chip vending machine."

Getting a toehold in grocery stores would not be easy, which General Mills seemed to recognize based on the muscle it put behind Tom's Great American. Frito-Lay had come to dominate the chip aisle, and half the battle would be getting Tom's on the shelf in the first place. If successful, Great American faced the "Supreme Court"—consumers. In its brochure, General Mills tried to anticipate the questions a grocery store manager might ask, starting with the most obvious: "Why do we need another snack line?" It claimed that adding a new line in and of itself could hike sales 15 percent, that snack growth more than doubled total grocery store growth between 1970 and 1980, and that "growth should continue, as snacks play an even bigger part in the American lifestyle." Snacks also enjoyed a much higher turnover rate than condiments or canned goods and boasted a profit margin General Mills claimed was up to ten times the average of other foods. But why should grocery store managers stock Tom's Great American specifically? Here, the brochure admitted the lineup was being launched only in the Southeast, saying the region lagged behind the rest of the nation in snack and chip consumption. Tom's used the Tampa/St. Petersburg area as a test market ahead of the wider launch, and according to the brochure, "studies indicate an opportunity for an *immediate* snack market increase in this area of up to 25%! The Southeast lacks strong competition." The brochure didn't mention it, but the biggest regional competitors were Birmingham's Golden Flake, which was particularly strong in its home state thanks to ads featuring Crimson Tide football coach Bear Bryant, and Charlotte's Lance Inc., which was known for its cracker line but struggled with chips. Herman Lay, the founder of Lay's potato chips, was an Atlanta guy, and Frito-Lay was based in Texas, but it was a national rather than a regional brand.

General Mills thought it could break in with a good product line, strong service, free coupons, "gondolas" filled with chips provided at no cost to the store, and, in a first for Tom's, major television advertising. It drew up two thirty-second spots, both featuring slices of Americana such as children at a circus, marching bands on parade, a little girl and her grandfather playing checkers, a young couple strumming a banjo by a lake, little league baseball, clowns, and fireworks, all accompanied by a cheesy jingle:

There's a little Great American in everybody
Reaching for the good times, reaching for the sun
There's a Tom's Great American, to make the good times better,
For you—and me—and everyone
Tom's Great American, fresh and light and crispy
Come on along, come on and celebrate
Tom's Great American Potato Chips, the taste that makes
the good times great.

The spots ran for forty-two weeks in 1981 and 1982, hitting individual televisions more than 60 million times, or 107 times per household, according to the brochure. Southerners tuning in to *Archie Bunker's Place*, *M*A*S*H*, *Little House on the Prairie*, *The Phil Donahue Show*, *The Young and the Restless*, and *Password* were all treated to Tom's Great American commercials, provided they didn't run to the bathroom or kitchen at the start of each ad break. "Here comes another fine product, from the folks who have generations of experience at understanding and meeting the food needs of the American family," beamed the brochure. "With quality products, priced right, packaged beautifully. So don't miss out—on the excitement *or* on the profits. Join with us. Together we are going to make it happen."

No doubt some of this was fluffy sales speak, but enough effort was put in behind the scenes to make it clear General Mills was serious and expected success. Tom's completely rebuilt its Knoxville plant beginning in March 1980, developing a new 100,000-square-foot facility at the Byington-Solway Industrial Park in suburban Karns. It also built an entirely new chip factory in Perry, Florida, about fifty miles southeast of Tallahassee. Spanning 110,000 square feet and employing two hundred, the Perry plant opened in the fall of 1980 on Duval Street between Jefferson Street and U.S. 19. In yet another 1980 move, Tom's acquired Circus Time, a potato chip company in Portland, Maine, to facilitate chip production in New England, perhaps signaling future expansion plans. According to the sales brochure, the company spent $12.5 million on the three plants, which brought Tom's up to eight factories spanning three of the nation's four corners. That was supposed to be just the beginning. In speeches, Tracy told employees of a vision to keep expanding, with a new chip plant opening every two or three years as the Great American brand took off and became a staple of the supermarket aisle. Frito-Lay was going to have a run for its money.

But it did not turn out that way. General Mills learned fast that Frito-Lay wasn't going to lie down and let another firm bite its shelf space; instead,

Frito-Lay upped the ante with its own marketing promotions and challenged Tom's to keep up the fight. And whatever goodwill the Great American brand may have bought with its star-studded foil packages, its free coupons, and its sixty million television impressions, it did not seem to make much of an impression with consumers. In Midwestern author Dirk Burhans's history of the potato chip industry, *Crunch!*, the Great American potato chip launch isn't mentioned. Neither is Tom's as a whole, except as an aside in a passage about the relative lack of regional competition faced by Lance.

Not only was Tom's grocery store offensive a disappointment, it soon found itself losing ground on defense in areas that were supposed to be its core strengths. Disturbing Polaroid pictures started showing up at headquarters. Taken by field sales staff, the photos depicted Tom's vending machines, red triangle logos plastered on three sides, with bags of Frito-Lay chips hanging from the spindles. No doubt the work of a rogue route person, news of the offense would filter down through Tom's headquarters staff until someone called the distributor to remind them that everyone at Tom's is on the same team, and maybe mentioning too that corporate Tom's provided financing for the machine and for the distributor's truck. In other cases, a Big Tom's driver might make a delivery to Jackson, Mississippi, or Little Rock, Arkansas, and report back that they found a warehouse full of Nabisco product. With only twenty-two spindles available on each of the 150,000 Tom's vending machines, the loss of a single spindle to a competitor represented an existential crisis. What's more, because distributors were independent contractors, headquarters was severely limited in how far it could go to tamp down the problem.

Tom's began losing ground in vending equipment as well, partly due to circumstances beyond the company's control. Pat Stoltz, whose firm created the H-22, was convicted in 1974 of bribing Illinois Secretary of State Paul Powell in a bid to get the state's license plate manufacturing contract. Stoltz died three years later at age fifty-three, and his nine children began a decades-long fight over control of the company and a $9 million life insurance policy. Amid that struggle, Polyvend and Tom's lost their edge on the competition. When vending machines began featuring multiple price points, dollar bill changers, and auger-based shelving to replace the old spindle system, Tom's was not necessarily ahead of the curve.

It's hard to say why Tom's Great American chips failed to make it in grocery stores, though one reason could be that General Mills couldn't sufficiently answer the first question in its sales brochure, "Why do we need another snack line?" But the issue of Lay's chips or Nabisco Fig Newtons appearing in Tom's vending machines—often at customer request—reflected larger industry trends. In the late 1970s, American Canteen, the nation's largest snack vending firm, switched from private label to national name-brand products, saying that it made smaller profits on the name brands but they boosted sales enough to more than offset the difference. And while the Tom's product lineup had lots of originals like Tom's Toasted Peanuts, the Full Dinner bar, Coconut Slice, Peanut Plank, and the Peanut Butter Log, much of it by that point was simply copycat products of national name brands anyway—the Park Avenue bar looked and tasted like a Snickers, the Salted Nut Roll resembled a Payday, My Buddy bore a striking resemblance to a Baby Ruth. Tom's even tried a York Peppermint Pattie look-alike—until it got a cease-and-desist letter.

It's possible that General Mills anticipated some of the issues with vending, which is why it brought in Mike Tracy and made a go with the Great American chip line. Whether it did or not, by 1983 General Mills had seen enough. It decided to refocus on its core business and offload some of its many subsidiaries, and in April of that year General Mills sold Tom's to a York, England–based candy company called Rowntree Mackintosh, which made Kit Kat bars and other chocolate goodies like Rolo and Aero. The deal was for $215 million in cash, only slightly more than Tom's Foods' $200 million revenues in 1982. "General Mills Chairman H. B. Atwater said that Tom's Foods did not fit the company's growth strategy for consumer food," explained the *Minneapolis Star Tribune*, "which calls for continuing emphasis on the company's established supermarket distribution systems." General Mills brought in $5.3 billion in 1982, making Tom's a pretty small fraction of its portfolio. For Rowntree, which made $1.1 billion that year, Tom's was a bigger deal and was its first foray into the massive U.S. salty snacks business. Rowntree also felt that it was making a safe bet, since Tom's still raked in about $20 million a year in profit. It pledged not to interfere in the basic operations of the business or to push its English products into Tom's machines. "The British are coming to Tom's Foods," the Associated Press wrote when the sale was finalized in August 1983, "the Georgia-based snack manufacturer whose red triangle trademark is as much a part of the South as the peanut that spawned the company."

While not colossal by historic standards, Rowntree's purchase of Tom's proved to be the largest food industry acquisition of 1983, and Rowntree borrowed heavily to finance the deal. Tracy was allowed to stay on as company president, emphasizing that Tom's would continue producing exclusively for its seven hundred distributors and that there was "no need" for them to look elsewhere. "They [Rowntree] are a company that honors tradition. So is Tom's. Our philosophies mesh very well," Tracy said. "We can build on our past, but we can't live in the past. The entire snack business is far more sophisticated now than it has been." It does appear that Rowntree let Tom's operate more or less independently, not least because it was located in a country thousands of miles away in a pre-internet world. After the sale, to showcase its resilience and demonstrate that it remained a corporate power in Columbus, Tom's hosted a big-budget extravaganza dubbed "Homecoming '83" in September of that year. The company invited all distributors and sales staff and their spouses to Columbus for the convention, letting them tour the home office and do some "Tomfoolery." Held at the Columbus Iron Works Convention and Trade Center, the three-day event brought in people from all fifty states, Puerto Rico, and the Bahamas. The visitors filled five hotels and were shuttled to various events, which also included a barbecue at the Harris County lake. What's more, Tom's brought in entertainers and speakers including broadcaster Douglas Edwards (forerunner to Walter Cronkite at CBS News), motivational speaker Herb True, economist Arthur Laffer (who would later win the Presidential Medal of Freedom for popularizing the Laffer Curve concept), "Georgia on My Mind" singer Ray Charles, the Preservation Hall Jazz Band, and the Florida State University marching band. Tom's did not say how much all of this cost, but it would not have been an inexpensive venture.

Tom's expanded its revenues throughout the mid-eighties, but only marginally, and increasingly by using its facilities to make products for outside companies. This practice started with contract packaging for General Mills, Tom's former owner, in the Macon plant, and in 1984 Tom's hired about fifty new employees in Columbus to manufacture things for General Mills at the home office. "This will not be a Tom's product," Tracy explained. Sales of the Tom's brand weren't so hot around this time. By late 1985 Rowntree chairman Ken Dixon admitted its acquisition was "not spectacular" but defended it as a steady business producing lots of cash. Making another go, in 1986 Tom's launched another chip line, the thick, rippled "Country Style" brand, which came in plain, mesquite barbecue (which Tom's claimed was an industry first), zesty ranch, spicy cajun, and au gratin flavors. Country Style was a second shot at supermarkets, but by the end of that year there was no denying Tom's was in trouble. "If you are a Tom's salesperson, I need your help and so do 2,000 Tom's employees," wrote new Tom's president Mike Dillon in the October 1986 *Toaster*. "We just survived the strongest competitive attack in the history of the company within the past three months, but Tom's didn't back away from the increased promotions." The source of the attack wasn't named, but Dillon felt the need to stress that "we need increased unit sales" and to repeat that the 2,000 employees "are depending on your sales increase to give them a full week's work."

No doubt the sales staff was working as hard as ever, but the bottom line did not improve, and high-level churn continued. Dillon had replaced Tracy as Tom's president in May 1986, with Tracy becoming chairman; in January 1987 Tracy left the company for good after just seven years, a vastly shorter tenure than the decades-long runs of Richards and Feighner, and retired at age fifty-nine as part of a "management restructuring." He reportedly handpicked Dillon, then forty-eight, to be his successor, while Rowntree executive Roy Sugden became Tom's chairman. Dillon was born in Detroit and raised in Jacksonville, Florida, and also came to Tom's through General Mills, though much earlier than Tracy, joining Tom's to launch its marketing department in the heyday of 1971. Dillon was behind the logo revamp in 1975 and had high hopes of bringing Tom's back, somehow, to the successes it enjoyed in that decade. "Tom's needs to get more aggressive," Dillon told *The Columbus Ledger*. "We've got to take an active role in assuring that our distributors are getting more volume."

Mike Tracy did not fully retire. He became president and CEO of a conveyor equipment manufacturer called Northstar Industries, though his tenure would be short. Sadly, he developed cancer, succumbing to the disease in April 1989. His last visit to Tom's came three weeks before his death. Tracy left the hospital to attend a ceremony in which the maintenance department, the place where he enjoyed all those coffees with the crew, was renamed in his honor. Tracy was buried in his birthplace of Ogden, Utah, and was remembered in Columbus as "a high-powered executive who never lost his common touch or his interest in the community."

Turmoil continued on both sides of the factory walls after Dillon became president. In the fall of 1986, a man named Dale Nichols took a trip from Washington, D.C., to Columbus, where he remained for the next six months. Nichols was a staffer at the Bakery, Confectionery, and Tobacco Workers Union, and he was there to organize Tom's. There were three other bakery-type facilities in town, Sunshine Biscuits, Dolly Madison, and Colonial Bakery, and all of them were unionized. Nonunion Tom's was the exception. Dolly Madison had gone on strike earlier in the year, which might have brought attention to the discrepancy. In any case, Nichols and his union sought to change things by making six hundred Tom's workers a part of BCTWU Local 435. Management, of course, thought unionization was unneeded, saying the company's long-tenured employees had no trouble speaking their minds. Dillon admitted that communication between management and workers needed to improve, and he took some blame on that front for the union drive, which became one of Columbus's biggest labor organizing efforts ever. But a union, he warned, "thrives on adversity," and he hadn't seen any specific labor problems that a union would address. "If we do our job, we shouldn't have a union," Dillon said. "If we don't, we'll deserve one."

Did Tom's need a union? Paul Massey thought so. He was the BCTWU's local office manager and a former Tom's employee. Massey didn't share any horror stories, but he said Tom's workers needed "layoff and recall rights. They work 30 years and retire at less than $300 a month. At Sunshine Biscuits (which is unionized), you work 30 years and retire at more than $700." A Tom's employee interviewed by *The Columbus Enquirer* agreed. "We need it," he said, while refusing to give his name. "There's a lot of injustice going on here—unfair wages, that kind of stuff. And we don't have anybody on the inside that can get to the bottom of it." But seven other employees who spoke to the newspaper all said they voted against organizing, and in the end the union was soundly defeated by a vote of 357 to 179 on March 25, 1987. "Our job now is to work hard to show we are deserving of this type of support," Dillon said. Nichols, the union rep, was undeterred. "Oh yeah. We'll be back," he said. "Companies make a lot of promises during campaigns like this that they don't keep, and that's when [workers] find out [the union] wasn't as bad as they were told it was." Nichols predicted BCTWU organizers would return to Columbus within eight months to lay the groundwork for another campaign. It doesn't appear that ever happened, and unions generally faced an uphill battle in the Southern city. The unionization effort at Tom's was one of eight consecutive failed union drives in Columbus during the 1980s.

The management restructuring that led to Tracy's ouster did not turn things around financially at Tom's. In April 1987 it laid off thirty-eight people at its Virginia plant, or roughly 25 percent of the workforce there. That summer, Dillon warned again in the *Toaster* that times were changing and Tom's would too. "As you know, the marketplace has been changing over the past five to 10 years. Competition has also been changing," he wrote in the president's letter. "No, Tom's will not be the same old company it was 25 years ago—I don't believe that kind of company could make it in today's market." Yet he also claimed that sales had increased over the previous

Mike Dillon.

eleven months, trying to reassure any nervous employees that things would be okay. If this assurance worked, the balm didn't last long. On January 4, 1988, Rowntree told Dillon it was selling Tom's after less than five full years of ownership. Tom's revenue did climb between 1983 and 1988, but only marginally, from $225 million to $247 million, and the growth was only on paper. When adjusted for inflation, revenue had hardly budged since the early 1970s, and by 1988 Tom's found support slipping among its own distributors, who represented 90 percent of its business. Rowntree had other incentives to sell Tom's, namely that it was fending off a hostile takeover from Nestlé S.A. (a defense effort that ultimately failed, as Nestlé purchased Rowntree for $4.5 billion later in 1988).

The news that his company was being sold again weighed on Dillon, who had to rally the troops into battle against an uncertain future. Yet by his own account, he also was immediately struck with a game-changing idea, one that would allow him to take charge and place matters into his own hands in a way not seen at Tom's since the 1930s. If anyone was going to turn Tom's around and bring back the good old days, it wasn't going to be some number-crunching executive in faraway Minnesota or England. No, Tom's should be in the hands of the people who knew it best and cared about it the most, the ones who saw it firsthand and inhabited its walls each and every day of the week, and the ones who had the most invested in the company—literally. Dillon said the Rowntree sale came as a "complete surprise," but his reaction was instantaneous. "I remember my first words were, 'Can we do a management buyout?'" he said. In doing so, he put Tom's on a collision course with two of the biggest business trends of the 1980s. The first was the hostile takeover, which triggered the sale. The second was the leveraged buyout, a Wall Street fad that was peaking right when Dillon heard the news.

A leveraged buyout, or LBO, as it's called in the business, is basically what the name implies. Investors buy a company using as much debt as possible, often with the company's own assets used as collateral, and try to make money either by paying down the debt to create equity, by engaging in aggressive (some would say ruthless) cost cutting to grow profits, and/or by selling the company at a gain a few years down the road. Leveraged buyouts exploded into the mainstream in 1982, when a former U.S. treasury secretary named William Simon took Gibson Greetings private for $80 million. Simon invested just $330,000 of his own money in the deal, yet when he took Gibson public eighteen months later, the company sold for $290 million, and Simon's stake was suddenly worth $66 million. Simon's experience was definitely not typical, but it turned heads on Wall Street, and the trend took off. The LBO craze was near its apex in early 1988 when Dillon proposed his idea to Rowntree. The concept was controversial then and remains so now, as an LBO often leads to layoffs and to a company that crawls along under a mountain of debt, unable to focus on marketing or growth. Profits, if they come, are doled out mostly to a small group of Wall Street types who led the deal.

For Tom's, some of the fear over undertaking such a maneuver was mitigated by the unique set of circumstances it faced. For one, the company was going to be sold no matter what, and management worried an outside owner would break it up and sell it for parts. In addition, the investors in this case were Tom's management and some Columbus boosters, beginning with Dillon and filtering down to mid-level supervisors, all of whom carried strong local and emotional ties into the deal. They hoped to save Tom's and take it public in a few years by selling stock to employees and distributors. It was a novel if highly risky idea.

Dillon may have drawn inspiration from a man named Ron E. Doggett, who was close with Mike Tracy during Tracy's time at GoodMark Foods in North Carolina. Tracy had helped launch GoodMark, but after he left, General Mills put the subsidiary up for sale in 1982, and Doggett bought it through an LBO. Doggett ran and repositioned the company as its president for three years, then took it public in 1985. The firm's Slim Jim brand surged in popularity, Doggett sold 300,000 shares in the company at ten dollars each while remaining a majority owner, and he wound up in the North Carolina Business Hall of Fame. Doggett described Tracy as a mentor and remained close with him throughout this period, and when Tracy passed away, Doggett gave a eulogy at his funeral. Given that Tracy and Dillon worked together between 1979 and 1986, Dillon was likely familiar with the GoodMark success story. Either way, in 1988 Dillon was ready to take Tom's down a similar path. Rowntree supported the idea, though it wouldn't be easy. Dillon had to convince a bank to finance the deal, line up a team of co-investors, and outbid any would-be buyers.

A few other firms took a glance at Tom's, but it quickly became apparent that Dillon could buy it if he could secure the capital. To do this, he linked up with Citicorp, which was one of three banks that dominated the 1980s LBO market, and then signed up about fifty people to help front money on the management side. Dillon took the lead with a six-figure investment of his own, some local businesspeople and retirees pitched in, and mid-level managers contributed $10,000 each to become part owners of their employer. In total, the Columbus people put up about $2 million, but that was just 1 percent of the $200 million Tom's sold for when the deal closed and papers were signed in New York on June 27, 1988. Dillon and his co-investors had leveraged 99 percent of the purchase. In truth, just as in the 1930s when the Trust Company of Georgia owned Tom's, the bank was in control. Citicorp officially held 60 percent ownership, giving it a controlling share, and it claimed five of eight seats on the reconstituted Tom's board. Dillon became chairman, adding that title to his president and CEO roles. He was permitted to pick two board members, choosing longtime Tom's attorney Alan Rothschild and J. W. Feighner, his old boss. Citicorp named Tom Darling, John Luby, Henry Mueller, Jim Hong, and Clement Woods, all current or retired bank employees, to the Tom's board.

The new local owners put on a brave face and pitched the deal as a triumphant homecoming. Employees were told at the Family Day picnic in May and were immediately handed T-shirts and bumper stickers bearing a new slogan: "Tom's: Back Home Where We Belong." A banner went up at headquarters reading the same thing, and Dillon tried to play up the occasion by focusing on the firm's rich history. Company officers met with eighty-two-year-old Minnie Huston and commissioned a company history book, also called *Tom's: Back Home Where We Belong*; copies were sold to distributors for fifteen dollars. Continuing the nostalgia theme, Tom's launched the "Classic Collection," in which some of its oldest products, such as Tom's Toasted Peanuts, peanut brittle, and the Peanut Butter Log, were sold in packages bearing photos of old Tom's trucks and glass jars. But behind the scenes, the harsh reality of debt settled in fast. "Tom's did a leveraged buyout with about fifty investors," Jack Warden later recalled. "It was management, and local people, and a lot of debt. A huge amount of debt. I was part of it, although you can't measure the percentage that I had, but I was one of the fifty. It was very, very heavily leveraged." Not only was Tom's on the hook for nearly $200 million, but it was committed to paying interest rates as high as 14 percent a year for the privilege. As such, the company struggled to meet payments almost from the start, even as management carved out plans to jump-start growth.

In the short run, Tom's cut costs. The Salem, Virginia, plant was closed in October 1988, and 120 people lost their jobs. The Macon plant was put up for sale. Maine was already gone by this point, so the Salem and Macon closings pared Tom's back to five factories—in Columbus, Knoxville, Corsicana, Fresno, and Perry, Florida. Tom's also sold a small number of corporate-owned distributor routes it had built up over the years. At the home office, the *Toaster* went from monthly to bimonthly and then to quarterly, and at some point *Family Weekly* disappeared entirely. Columbus was mostly spared otherwise, being hit with about a dozen layoffs. (Personnel head Paul Serff said that management's motto was "Tom's will be lean, but we will never be mean"—the people let go may have felt otherwise.) But the headquarters workforce was allowed to gradually shrink through attrition. Tom's overall workforce shrank from 2,200 to 1,850 employees. That figure included the departure of several top executives, though Dillon said what bothered him most was closing the company cafeteria, housed in the old shack where Tom's was founded, and laying off a couple of women who worked there.

Was Dillon stressed? Here's how *The Atlanta Journal-Constitution* began an article about Dillon and the buyout in May 1988:

> "The buyout hasn't affected me at all," he chuckled nervously as he fumbled with his first pack of Marlboro Lights in five years.

Tom's employees were showered with "Back Home Where We Belong" T-shirts and bumper stickers to boost morale following the leveraged buyout. Here, employee Jimmy Elias sports one of the shirts in 1988.

How could he turn things around? Dillon saw his first task as shoring up the relationship between corporate Tom's and its army of distributors. Rowntree had invested lots of money in new equipment at the factories—a plus considering Tom's would have so little working capital in the next few years—but Dillon and the new management felt the British firm had neglected distributors. He created the Tom's Distributor Council after becoming president, with the goal of improving communication between the company and its nonemployee sales force. South Carolina distributor Charles Timbes helped hatch the idea, and twelve distributors ultimately made up the council. After the buyout closed, Dillon sent Tom's management out to large distributors to work with them for a week, a symbol of goodwill to show that he was listening to their concerns. Tom's also tried to restructure the relationship by having distributors sign "franchise" agreements. In years gone by, both Walter Richards and J. W. Feighner had informally referred to Tom's distributors as franchisees, but Dillon tried to formalize the notion that they were running something akin to a restaurant franchise and had them each sign a ten-year contract outlining the terms. As Tom's vice president Stewart Lyman said, "There are a lot of people out there today with money who are not able to buy a McDonald's franchise or a Burger King or a Coca-Cola Bottling Company, but they would be good prospects for a Tom's distributorship." There is little evidence the franchise pitch stopped the bleeding of distributors seeking products from outside sources.

Management also believed the product lineup had become bloated and unfocused. According to a 1987 distributor invoice, Tom's was offering six varieties of peanuts—Tom's Toasted, Spanish Redskin, roasted, dry roasted, hot, and honey toasted, along with sunflower seeds and sunflower kernels, pistachios, and cashews. Each of these was offered in at least three different sizes. Ten varieties of crackers included Eat-a-Snax, butter toast, Cheezers, cheese crisp, wheat cheese and wheat peanut butter, butter malt, chocolate creme, vanilla creme, and peanut butter squares (known as "Sweeties" until consumers became more health-conscious during the 1980s). There were fourteen types of "baked rack goods": chocolate pies, chocolate double decker pies, banana double decker pies, oatmeal pies, fig bars, brownies, peanut butter wafers, vanilla cream wafers, pretzel sticks, pretzel twists, cheese bites, animal cookies, chocolate chip cookies, and vanilla wafers. The candy lineup featured the veteran Peanut Butter Log, the Peanut Plank, Coconut Slice, My Buddy bar, the Peanut Roll, an almond coconut bar, Peanut Butter Pals, lemon drops, candy peanuts, spice drops, orange slices, jelly beans, cherry candy, gummy bears, candy corn, and red hots.

The various types of Tom's chips came in four different sizes and included the five-flavored Country Style lineup, plus hot, spicy, and original pork rinds, onion rings, nacho rings, Bugles, nacho Bugles, hot fries, bacon cheddar fries, cheese popcorn, natural popcorn, Puffed Cheezers, corn chips, barbecue corn chips, nacho tortilla chips, rippled chips, hot chips, vinegar and salt chips, sour cream and onion chips, barbecue chips, and plain chips. There were canned nuts along with bagged nuts and a line of dips including picante sauce, hot bean dip, jalapeño and cheddar dip, and sour cream and onion dip. Looking further down the product sheet, one could find a section titled "Miscellaneous," with another fourteen products listed: "candies in jars," thirty-six-count candies, take home bag/slab candies, the Full Dinner and Park Avenue bars, caramel corn, soft chocolate chip cookies, donut sticks, pecan twirls, multipack potato chips, and peppermint balls, logs, and suckers. Also on offer were three varieties of Donruss Super Bubble gum and ten varieties of the Goodmark Slim Jim brand—Big Slim, Big Jerk, Red Hot, Super Slim, Super Jerk, Nacho, Firecracker, Beer, Barbecue, and Pemmican Jerky. In total, there were almost two hundred items listed on the page. Which were the most important? Which, if any, could be ignored?

A rough road lay ahead. The leveraged buyout put Tom's in the care of Columbus people for the first time in more than two decades. It gave employees, or at least upper management, a sense of ownership and a chance to set things straight after the rocky 1980s. Dillon harbored visions of becoming a Walter Richards–style stabilizer and buying the company back from the bank in as few as two years, selling stock and a piece of ownership to Tom's employees and distributors. But on the flip side, the LBO also represented the end of Tom's as a Columbus corporate giant. It suddenly had much less spending power for things like Family Day or for sponsoring events or charities in town. There certainly wouldn't be another Homecoming '83, with Ray Charles and college marching bands descending on the Chattahoochee Valley. It was going to be a tough few years one way or the other. Dillon saw even more cutting ahead, not just of people and plants but of products too. Tom's was making a total of 289 different items inclusive of size differentials, and he knew more difficult decisions loomed so that the company could focus on core products like chips, crackers, and peanuts. "We've weakened ourselves competitively on product lines that are our real strengths," he wrote. "We must reach an agreement as to what items we want to support. Let's try to become a quality company with manufacturing efficiencies that make us a leader in the marketplace and not a follower. We must focus on what we do best and not try to be all things to all people." Dillon was named the Columbus Chamber of Commerce's Business Leader of the Year in 1989 for driving the LBO. But in accepting the award he used a two-word phrase to describe the buyout experience: "very humbling."

CHAPTER 8

The Turnaround Guy

Tom's Foods entered the 1990s in a much different place than where it had been the previous decade. In 1980 Tom's was a large and profitable subsidiary of General Mills and believed to be stable, and with a new president at the helm, it was aiming to finally break into America's grocery aisles and become a direct competitor with Frito-Lay, the top player in the salty snack game. By 1990, the scale of those visions was vastly diminished. Tom's was sold twice in the eighties, revenues were stagnant or even falling, and while it could brag about being locally owned again, pulling on emotional ties to the community and the company's rich history, Tom's began the twentieth century's final decade inching along under a mountain of debt and hoping to regain stability. With Mike Dillon serving as president, CEO, and board chairman, Tom's dutifully made its interest payments to Citicorp through the end of 1988 and all of 1989 and into the early 1990s as it sought better days.

Dillon, the former marketing department head, was brimming with ideas. He launched a holiday fundraiser program featuring old staples like peanut brittle and hatched a concept called "snacks to pack" in which Tom's Toasted Peanuts and Eat-A-Snax crackers were sold in large packages for schoolchildren, part of yet another attempt to sneak into the grocery aisle. Dillon looked into selling table crackers and melba toast to mom-and-pop restaurants and at having Tom's distributors move Coca-Cola or Royal Crown soft drinks as a tie-in (not Pepsi, though—it owned Frito-Lay), and he even tried coffee vending to boost pastry sales. Despite the debt load, he splashed cash on a few extras, including a package of commercials during ESPN college football games in the fall of 1989 as part of a $500,000 ad buy. In 1990, Dillon got a car phone so he could jawbone his deputies during the eight-minute drive to work.

But at least three different trends worked against the LBO version of Tom's, with each threatening the already imperiled company in a unique way. First, the entire LBO phenomenon flamed out just a few months after Dillon closed the Tom's deal in June 1988. That fall, a conglomerate called RJR Nabisco sold for $25 billion to an LBO specialist firm known as KKR. It was the largest LBO in history, and it followed a bidding war that became legendary on Wall Street, as RJR head F. Ross Johnson and KKR's Henry Kravis fought for control in a battle that seeded a best-selling book and an HBO miniseries, both titled *Barbarians at the Gate*. It was all very exciting, but when the ink dried, RJR Nabisco became just another company that couldn't focus on marketing or growth because it was throwing all its money at debt payments. The saga was a bad deal for all involved, and the publicity, along with a series of high-profile LBO failures, soon gave leverage a bad name.

The second problem was more direct. When Tom's and its then-owner, General Mills, launched the Great American snack line in 1981, they landed on the front edge of another 1980s trend. Tom's was not successful in its attempt to rival Frito-Lay on America's grocery shelves, but that didn't stop a host of other companies from trying. By the end of the decade, Nabisco and Keebler had created their own national chip lines, and a company called Borden Inc. tried to go national by buying up regional chippers and incorporating them under a unified parent company. Borden at one time owned the chip brands Wise, Buckeye, Snacktime, Laura Scudder, Clover Club, Guy's, Jays, Seyfert's, and Southwest Snacks, and it looked at buying Tom's when Rowntree put it up for sale. Most notably, Anheuser-Busch got into the game with its Eagle snack line and started pouring money into the venture.

Pouring Tom's Toasted Peanuts into a bottle of cola became a regional custom and allowed Tom's to cross-promote with Royal Crown, another Columbus-based firm, as shown in this 1987 billboard.

Eagle first launched in 1979, and Busch was unafraid to lose money in order to get a foothold in the market. The company gave away honey roasted peanuts on airlines and later took it to Frito by paying money directly to grocery stores for shelf space. The controversial practice became known as "slotting fees," and Eagle got it started on the snack aisle, which spelled trouble for Tom's and anyone else who couldn't afford to pay the fees. By the end of the 1980s, a foot of space in one grocery store could cost up to $500. U.S. Senator Christopher S. "Kit" Bond once called slotting fees the "dirty little secret in retailing," in part because the fees were done mostly by word of mouth, with no written account of the transactions. In any case, Eagle used its beer profits to buy shelf space, and Frito was already national and aligned with Pepsi. Tom's? As an LBO, it was doing all it could just to stay above water, even as executives continued dreaming about grocery aisles. Anheuser-Busch was willing to lose money on chips, while Borden, Nabisco, and Keebler all jumped into the game at a time when Tom's simply could not afford it. By the early 1990s there was a national potato chip war of attrition going on, with Dillon and his team caught in the crossfire.

The third problem was that a recession hit the U.S. economy in 1990. It technically ended in March 1991, but unemployment kept rising through June 1992, leaving people with less loose change in their pockets for things like peanuts and chips. While the recession was relatively mild and is remembered mostly for helping Bill Clinton get elected president, it was just one more ill-timed pressure point weighing down on Eighth Street in Columbus.

There were lots of goals and projections emerging from the Tom's boardroom: Go public by 1992; reach twelve hundred distributors by 1994. The company even gave employees one hundred shares of performance "stock" plus one share for each year of service, a motivational technique that workers could trade for common stock if Tom's ever did go public. Tom's heavily promoted the franchise concept in newspaper stories and classified ads, predicting big things in that space. "In five years, you are going to read about us on the front of *Business Week, Time*," Dillon said. "It's going to say that Tom's Foods is the largest, most successful franchiser in the country." The push convinced at least one New York corporate executive to leave his upper-crust life for Charlotte, North Carolina, where he bought an eleven-route Tom's franchise. Ironically, the sluggish economy helped out in that regard, as corporate layoffs were thought to make white-collar workers more open to the idea of going into business for themselves. But by the end of 1991, if not earlier, it was clear that the one-two-three combination of heavy debt, fierce competition, and a recession were too much to handle. And for all of Dillon's work, Tom's, by then a sixty-five-year-old company—old enough to collect Social Security if it were a person—remained largely the same place it had been before Dillon's tenure. It sold the same products using the same business model, only now with diminishing returns, in spite of plans to change, a common fate in business and politics that some scholars refer to as path dependency. The LBO was not going to work. In December 1991 Tom's creditors brought in a turnaround specialist named Michael E. Heisley as a consultant. Just over a year later, in early 1993, Tom's management defaulted on an $80 million loan from Citicorp; the company was put up for sale for the third time in a decade, and Heisley emerged as the buyer.

"The saddest day of my life was when they called us into a big room and said, 'The banks are not going to be able to help us anymore,'" recalled Glenn Seawell, a Tom's salesman from 1975 through 1995 who was among

Tom's launched two potato chip product lines in the 1980s, "Great American" and "Country Style," while trying to take on Frito-Lay in grocery stores. Both lines were featured on the cover of the Fall 1989 issue of the *Toaster*.

the owner-managers. "A banker got up and said they'd done everything they could and that effective on a certain date there'd be a new owner. . . . I think I even said something in the meeting like 'Give us another chance.' I was very disappointed. I knew what would happen. I sat there that whole meeting and thought, 'This company will never, ever be the same.' All this is happening in like an hour, you're sitting there going, 'Oh my God, this is probably the end of Tom's Foods.'"

Heisley, at least at first, tried to prevent that from happening. Born in Alexandria, Virginia, on March 13, 1937, he had grown up eating Tom's Toasted Peanuts in a working-class family, which sparked some of his interest in the company. After graduating from Georgetown University, he began his career in Chicago. Heisley joined RCA Corporation, ascending quickly to vice president of its computer division. From there, he joined SI Handling Systems Inc., a maker of automatic conveying equipment, where he served as president for five profitable years. That company struggled after Heisley left and later sued him, alleging that he stole trade secrets, nabbed former employees, and used his business contacts to build a competing firm. The case was settled out of court. In 1979 Heisley bought his first company, Illinois-based sewer and drain equipment maker Conco Inc., using $150,000 in profit from selling his house and $10 million in bank debt. He renamed it Heico. It was a risky play for a troubled and decidedly unsexy business-to-business company, and it became a model he'd use for the rest of his career.

Heisley made a habit of buying distressed companies, typically manufacturing concerns in the Rust Belt, stabilizing them, and, crucially, keeping them. He rarely sold anything, choosing instead to attract other investors to the newly profitable firms and pulling out his money for other acquisitions. By 1988, Heisley's net worth was estimated at between $25 million and $50 million. But that was only the beginning, as his unique turnaround model was a perfect fit for the LBO fallout. Suddenly there were struggling, over-leveraged businesses all over the place, and banks were constantly calling to make him offers on troubled assets. He often paid as little as ten to thirty cents on the dollar to take the problem off the bank's hands and was once described as a "master of bottom fishing." When he bought Tom's in 1993, Heisley reduced the company's debt burden by $70 million, and its annual interest payments dropped from $21 million to $6 million. Dillon and his co-investors got roughly 75 percent of their initial investment back, not accounting for inflation, and the 1988 deal was described as a "badly executed" leveraged buyout that "went awry." Dillon acknowledged as much in saying, "We weren't in the LBO but a year or so when the recession hit and the snack food war started." It was believed that lifting the debt alone would get Tom's cooking again.

Yet even if distressed companies were Heisley's specialty, Tom's was a different kind of animal. Heisley usually bought businesses that made things like copper wiring or drainage pipes in the states around Chicago. His last deal before Tom's was the purchase of Akron, Ohio–based NRM Steelastic, Inc., a manufacturer of steel belting for tires. Heisley had never bought a food company before, and he hadn't bought anything in the South. But Tom's did have some things in common with his other holdings: It was a business-to-business enterprise selling to distributors, and at its core it was a manufacturing firm. So he decided to make a go of it, and the deal closed on May 14, 1993. "When I looked at the company—having grown up in the South I knew the brand name—I was interested," Heisley said. "I felt very strongly that if the company could be restructured and debt removed, it could go a long ways." He also planned to restructure the franchise operations, musing about corporate taking them over, getting them in shape, and reselling them.

Technically, Tom's was not the first food company that Heisley bought. Just two days earlier, on May 12, he bought Nutri/System Inc., a distressed weight-loss business that sold low-calorie meals. Of the two, Tom's was considered the safer bet. "Mike is very good at studying the underlying value of a company," Gerald Hosier, a Chicago lawyer who put $9 million into Tom's as a co-investor, told *Crain's Chicago Business*. "Tom's, for instance, has a stable, viable business, but its owners clearly took on more debt than they should have in a leveraged buyout in the late 1980s. Nutri/System looks like a riskier investment, but it also carries the potential for a far higher return." Heisley tried to downplay the significance of his big departure from the Midwest, playing up the similarities among Tom's, Nutri/System, and his older businesses. "The process of restructuring distressed companies is something I've done for 15 years," Heisley told *Crain's*. "The fact that I'm doing it with food companies is very different for me. But my focus has changed somewhat. I don't intend to operate these companies myself. The key is finding the right management to do that for you." In Columbus there were high hopes. Crippling debt was no longer going to be a problem, and Heisley's track record of fixing up companies and holding onto them in a newly profitable state sounded promising. Maybe the good old days would return after all. Dillon was allowed to stay on as president for a time, while Heisley became chairman.

But if the LBO marked the end of Tom's as a Columbus corporate power, the Heico takeover marked the end of its time as a company with a local, family-oriented ethos. Johnny Johnson, a Tom's employee who joined the company in 1970 and stayed at the home factory for more than fifty years, described Heisley as a "foreigner" to the area who took little interest in learning about its history or its people. Mike Tracy–style chats with the maintenance crew were long gone. "We lost some of that loyalty," he said. "It became just an hourly job." Even little changes, such as switching from a Columbus-based health insurance broker to one based in Chicago, were alienating to the Southern workforce. Still, it could all be worthwhile if Heisley helped the bottom line.

His first big change was to bring in Peter Rogers, a longtime disciple and understudy of RJR Nabisco CEO F. Ross Johnson. Rogers and Johnson linked up while the two men worked together in Canada. Johnson's off-the-wall management style included hosting all-night drinking sessions with his top deputies, and he dubbed Rogers "The Rook," short for Canadian Olympic Drinking Team rookie. The nickname stuck for more than ten years. Rogers was an eccentric Englishman who listened to Winston Churchill speeches on tape and refused to wear shoes in his office, but he did well under Johnson's tutelage, rising to become the president of ten different snack businesses, including Nabisco, Planters, and the Curtiss Candy Company. He developed into something of a corporate pinch hitter, staying with each company for only a year or two before moving on. Rogers joined Tom's in July 1993, was named a director that December, and then became Tom's new CEO in June 1994, while Dillon rotated into the role of chairman and official liaison between headquarters and distributors. Even as CEO, Rogers was a contractor paid on an hourly basis, and he continued living in Chicago, staying in hotels while in Columbus for two weeks each month. "This is not a quick-fix business," he warned as he pored over the company's finances. "It took 10 years to get into trouble, and it's going to take a lot more than one year to get out of trouble."

Rogers's caretaker presidency ended after just six months. He remained a director through June 1995 and then left for good, along with Dillon. To replace them, Heisley chose a Kansas State University graduate named Ron Divin, who was a turnaround artist in his own right. Divin made his name as the CEO of Chun King Limited Partnership, a brand of canned Chinese food products that had gone through its own series of ownership changes during the 1980s. Divin led Chun King from 1992 through the end of 1994, after which it was sold to Hunt-Wesson, owner of the rival La Choy brand.

Chun King was later discontinued completely, but Divin's repositioning of the brand was considered successful, and Tom's was his next task. Divin, then forty-eight, became Tom's president on January 16, 1995, and there were lots of growing pains as the Midwesterner moved in. He was aware of the Tom's "family" mantra, which he saw as something less than a warm and fuzzy ideal.

"It was a very, deeply Southern company," Divin said. "The influence of the original founders of Tom's was still there. It had a deep history, and I had to take that into consideration as I made changes. I had to go slower than normal simply because of that. . . . I had come from a faster-paced history, a more aggressive business approach, and that wasn't what I found [at Tom's]." One of the first moves Divin made was to freeze and then replace the pension plan Tom's created after World War II, a move many companies made across the 1980s and 1990s. He described the new retirement program as "much more beneficial," though employees had to put their own money into it, and he said the pension plan had been managed quite conservatively with a too-heavy mix of bonds versus stocks. In any case, the pension was frozen, which Divin said was controversial but inevitable. "The company was a good company, the people were in large part good people. Very loyal," he said. "They wanted the company to win. But they were very upset that it didn't stay like it was back forty years before. That's just the Southern way." The tension ran both ways. Longtime employees, many now working under their fifth CEO, saw the red Tom's triangle as a symbol of the South, as important to the region as the peanut itself, with a legendary history to preserve and maintain. The new ownership saw this type of "old ways" thinking and sentimentalism as the problem they were brought in to fix.

Divin also worked on repairing the Tom's–distributor dynamic, saying the route men "had to be influenced to do the right things for the brand, rather than just for themselves." Vending machines by that point were a dying part of the business, and management finally let distributors go their own way on that side. Instead, the company mostly pursued convenience stores, the original point of sale dating back to the days of Tom Huston. According to Divin, Tom's was unusual in even maintaining an independent distributor network, particularly because the company often assisted distributors with financing their businesses. Lance Inc. and Frito-Lay, for example, used company-owned routes that gave them heavy control over their distribution networks.

Heisley's big-picture turnaround plan emerged quickly once Divin took control—Tom's was going to launch a line of health food products. If that seems like an unusual strategy for a company that made salted peanuts, potato chips, and candy bars, it wasn't in the mid-1990s. The U.S. government was pushing the public to cut fat intake, and food companies battled to meet demand. Nabisco was first out of the gate with its Snackwells brand of low-fat cookies. Released in 1992, they sold very well and launched a kind of gold rush, as other snack makers got in on the game. This may have been Heisley's plan all along. It was probably not a coincidence that Heisley bought the health food company Nutri/System at the same time as Tom's. Rogers, a former Nabisco president, was also the owner of Greenfield Health Foods, a maker of fat-free cookies and brownies. Divin created a line of low-fat noodles during his run at Chun King. And Tom's did have some history of dabbling in healthy snacks. It tried out a low-fat peanut as early as 1966, and in the 1980s it experimented with white cheddar popcorn, which at the time weight-conscious consumers considered a healthier alternative.

In February 1995, Tom's went all in. Under Divin's guidance, it launched forty-eight new products all at once and drew up a new diamond-shaped logo reading "Tom's, less fat, Great Taste!" Most of the line consisted of existing products with some or all of the fat content removed, with the new logo topping green and white bags with gold trim. There were low-fat animal cookies, no-fat pretzels, no-fat tortilla chips, less-fat hot fries, low-fat mesquite fries, less-fat popcorn, less-fat crackers, and no-fat fig bars. Some products, such as pretzels, had always been low in fat, and so the new labeling was mostly a marketing exercise, but there were federal regulations in place regarding what could be called what. For a bag to read "less fat," the product needed to have at least a 25 percent fat reduction compared to its original form. "Low fat" products had to have fewer than three grams of fat per serving. Executives retrofitted some Tom's vending machines with the "less fat" logo and took out ads featuring a slender woman in workout gear next to bags of low-fat and less-fat products. The idea was that calorie-conscious women, who traditionally didn't buy salty snacks, might take a look at the new Tom's offerings the next time they were out, and if the product line worked, it might finally pry open the door to supermarkets as well. Of the forty-eight low-fat and no-fat offerings, twenty-four were for vending machines, and the other half were explicitly designed for grocery stores. Tom's had never released that many new products simultaneously. "We think it has a lot of potential," Divin said in April 1995. "We don't know how big it will be, but we have hopes for it."

Items like the unaltered "low-fat pretzels" sold well for a time, but two factors ultimately doomed the venture. One was that the low-fat fad fizzled out as the nineties wore on, and competitors, including innovator Nabisco, abandoned their reduced-fat lines. The other, perhaps more important factor was the simple lack of overlap between health-conscious consumers and snack food junkies who bought chips and pastries from vending machines or gas stations, the very locations where Tom's was established. Within a year of the big launch, Tom's canceled almost all of the low-fat line.

On March 12, 1996, the company lost the last living link to its founding when Minnie Huston died just after her ninetieth birthday. She had remained in Miami after Tom Huston's death, though she visited Columbus frequently and met with the Tom's board in 1988 as it began work on a company history project. Minnie Huston's graveside service was held at Linwood Cemetery, where she was buried next to her husband.

After the failure of its health food venture, Tom's was once again left searching for answers as it entered the latter part of the 1990s, and it wasn't alone. Lance laid off five hundred people and closed two plants, several other regional competitors went bankrupt, and all of the national players quit the chip business completely—with one very notable exception. Frito-Lay had taken a beating when Nabisco, Keebler, Borden, and especially Anheuser-Busch's Eagle snacks went national with their chip lines and were happy to lose money doing it. Eagle threw cash at grocery stores for shelf space and paid for it with Anheuser-Busch's beer money, leaving Frito-Lay scrambling. In 1991 Frito got down to a 38 percent market share. But it took action by hiring former Pepsi CEO Roger Enrico, a veteran of the "cola wars" with Coke, for a refresh. Enrico changed the formula for Lay's chips to make them less greasy, laid off 1,800 employees and replaced them with hipper, younger ones, switched up the company's packaging, cut prices, and trotted out celebrity-filled television advertisements with big-time athletes like Larry Bird and Kareem Abdul-Jabbar. Enrico didn't call it this, but his work could rank among the most successful five-year plans in business history.

By 1996 Frito-Lay's national market share topped 50 percent. The company was so dominant that would-be national competitors Borden, Nabisco, Keebler, and Anheuser-Busch all gave up, and about two dozen regional players went bankrupt. Eagle, Frito's largest competitor, lost $25 million in 1995 alone before calling it quits at the end of that year. Tom's stayed in the fight after its health food failure and got major breaks, or so it hoped, from the sudden drop in competition and, surprisingly, from the federal government. When Eagle went under, it closed all of its plants and struck a deal to sell four of them to Frito, which made sense from a business standpoint, since Frito was eating everyone's lunch anyway and needed the space. But there are always losers in such a deal. Eagle used the Tom's-style independent distributor model for some of its chip routes, and because Frito used company-owned routes, the deal put Eagle's independent distributors out of business. Eagle distributors in California shrewdly hired a legal team to argue that Frito was violating the Clayton Antitrust Act, and their case caught the attention of the U.S. Justice Department. The DOJ opened an investigation in May 1996, and on Memorial Day weekend the case made national news, with NBC's Tom Brokaw and ABC's Peter Jennings telling America's television viewers that Frito-Lay was in the government's crosshairs, accused of being a monopoly.

Divin paid close attention to the probe and kept Tom's distributors apprised of new developments. He was optimistic that the exit of the four money-losing national competitors would ease pressure on regionals, and if the federal government forced Frito to sell some of its plants or to stop paying for shelf space, it could open new opportunities for growth. This was always an unlikely outcome, but amid so many struggles, it provided hope. Frito-Lay didn't slow down amid the probe. It forced Tom's out of the RaceTrac convenience store chain while the investigation was ongoing by paying what Divin described as an exorbitant up-front price for exclusivity. A few folks from the Justice Department made a trip to Columbus to speak with Divin, though even decades later he said he was "not at liberty to talk about" specifics. In its investigation, the DOJ focused mainly on the controversial slotting fees practice. The feds correctly noted that smaller companies like Tom's couldn't afford to pay slotting fees, and thus size alone often determined who got shelf space. Frito, needless to say, disagreed.

There was a wide variety of opinion as to whether Frito was competitive or cutthroat. Tom Bigham, a vice president of Texas-based Tejas Snacks, shrugged the whole thing off. "They are just real good at what they do," he suggested. Peter Sprecher, president of Kentucky-based Louise's Inc., a fat-free snack maker, had a different take, comparing Frito to another 1990s giant that got on the wrong side of a DOJ probe: "This is a company that makes Microsoft really look like a pussycat." In another era, Frito-Lay might have been in trouble. When it merged with Pepsi-Cola in 1965, Frito-Lay was ordered to sell ten of its plants amid antitrust concerns. Similarly, when General Mills bought Tom's in 1966, it was restricted for ten years from buying other snack food businesses. By the 1990s, the government's heavy-handed, structure-focused approach gave way to the free-market "Chicago School" of antitrust. The issue with monopolies was that they had power to raise prices and harm consumers, the new thinking went, so as long as prices did not rise, the government had no place telling private businesses what to do. If Eagle or another company was willing to sell chips at a loss, that was even better for the consumer, as they got the sheer benefit of the discount. The fact that smaller companies like Tom's couldn't afford to lose money year after year or pay exorbitant up-front fees wasn't a consideration, nor was the fact that their employees stood to lose their jobs.

"What a number of economic studies have shown is that predatory pricing, or actions alleged to be predatory pricing, generally benefit consumers because the consumer has the sheer benefit of that forty-nine-cent bag of potato chips," attorney Jonathan Jacobson told National Public Radio amid the Frito probe, explaining the logic. "Whether Frito-Lay in two years will be able to charge three dollars is speculative."

In 1997, Frito-Lay controlled 89.6 percent of the corn chip market, 79.4 percent of the tortilla chip market, 55.4 percent of the potato chip market, and 49.5 percent of the market for extruded snacks such as Cheetos. In 1998, the government dropped its probe without taking action and without even formally saying why. "We are very pleased with their decision," Frito-Lay spokeswoman Lynn Markley said dryly in reaction to the news. "We were never accused of any wrongdoing."

Tom's, along with other regional snack food makers across the country, was back at square one. Divin put a brave face on the situation, encouraging distributors and employees through a rebranded quarterly magazine called *Tom's Today*, and under his leadership Tom's rolled out new products at a high clip throughout the late 1990s. It launched Gold Rush pretzels, a cookie brand called Mt. Chocolate, a Hispanic-focused line dubbed Señor Tom's, a brand of gummi worms called Electric Willies, and lots of new flavor combinations like loaded spud chips, zesty lime chips, salt and pepper chips, honey mustard chips, dill pickle chips, French onion chips, caliente fries, chili cheese fries, four-cheese tortilla chips, ranch tortilla chips, pizza tortilla chips, and taco tortilla chips. It also brought back old favorites as a nostalgia buy. Peanut Butter Logs came back with a message on the bag reading, "Remember when you were a kid?" If new stuff was the goal, it was met. Tom's created fifty-one new or revised products in 1996, and even more than that in 1997. It tested out ideas on soldiers at Fort Benning and on Muscogee County schoolchildren.

But longtime employees noticed that big-picture investments were not being made. A new flavor of chip only involved switching up seasonings and graphics. The kind of game-changing innovation that required more money was not in the works, and often it seemed like basic factory maintenance wasn't happening either. "They just skimmed the cream off of the top and quit investing any money," said Johnny Johnson, the employee with a fifty-plus-year tenure. "They reaped the benefits and wouldn't invest any money back into the plants. They weren't upgrading the machinery. That's what happened, they just wanted the money."

After the first turnaround attempt by Michael Heisley failed—and he had bet heavily on the "Tom's less fat" line—he appeared to lose interest. Heisley owned twenty-six companies bringing in more than $1.2 billion a year combined. Tom's wasn't thriving, and Heisley seemed uninterested, indifferent, or at times actively hostile toward it. The company was not profitable, though Divin pointed to a different metric—earnings before interest, taxes, depreciation, and amortization, or EBITDA—which he said improved for thirty-four straight quarters. But the problem with using EBITDA as a metric is that it ignores the need for capital expenditures, the funds companies use to acquire, upgrade, and maintain plants and equipment. It's no way to evaluate a company's performance on a long-term basis.

Sharon Sanders, who joined Tom's in 1982 while still in college and rose to become its final chief financial officer, often called Heisley to ask for money to pay the company's bills. She flew with Divin to Chicago for Tom's board meetings as well and recalls a lot of "posturing" between Divin and Heisley, neither of whom wanted to bow to the other. "You can't tell me what I can and can't say. That just isn't gonna work for me," she said years later. "Before going into a board meeting, Ron Divin would say, 'You can only say this and I don't want you to say that. If you're asked a question you do not answer it.' He'd read me the riot act about what I could and couldn't do. And when you get up there and get peppered with questions, you feel like you have to answer them! It's his boss [Heisley] and he's not saying anything. Then you'd get yelled at the whole trip back. These weren't inflammatory questions either; it was the simplest little questions he didn't want you to answer. [Divin] was a character all by himself." At the same time, Sanders acknowledged it was Divin who promoted her up into the top echelons of the company during his tenure.

By the end of the 1990s, Heisley's mind was clearly focused elsewhere. In 2000 he went from a rich man who wouldn't be recognized walking down the street in his own neighborhood to a man making front-page headlines after purchasing the National Basketball Association's Vancouver Grizzlies. The team had joined the league as an expansion franchise in 1995 and struggled to attract fans or players to its Canadian arena. Heisley saw the

Grizzlies as another turnaround project and, at age sixty-two, maybe a way for him to have a little fun. "I'm sure that few, if any of you, have heard of me," he told the Vancouver media after the sale closed, "but that is about to change." Heisley said he'd keep the Grizzlies in Canada, even while admitting he'd bought the franchise largely because it was cheap and available at $127 million. Unfortunately for the locals, Heisley's turnaround plan was revealed just one year later—he went back on his word and moved the team to Memphis. The Grizzlies kept their name despite the lack of grizzly bears in Tennessee, and Heisley attracted a measure of infamy for breaking his promise. As a business venture, however, it worked. Heisley got his team a brand-new arena, it made the NBA playoffs for the first time ever under his ownership, and he later sold the Grizzlies for $377 million, more than doubling his investment. "If making a lot of money is the mark of a self-made man," he once said, "then I guess I'm a self-made man."

The city of Columbus could also be forgiven for ignoring troubles at Tom's. Luckily, this was not a case in which a struggling factory crippled the community. No doubt Columbus would have been stronger if Tom's had continued to thrive and prosper, but thanks to other big businesses, the city kept growing throughout the 1990s even as Tom's faltered. By 1993, Total System Services, Inc. (TSYS), a spin-off of a local bank, had become the world's largest credit card processor, dominating the market not only in the United States but also in Europe and China. That same year, Columbus College began offering computer science degrees to meet growing demand, sending 99 percent of its graduates to TSYS. Columbus-based Carmike Cinemas grew into the second-largest movie theater chain in the United States by 1996, the same year that Columbus hosted Olympic softball as part of the Atlanta Games, building out infrastructure that helped it attract sports tournaments for years to come. The city's civic life improved as well, with the first leg of the Chattahoochee RiverWalk opening in 1992, the Coca-Cola Space Science Center opening in 1996, and the 7,500-seat Columbus Civic Center debuting in 1996. The venerable Springer Opera House, Georgia's official state theater and a shining symbol of Uptown's revitalization, was renovated in 1998. The change from an industrial to a postindustrial world was on: 1998 also marked the closure of the Bibb City Mill, the last of the textile mills that dominated life in Columbus for so many decades.

Columbus College was renamed Columbus State University in 1996, and its Uptown music school began a revitalization of the area. In a fitting symbol of the city's transformation, the clock tower that serves as CSU's logo is built from the bricks of an old textile mill, representing the city's transition from a gritty factory town to one with a service-based economy. TSYS headquarters was also located in a converted mill along the Chattahoochee. Along with TSYS and the university, the city's other corporate giants, regional bank Synovus Financial Corp. and insurance provider Aflac Inc., fueled Columbus's improvement. Already earning $2.7 billion a year in 1991, Aflac grew throughout the decade and launched its mascot, the Aflac Duck, in 2000, which became an advertising sensation with star-studded television commercials. The company's annual revenues went on to top $20 billion, making Aflac by far the largest private enterprise in Columbus. Amid all of this, Tom's hobbled along toward the twenty-first century, still employing 800 people locally and 1,600 in total at the end of the 1990s, even if it was no longer a major player in the Columbus civic scene. The year 2000 marked a big milestone, as Tom's celebrated its seventy-fifth anniversary. It still had some cultural clout too. The first "millennium baby" born in Columbus in 2000 was the son of a Tom's machine operator. The family got a write-up in the local newspaper. Phenix City, Alabama, Mayor Peggy Martin worked at Tom's until her retirement in 2001. Tom's products even appeared in a couple of movies, 1997's *Midnight in the Garden of Good and Evil* and the 2000 film *My Dog Skip*, both Southern-fried tales with a heavy regional flavor.

The Columbus factory's biggest successes at the turn of the millennium were mostly in contract work. Tom's expanded its home factory one last time at the end of the nineties. Four days before Christmas 1998, Tom's executives joined civic leaders such as Columbus Mayor Pro Tempore A. J. McClung to announce a $6 million, 33,000-square-foot bakery expansion scheduled to open in June 1999. More than four dozen employees were on hand as well. The bakery produced enough crackers every day to stretch the one-hundred-mile journey from Columbus to Atlanta, but not all of those crackers wound up in Tom's-branded bags. Many were made for Keebler, Golden Flake, or even Frito-Lay.

By 2001 Tom's was making 1.5 million Slim Fast bars a week, one of which made it onto *The Rosie O'Donnell Show* for an advertising spot. "You never know who is going to open the product you just made—maybe even on national TV!" Tom's boasted in the company newsletter. Even bigger was Dunkaroos, a General Mills cookies-and-frosting treat in demand with America's toddlers. Tom's made every Dunkaroos package in the United States, running a factory line twenty-four hours a day in the early aughts. Contract work kept the lights on, though it came with significant drawbacks.

The profit margin was lower, the end product did not bear Tom's branding, and in some cases Columbus churned out products that competed directly with its own on store shelves. Still, if the work brought in revenue and kept people employed, it was considered worthwhile. Divin gamed up new ideas in the meantime. There were talks of making an acquisition to switch things up. Tom's looked at buying Pennsylvania-based Wise Foods, Inc., and there were some preliminary talks toward a merger with Lance Inc.

There were hundreds of Tom's distributors across the South still plugging away, many of them long-tenured and loyal. For example, in 1999, Paducah, Kentucky, distributor W. J. Word turned seventy years old while still driving his Tom's truck every day. Customers called him "Mr. Tom." He had been in the business since 1957 and had taken only one vacation in forty-two years. He was on his fourth Tom's truck, which had 232,000 miles on it, and still handed out paper receipts in a rapidly digitizing world, and he had no intention of retiring. Word's wife, Norma, did the bookkeeping; his son Mike had joined the family business in 1976, and they sold Tom's Toasted Peanuts by placing them at the eye-level no. 19 spot in the H-22 vending machines they still stocked every week. It was a charming story replicated over and over again across the history of Tom's, but by the late 1990s it was becoming too common. Tom's thrived increasingly in rural or midsized Southern towns with little competition and with established distributors who'd joined during the glory days.

Overall revenues at the company did not improve or even stabilize. Tom's brought in $220 million a year as late as 1993, the year Heisley bought it. After the health food experiment, things stagnated and then slowly declined. By 2002, revenues were down to $209 million, and in 2003 they fell below $200 million. In 2004 Tom's earnings fell sharply from the year before, dropping from $196 million to $181 million, and its operating loss more than doubled, from $3.3 million to $6.4 million. When adjusting for inflation, Tom's was bringing in less than half of what it did in the early 1970s. Something had to give. In the early 1960s, Frito-Lay was a little more than three times the size of Tom's, and Tom's was actually growing at a faster rate. By 2005 there was no comparison. Tom's earned less than $200 million that year, while Frito made $8.2 billion. Tom's defaulted on a $60 million loan from Bank of New York in early 2005, calling its future into question once more. Officially, Heico proposed spending $15 million to pay down the loan and extend the maturity date. But Tom Hill, a turnaround specialist interviewed by *Crain's Chicago Business*, had his doubts. "[Heisley has] done really well, but when you take risks, sometimes you hit home runs and sometimes you don't," he told the outlet. "If I had a $60 million loan called, I wouldn't put good money after bad."

Heisley didn't. On April 6, 2005, Tom's filed for Chapter 11 bankruptcy protection with the U.S. Bankruptcy Court for the Middle District of Georgia in Columbus, listing $93.1 million in assets and $79.1 million in liabilities. Tom's hadn't turned a profit in any year since Heisley bought it. Chapter 11 is a form of bankruptcy that allows for reorganizing, meaning Heisley could try to restructure the debt down again and give it another shot. In reality, with falling revenues after more than a decade under the same leadership, that was not a smart idea. Heisley was already refusing to put capital into the company for marketing, personnel, or equipment, so doing so to secure a loan was unlikely and unwise. It was a painful time at the home office. The accounting department wrote checks that it couldn't mail out and asked for extra time to pay for basics like sugar and flour, just like in the early 1930s, when Tom Huston's big bank loans coupled with the Great Depression to wreck his own company's finances. Tom's had been shedding employees, many with a lifetime of experience, since the mid-1980s. With the bankruptcy filing, they left at a faster clip than ever.

Heisley, looking to recoup some of his losses, sold off the Harris County lake property. Before the sale closed, he met Tom's general manager Jack Warden at the site to see if there was anything there he wanted, showcasing his frugal ways in the process. Heisley being a billionaire, Warden expected him to arrive in a helicopter or at least a limousine. Instead, Heisley left a Grizzlies game the night before in Memphis and drove all the way to Columbus in a rented sedan, then proceeded to go through the minutiae of materials himself—old chairs, old mattresses—poring over which he might want to keep. The headquarters situation deteriorated further throughout the year. In August 2005, Tom's told employees and retirees that it would no longer pay for their pensions, joining four Columbus textile manufacturers who'd recently done the same. All of them turned to the federal Pension Benefit Guaranty Corporation looking for a bailout. Tom's pension plan had about 3,500 pensioners at the time and was underfunded by $43 million. By October, Tom's had stopped trying to reorganize and was desperately searching for a buyer, as it expected to run completely out of cash within weeks. A bidding deadline was set for October 14, with a final decision to be made October 19. If no one made a bid, the company could be liquidated out of existence. Even if a buyer emerged, Tom's was going to be sold for the fourth time in twenty-two years, and decline and uncertainty must have started to feel like a way of life for those who stuck through all the changes. Divin once again put on a brave face. "We have a long list of potential buyers," he promised, claiming he even looked at buying Tom's himself. "There is no question, in my view, that the company will not be liquidated or closed down. I believe the company will be sold and at a good price, actually."

In the end, Tom's was sold to a bidder using the bankruptcy process, and at a very high price indeed.

CHAPTER 9

Letting Go of the Legacy

Lance Inc. had always been something of a cousin to Tom's, with a similar history, geography, product line, size, and culture. Philip L. Lance started the company in Charlotte, North Carolina, in 1913 due, mostly, to a shipping mix-up. Lance was a food broker, and as legend has it, he got stuck with five hundred pounds of unwanted peanuts after someone canceled a big order—similar to how Tom Huston got stuck with peanuts when farmers couldn't afford his shellers. Also like Huston, Lance started out by toasting the peanuts and selling them for five cents a bag. Some of the similarities end at that point. There was nothing particularly innovative about Lance's operation, and his firm remained a one-person unit until 1915, when his son-in-law, Salem Van Every, joined up and doubled the workforce. What proved to be the big break came that same year, when Lance's wife, Mary, and his two daughters suggested spreading peanut butter between two sandwich crackers. It seems like an obvious idea now, but the women's innovation created the world's first sandwich cracker and cemented Lance's place in the market from that point forward.

While Tom's Toasted Peanuts exploded onto the scene in 1925, Lance crackers grew gradually. It wasn't until 1939 that the company launched the cheese cracker and peanut butter combination, ToastChee, that became its signature product. Van Every's son, Philip Lance Van Every, was Lance's answer to Walter Richards. He joined the company at the age of nineteen in 1932 and became its president at age twenty-nine when Salem Van Every died on Easter Sunday 1943. Philip Lance Van Every then led a period of steady growth over several decades while also serving two terms as Charlotte mayor, just as Richards had led the Columbus city government. Lance and Tom's were roughly the same size for much of the twentieth century and were located just 350 miles apart, with Tom's being the slightly bigger cousin through the 1970s thanks to its vending innovations (Lance didn't get its first vending machine until 1954—four years after Tom's). Their paths began to diverge in the 1980s. Tom's went through its series of ownership changes following an unsuccessful pivot to potato chips, and while Lance had even less luck getting into chips, its strong cracker line kept it competitive. Lance broke into grocery stores during the 1980s and sold millions of dollars' worth of stock as a publicly traded company, two goals that had eluded Tom's.

The divergence grew over time. Tom's annual revenue fell below $200 million a few years into the new millennium, while Lance's surged past $500 million, eventually reaching $600 million. Lance was an entrenched presence in mega-retailers like Walmart, boasted a distribution network extending northward into Canada, and was healthy enough to sponsor a NASCAR team. One cousin was clearly outperforming the other. Lance was bringing in three times the revenue of Tom's by the mid-aughts, anchored by a flagship product that was in demand pretty much anywhere somebody wanted a cracker. As luck would have it, Lance also got a new CEO in 2005. Paul Stroup III was forced out of the job amid sagging profits, and the powers that be replaced him with David V. Singer, who had been a member of the company board since 2003. Singer was an acquisitions man. He'd spent nineteen years as chief financial officer at Charlotte-based Coca-Cola Bottling Co. Consolidated, overseeing twenty separate acquisitions during that time. He took over as Lance CEO in May 2005 and was expected to do more of the same in his new role.

Tom's put itself on the market that fall. The bankruptcy sale was authorized in September, with a bidding deadline set for October 14, giving anyone interested just a few weeks to decide on a nine-figure purchase. Lance got even less time than that. Singer didn't find out Tom's was for sale until October 5, leaving him just nine days to put together a bid for his first major acquisition as the head of Lance. But Singer had a clear vision and determined right away that he should pursue it. Singer and Lance made an attractive bid ahead of the deadline and were announced as the winners on October 21. The final purchase price was $37.9 million—plus the assumption of $63 million in debt. Lance did not have to take on Tom's $43 million in unfunded pension liabilities, which were handed over to the federal government's Pension Benefit Guaranty Corporation. Even with the debt service included, the cost was much less than the $215 million Tom's sold for in 1988 (the price for Heisley's 1993 purchase was never publicly disclosed), and that's without accounting for inflation. Industry analysts were impressed, describing the buy as low risk with a high upside. "Tom's has got a lot of committed, local employees," Singer said after closing the deal. "It's got a great customer base. It gives us some capacity to grow. . . . Our shareholder value is about $500 million and we have almost no debt. So this transaction is not a financial burden to us."

Ron Divin, as usual, put the best possible face on the transaction. "GOOD WORK!" he wrote in the subject line of a memo sent to all Tom's Foods employees the day the sale closed. "The bankruptcy and recent sale were a result of many factors, most not under our control or operationally driven. You took Tom's from its worst financial years in the company's history in '93–'95 to its best in over 80 in 2002." Since Tom's was not quite eighty years old in 2002, this statement would suggest that 2002, a year the company lost $20.9 million, was its best year ever. This was not the case. Divin listed "lost co-pack volume," high agricultural commodity prices, high energy prices, and the impact of five major hurricanes as the reasons Tom's went bankrupt. He continued:

> What you have accomplished set the stage for an excellent sale price and assured continued operations rather than an asset liquidation. You did an excellent job! I believe the acquisition by Lance is the best outcome for the future of the Company. Lance has a strong balance sheet and there are many synergies between the two companies that, once captured, will make the two brands much stronger. In fact, I have attempted to get Lance and Tom's together in some fashion for more than five years. I just didn't think it would happen this way, but no matter. It is a great opportunity for both companies which will provide more certainty and stability for employees, which you have not had since the late '80s. . . . I must say this is the first company I fell in love with. All the others were good companies with good people, but Tom's turned out to be very special for my family and me. It allowed Pam and me to put both our sons through high school

> and college and kept us in one place for ten-plus years. I passed on a number of better opportunities and stayed.

The note was issued on company letterhead that had not been updated since the 1970s.

Divin also announced that the email marked his final day at Tom's. But at first, he was the only person asked to leave. "Everybody except the CEO will be offered a job" is how Singer put it, saying the Tom's plants in Columbus, Florida, Tennessee, Texas, and California were "strategically located to help reduce our transportation costs." Several higher-ups at the Columbus factory elected to stay on after meeting with Lance leadership, finding them to have the same family-oriented, Southern-style approach to business that drew them to Tom's in the first place. "The period of time when Lance owned us was really fun," longtime Tom's peanut operations manager Ben Smith said. "Lance's history and Tom's history were very similar. Their philosophy of businesses was similar, and so they meshed together very well." Jack Warden had already put in his notice to leave but decided against it after a conversation with Singer. He became general manager and the top dog in Columbus after that. Lance and Tom's had strong regional overlap and could combine the best elements of their two product lineups to match strength with strength. Thanks to the Columbus factory's location in the middle of the peanut belt, Lance began processing the peanut butter for all its crackers nationwide at its old rival's headquarters. But for Tom's Foods as an entity, as a corporation, as a business, as a going concern, the price of the Lance sale was very high indeed. It meant nothing less than extinction.

While Tom's was owned by General Mills from 1966 to 1983, by Rowntree Mackintosh from 1983 to 1988, and by Heico from 1993 to 2005, it operated more or less as an independent entity throughout. The Tom Huston Peanut Company, and later Tom's Foods, always had its own president, its own board of directors, a headquarters building in Columbus, and a full office staff. Following the Lance sale, Tom's as a company ceased to exist. Lance created the trade name "Tom's Snacks Co." to carry on the brand going forward, but it opted to continue printing the Tom's logo only on potato chips and pork rinds, the products Tom's had promoted most heavily since the 1960s. Tom's never found the success it sought with chips, but it did fare better than Lance, and most Lance-branded chips and extruded products were discontinued. This meant, ironically, that none of the remaining Tom's-branded products would be made in Columbus. The items Columbus did make, including salted and candied peanuts, crackers, and pastries, would carry Lance logos going forward. Tom's Toasted Peanuts, the company's first product and for decades its "papa product" and best seller, was discontinued. Or rather, it and many other old Tom's favorites continued production but with Lance labels placed on the bags.

There were other growing pains during the transition. Despite initially keeping all Tom's employees on board, Lance later moved most of the Columbus office jobs to Charlotte, shut down the 149-person Knoxville plant at the end of 2006, and sold off the Fresno, California, plant to a plastics manufacturer called Prinsco Inc. in 2007. That left only the plants in Corsicana, Texas, and Perry, Florida, and the old Tom's headquarters in Columbus still operating as part of Lance Inc. The Columbus workforce dwindled from 600 workers all the way down to 165 before it began to rebound upward. But sales at Lance Inc. grew rapidly in the latter part of the twenty-first century's first decade. Singer placed a strong emphasis on reducing complexity, envisioning a unified company centered on its three brands: Lance, Tom's, and Cape Cod kettle chips, which Lance had bought from Anheuser-Busch in 1999. This meant streamlining and simplifying the product lineup. Tom's alone was making 400 different items as it fell into bankruptcy. Under Singer, the combined lineup of all three brands was trimmed to 350. "That's one of the things in the turnaround you do, is you try to get your business to be a lot less complex," he said.

Tom's focused on its strongest products such as vinegar and salt chips and hot fries, Lance churned out its industry-leading cracker line, and Cape Cod exclusively manufactured its niche brand of kettle chips. The Tom's logo got its first refresh in thirty years, with a bold outline edged by a dash of yellow trim and the "Tom's" script brought outside of the red triangle for the first time. Many former Tom's employees began to buy into the idea that a Tom's/Lance partnership was a smart idea, even if Lance was in control. "The people with Lance seemed like the old Tom's people," said Jernigan Gresham, a Tom's manager with more than three decades of experience. "Their stories sounded so much like our stories, how the company grew and what happened with them. It felt like a good fit, and it was for a time." As judged by revenue figures, the public agreed. Lance made $600 million in 2004, the year before it bought Tom's. By 2007, revenue had shot up to $762.7 million. By 2008 it reached $852.5 million, up 12 percent year-over-year even as the Great Recession settled in, and in 2009 it climbed up to $920 million. The recession actually boosted Lance, officials said, because cash-strapped consumers were spending more time at grocery stores and less at restaurants.

Lance Inc. updated the Tom's logo for the first time in thirty years after buying the company out of bankruptcy in 2005.

Another threat emerged when a nasty salmonella outbreak was traced to a peanut butter plant in Blakely, Georgia, in 2009. Lance wasn't impacted, but the public didn't necessarily know that from listening to all the news reports about tainted legumes. Singer turned to the then-new medium of YouTube to reassure the public that Lance products were safe. "At Lance, we make 100 percent of the peanut butter we use in our crackers," he said in the clip. "No peanut butter or peanut butter paste from the supplier at the center of this investigation is in any product carrying the Lance brand." What he didn't say specifically was that 100 percent of that peanut butter was made in Columbus, where Lance took advantage of the in-house shelling operation to shift production after it bought Tom's. Sales still took a modest hit due to fears from the nationwide product recall, but not enough to curb Lance's overall growth trend.

In May 2009, Lance invested $10.5 million to hire 70 more people at the Columbus plant, bringing the local workforce up to 520, almost as many as the 600 who worked there during the last days of Heico's ownership. "We all knew it was something special when Lance bought us," Warden told *The Columbus Ledger-Enquirer*. A fun perk of the Lance deal was that the company included Tom's in its NASCAR sponsorship, placing the restyled Tom's logo on the back fender and sometimes the hood of the No. 47 car driven by Michael McDowell in 2009, by Marcos Ambrose in 2010, and by Bobby Labonte in 2011.

It was a lot of fun for the old Tom's folks who had known nothing but struggles for twenty-five straight years. At the same, they knew that Tom's, to the extent it continued to exist, was not in control of its own destiny and was subject to the whims and desires of ownership that had no real connection to the brand. Singer was doing well leading Lance and reviving Tom's, but he was an acquisitions man, and that success positioned him to continue buying up other companies and brands. In November 2008 he bought up Archway Cookies, an Ashland, Ohio–based firm that had also gone bankrupt. Lance got Archway for the relatively small sum of $30 million and took over its plant in a maneuver similar to the Tom's deal. The next year, Lance bought a New York City–based company called Stella D'oro that manufactured Italian-style cookies and breadsticks. Workers at its factory in the Bronx had spent ten months on strike when the previous ownership said it needed to cut wages and benefits to make the firm profitable. After Lance bought Stella D'oro for an undisclosed sum, it closed the New York factory and moved production to the nonunion Archway facility in Ohio.

Amid all of these acquisitions, Columbus began churning out products for another Lance-affiliated brand called Late July, which gave the factory a star turn on the Food Network in 2008. But Tom's was becoming a smaller and smaller fraction of the lineup all the time. Singer's next move accelerated that process. On July 23, 2010, Lance announced a merger with Pennsylvania-based Snyder's of Hanover in a deal that created the nation's second-largest salty snacks business, with combined annual sales of $1.6 billion (still pretty minor compared to Frito-Lay, which brought in $13.2 billion in 2009). Snyder's was the nation's top brand of pretzels and had bought another chip company, Jays Foods of Chicago, out of bankruptcy in 2007. Both Lance and Snyder's dubbed it a "merger of equals," and in that spirit they forged an unusual power-sharing structure. Charlotte would remain the company headquarters, and the company would still be publicly traded under the ticker symbol "LNCE." Singer retained the title of CEO. But Hanover, Pennsylvania, was described as an "additional headquarters," and Snyder's president Carl E. Lee Jr. got the titles of president and COO. The combined firm was named Snyder's-Lance.

Singer stood to make as much as $3.6 million for closing the deal while maintaining a leadership role in the combined firm. However, the merger marked the end of his run of successes, as Snyder's-Lance proved to be an awkward fit in the market and stumbled through much of the next decade. The combined company lost $3.84 million in the second quarter of 2011 after buying yet another firm, George Greer Company Inc. of New England. A story in *The Charlotte Observer* about the disturbing news did not mention Tom's in a list of brands that Snyder's-Lance owned. That fall, Snyder's-Lance announced it was shutting down the Corsicana, Texas, plant that Tom's had opened in 1963. About one hundred people were still working at the plant when it closed; all of them were laid off with severance pay and support services toward finding a new job.

After another sluggish year in 2012, Singer announced his departure in January 2013, as Carl Lee Jr. unified the company's leadership roles of president, COO, and CEO. Things didn't improve from there. In 2014 Snyder's-Lance closed two more plants and sold off its private brands. It made another pair of acquisitions in the middle of the decade, Baptista's Bakery and Diamond Foods, neither of which seemed to make much of an impact. Lee made a surprise announcement in April 2016 that he was retiring, to be replaced by Diamond Foods CEO Brian Driscoll. That action was followed by dozens of layoffs at the Charlotte headquarters. In the middle of 2017, Snyder's-Lance closed the Perry, Florida, plant that Tom's had opened in 1980, leaving only Columbus still operating among the five plants Lance inherited when it bought Tom's. About 100 people were still working at the Perry facility at the time of the closure, and 250 other Snyder's-Lance employees were laid off simultaneously.

At the end of 2017 yet another sale emerged. Campbell Soup Company, based in Camden, New Jersey, just across the Delaware River from Philadelphia, announced an agreement to buy Snyder's-Lance for $4.9 billion. The deal had been rumored for a few months and came at a nice premium of about 27 percent for Snyder's-Lance stockholders. Campbell already owned several snack brands, including Pepperidge Farm, which made Goldfish crackers and Milano cookies, among other things. Of course, this sale made Tom's an even tinier portion of its parent company's portfolio. The old Lance headquarters in Charlotte was shuttered, with administrative functions handled in New Jersey, a place where few people knew of Tom's. The Snyder's-Lance deal was part of a buying spree in which Campbell CEO Denise Morrison made six acquisitions in five years. Campbell took on a lot of debt to buy Snyder's-Lance, so much so that its credit rating was downgraded in the process. In May 2018, just six months after Campbell announced the Snyder's-Lance acquisition, Morrison abruptly retired—on the same day that Campbell announced a $475 million quarterly loss. She was replaced by an interim CEO named Keith R. McLoughlin, who himself was replaced by permanent CEO Mark Clouse in December of that year. Even as a brand, stability proved elusive for Tom's Snacks. Between the 2005 Lance buyout and the end of 2018, it had seen three different ownership groups and six CEOs.

Clouse focused on revitalizing Campbell's core soup business, a nearly opposite tack from Morrison. He had plans for the snack division as well, but despite owning the nation's top-selling brands of pretzels and crackers, Clouse saw Campbell as a niche player that should concentrate on categories overlooked by larger competitors. "I'm not fighting it out in the big mainstream segments like potato chips," he told *The Philadelphia Inquirer*. "I'm in kettle chips. I'm not in crackers. I'm in kids' better-for-you crackers." Tom's at the time exclusively made potato chips and pork rinds. It did not make kettle chips.

The shuffling had decimated Tom's as a brand in less than a decade. From a heavily promoted chip line in 2005 through 2010 under Lance, Tom's became nearly invisible by the time of the Campbell purchase in 2018. Clouse's reshuffling and efforts to narrow Campbell's focus hit Columbus three years later. On January 13, 2021, Campbell announced it was closing the Columbus plant. While Tom's-branded products hadn't rolled off the line there since 2005, the announcement severed the last ties between what remained of the company and the city where it was founded. Employment at the factory had fallen from more than 500 in 2010 down to 326 by the time the closure was announced, and all of those employees were set to be laid off by the middle of 2022.

"Closing one of our facilities is a very difficult decision," Campbell Snacks president Valerie Oswalt said in a press release. "The Columbus plant is the oldest in our manufacturing network, making it difficult to retrofit. Our Columbus team is talented and dedicated, and we are committed to assisting them through this transition." The closure did not impact the Tom's brand as it existed in 2021, though it did come with the cancellation of three old staples from its peanut days: the Peanut Bar, Star Bites, and Boston Old Style peanuts. Each had been manufactured under the Tom's label originally, and under the Lance label from 2005 until 2021. The news wasn't a shock to Columbus, as the factory's decline was a story long since told. But it did bring finality to the saga at the local level, and it left a twenty-eight-acre site officials hoped to backfill one way or the other. "That factory has really done a lot for the lives of the people of Columbus, providing gainful employment for so many people for so many years,"

Columbus Chamber of Commerce President Jerald Mitchell said. "To the extent that we find a company that is considering Columbus and that footprint, whether the building, the land, or the workforce, we'll try to get them to locate there."

The closure spelled the end of Johnny Johnson's fifty-three-year career, every day of it spent at the old Tom's headquarters. But it also left 325 other people looking for work, marking one more step in the city, state, and country's march away from manufacturing as a means of employment. At its peak, Tom's operated eight factories in three time zones, with three shifts of employees working around the clock in a sprawling Columbus headquarters that spanned more than seven city blocks. Everyone in town knew at least one person who worked there, and most knew more than one. But from the mid-1980s onward, the company's slow unraveling commenced—never rushed, but never stopping. The little empire Tom's built slipped down to five factories by 1990, to three in 2010, and to one in 2020. Finally, the last and biggest closure came at the beginning of the 2020s, just four years shy of the company's one-hundredth anniversary.

But at least one thing hadn't changed between the days of Tom Huston and Walter Richards in the 1920s and the days of decay and layoffs a century later, and that was the factory's family atmosphere. Columbus television station WTVM caught up with an employee named Warren Brown Jr. in the factory parking lot on the day the closure was announced. Brown had worked there only since 2012 and had even left for a while, but he returned because "I had to come back home." In an impromptu interview, he returned to the word "family" again and again.

"Before it was Campbell, it was Snyder's-Lance; before it was Snyder's-Lance, it was Lance; and before Lance, it was Tom's. You're looking at a company that has been around here, as you reported, almost a century," Brown said, staring into the sunlight through the January chill. "When you've been at a place working with your coworkers for so long, you're no longer coworkers. You become family. . . . You have people there who have been there ten, twenty years. There are people who have been there over forty years. They've raised their family there. So it has affected us not just financially, but emotionally. We're family."

Conclusion

The factory did not close. Not completely anyway. Longtime Tom's workers Ben Smith and Johnny Johnson have told me it's still pulling in a crew of between twenty and twenty-five people who take in raw peanuts from the Georgia-Alabama peanut belt, shell them, roast them, and turn them into peanut paste, which is then shipped up to Charlotte for use in sandwich crackers and other products. Peanut paste is basically pure ground peanuts, whereas peanut butter includes certain additives to improve the flavor. The reason processing remains in Columbus is obvious enough—it's much more efficient than shipping unshelled loose peanuts all the way up to Charlotte.

In choosing to keep some production in Columbus, the Campbell Soup Company faced the same dilemma as peanut proprietor Henry Loomus in the late 1800s. Loomus initially shipped Virginia peanuts all the way to his shelling plant in Philadelphia before taking the practical step of moving his equipment to Suffolk, Virginia, for local processing. Nearly 150 years later, history repeats itself. There's also a bit of symmetry at play for the old Tom's factory, as the plant has come completely full circle. Tom Huston first moved to Columbus in the 1910s to set up a peanut-shelling operation, and a century later that's the function the business he launched still performs. Tom's was for decades the only major snack food company shelling its own peanuts, again owing to Huston's legacy, and it is doing the same thing today and for the foreseeable future. Lance initially moved its peanut butter production from Charlotte to Columbus after it bought Tom's in 2005, and here we have another Philadelphia-area firm (Campbell's Camden, New Jersey, headquarters is located just across the Delaware River from Philadelphia) learning the same lesson that Loomus did so many years ago.

As of this writing, the rest of the old Tom's plant is being sold off piece by piece. An entity called New Mill Capital bought the site, which included 510,000 square feet of space on 28.3 acres, in April 2022 for a price that wasn't publicly disclosed, then auctioned off the equipment inside that June. New Mill Capital owns the "peanut building" too, which it is leasing back to Campbell. I visited the plant in December 2023 with my dad and saw that some of the buildings had been rebranded as "Tom's Depot," owing of course to its history as the Tom's headquarters and also to its location on multiple railroad lines. A few of the buildings were already leased out to a printing company and a construction equipment rental business.

Having spent two full years researching the history of Tom's, it is hard not to look at the vacant, rusty architecture and question some of the decisions made along the way. A big one was the early 1960s choice to shift attention from peanuts to potato chips, which were never really a core Tom's product despite decades of efforts to the contrary. Could a tightly focused Tom Huston Peanut Company still be around, battling with Planters on America's store shelves? It's hard to say. I certainly understand the reasons leadership went toward chips—namely, they sell a lot better and represent a much bigger market. And to the extent that going chip-first was an error, Tom's didn't feel any negative consequences from that decision for more than twenty years. Still, the question of what might've happened, both at this juncture and at many others, will always remain.

Looking forward, I do wonder if some budding entrepreneur could make a go of reviving Tom's Toasted Peanuts. It's an iconic Southern brand with a great story that could be marketed any number of creative ways. There's the history of product innovation, the classic packaging and promotion schemes of Huston ("Society's Selection," "The Modern Way"), the George Washington Carver connection, and the simple fact that peanuts remain a miracle food high in protein, healthy fats, and other nutrients. They taste great, add nitrogen to soil and oxygen to the environment, and are both vegan and gluten free. Could Tom's Toasted Peanuts be marketed to an affluent, Whole Foods–type of crowd by playing up the health benefits and Carver history? Or maybe they could come back as an everyman's snack, their original market, playing on many of those same factors. Or perhaps time is up on a product as simple as salted, toasted peanuts, and any comeback attempt would fail against so many commoditized store-brand competitors. I don't know who owns the legal rights to the name or how much investment it would take to sprout a revival, but somebody ought to try it.

Separate from that, writing this history has convinced me that Columbus should make more of its peanut history. Despite their lowbrow reputation, peanuts remain an immensely popular food. More than 772 billion peanuts are grown in Georgia every single year, and they make their way into a myriad number of mega-brands like Snickers, Peanut M&Ms, Butterfinger, Baby Ruth, Reese's Peanut Butter Cups, Lance crackers, and literally thousands of other products. A few smaller towns in the region, such as Enterprise, Alabama, and Blakely, Georgia, play up their status as peanut hubs, but Columbus remains the biggest city in the peanut belt and still boasts an enormous set of fourteen-story peanut silos that sprouted up in one week seven decades ago. Columbus was the place George Washington Carver visited so frequently and where he made so many friends and connections. Columbus called itself the peanut capital of the Southeast in the 1930s, and that should be a bigger and more prominent part of the city's story.

While I'm selling my ideas, I must say that the Carver-Huston story is one that could be told more prominently as well, not just in the South but everywhere. I was born in Columbus, grew up with Tom's as a constant presence in my life, and learned about George Washington Carver almost every year in school, especially during Black History Month. Yet I knew nothing about the Carver-Huston connection before researching a 2021 *Atlanta Journal-Constitution* story on the Tom's factory closure. Theirs is an inspiring story of interracial friendship and achievement in the dark days of segregation. Their collaboration helped rescue the Southern economy and was hugely celebrated by Carver himself, who kept a jar of Tom's Toasted Peanuts on his office desk at all times once the product blew up. The story begs to be told more often, perhaps using Edith Powell's 2022 book *More Than Peanuts* as a model. The relationship that Carver had with Huston, his consulting work on Tom's Toasted Peanuts, and his brilliant presentation before Congress to secure a peanut tariff are arguably more impactful portions of his legacy than better-known facts like his three hundred uses for the peanut or his homeopathic peanut oil massage treatment for polio, and more people ought to know about them.

It's a little harder to draw conclusions from the post-1930s story of Tom's. My premise going into this project was that Tom's could be seen as an avatar of the wider twentieth-century Southern economy. Having written this history of Tom's, I still feel that is correct. Tom's certainly modeled the out-of-the-fields-and-into-the-factories movement of the early twentieth century as the region began to truly industrialize. Huston's peanut shellers embodied this trend, and his toasted peanuts were one of many mass-produced snacks invented during the 1920s. Tom's was part of many big-picture trends later on as well. It sent peanuts to soldiers during World War II, innovated the glass-front vending machine in the 1950s, faced the ravages of inflation and price controls in the 1970s, and then rode the Wall Street leveraged buyout wave in the 1980s and the low-fat craze of the 1990s.

The difference, after about 1970, was that Tom's increasingly found itself following those trends, rather than leading them as it had from 1925 though the 1960s. Tom's management executed its LBO just as that fad was about to fizzle out, then created a low-fat line three full years after Nabisco launched Snackwells. The final trend Tom's embodied, sadly, was the big trend away from regional manufacturing and toward knowledge work and services in the late twentieth and early twenty-first centuries. It was in this respect a bridge between agriculture and the office work people associate with today's economy. Tom's aging, rusting factory could be located most anywhere in the United States, from the South to the archetypical Rust Belt states to gritty neighborhoods in Philadelphia or even somewhere like Seattle, which was known for its ship and aircraft manufacturing in the days before Microsoft. Columbus made that postindustrial transition relatively smoothly, with Aflac, TSYS, Synovus, Columbus State University, and Fort Benning picking up the slack when Tom's and the old cotton mills faded out. Muscogee County's population continues to grow, as it has in every U.S. census since 1860. By no means was the transition painless, however. Layoffs hit Tom's at regular intervals between the early 1980s and the early 2020s when the old headquarters was shut down—or nearly shut down, as it turns out. Many of those let go did not have college degrees, making it hard for them to find a comparable salary elsewhere. Some had worked at Tom's for thirty years or more, making it difficult—and for some, practically impossible—to start over with a new employer so late in their careers. I saw it happen inside my own family and saw how damaging it was both financially and emotionally for those affected.

That's where the premise I began with, Tom's as the story of economic transition from agriculture to manufacturing to knowledge work, breaks down a bit. While it's accurate, an increasing number of people question whether it should be. There's no doubt that factory work employs a smaller portion of the labor force now as compared to the mid-twentieth century.

According to the Bureau of Labor Statistics, total U.S. manufacturing employment peaked in 1979 at 19.6 million jobs and then over the next forty years fell to 12.8 million—even as the population of the United States grew by more than 100 million. What doesn't hold up quite as well is the notion that this represents a natural change befitting a more educated, more enlightened workforce. In Washington, D.C., I'm seeing the idea of a postindustrial America challenged more and more frequently. For example, the student loan crisis has become a topic of campaign fodder, with roughly 45 million voting-age Americans holding a collective $1.7 trillion in debt. All of them entered school thinking college would be their path toward rewarding work in a white-collar job, and an untold number—somewhere in the tens of millions—have not found it.

Politicians from both major political parties have noticed and are again speaking about the upsides of manufacturing. For President Joe Biden, speaking about the CHIPS and Science Act in 2023, the promise of high wages held great appeal. "The focus of each of these investments is what [Congressman] Mike [Levin] is really focused on, training workers, hiring veterans, jobs paying a prevailing wage, union jobs, good-paying jobs that don't require a college degree," Biden said. "Intel says their average pay for running their factories—and they're employing thousands of people—the average salary where you don't need a college degree is $124,000." For Vice President JD Vance, speaking in July 2025, the focus was on the wider societal impact. "Our innovations—American innovations—revolutionized communications, medicine, and agriculture, extending human lifespans decades at a time," Vance said. "None of that would be possible if our citizens believed we lived in a postindustrial era."

A related piece of conventional wisdom holds that import tariffs are a relic of the 1930s that the United States wisely abandoned to open up free trade and allow cheaper products to reach our shores. In D.C., both the Trump and Biden administrations have implemented and then raised tariffs, mostly on China but to a lesser extent on other nations as well. This has a lot to do with upset Midwestern voters who saw their communities decimated by the loss of factories and, right or wrong, looked to the government for a solution. Sure enough, tariffs came up in my research, with George Washington Carver staking his claim to fame—launching his career, in the national sense—by lobbying Congress for a foreign import tariff on peanuts. Did that put a floor under the market that helped Tom Huston sell shellers and start a snack company? It would be hard to argue that it didn't, though there's no way to quantify the exact impact.

The lowering of trade barriers in the late twentieth century probably did not cause the downfall of Tom's. Tariffs and free trade damaged some domestic industries; food was not one of them. In fact, food manufacturing employment has mostly held steady since 1979. It was not foreign competition or cheap imports that put Tom's out of business, but rather regional rivals like Frito-Lay, Lance Inc., and Golden Flake. Most domestically consumed food products are still made inside the United States; it's just that Tom's is not one of those big brands still duking it out in America's grocery stores.

Yet in other ways Tom's is a perfect avatar of industrial decline. A third late twentieth-century notion being questioned again is the idea that anti-monopoly laws can mostly be ignored so long as prices remain competitive for consumers. Leaders from both major political parties are now asking whether this is wise, often focusing on "Big Tech" but also on other oligarchic industries like meatpacking or air travel. Here, Tom's could be Exhibit A in a presentation on how the dominant companies in a given sector cause harm that extends beyond simple store prices. Reading Dirk Burhans's 2008 history of the potato chip, *Crunch!*, I was shocked to learn just how many regional chippers went bankrupt around the same time as Tom's. That was not a coincidence, thanks to the slotting fees practice that forced so many regionals out of supermarket aisles, and anyone complaining today that a single company controlled 89.6 percent of the corn chip market and 79.4 percent of all tortilla chip sales, as Frito-Lay did in 1997, might find a more receptive audience at the Department of Justice.

The emerging, or reemerging, thinking is that people should be thought of as producers first and as consumers second, rather than the other way around. Here, too, Tom's holds up well as a model. For eighty years Tom's provided meaningful employment to thousands of people in Columbus and from places as far as fifty miles away in rural Georgia and Alabama, and that's on top of the factory workers in Macon, Tennessee, Florida, Virginia, Maine, Texas, and California who labored on the Tom's payroll, along with the army of distributors and Southern salesmen pushing the wares on their routes. While it will always be controversial to describe any company as a "family," that's the word I kept hearing in interviews with folks from the home office and in materials I read about Tom's, and it even came up in a few interviews I didn't conduct myself. You had the Tom's softball, basketball, and bowling teams; Family Day events at the company retreat; and literal family members hired and dispersed throughout various departments of the sprawling headquarters. I keep thinking about the folks who had the same coworkers for two or three decades and came to work smelling roasted peanuts every day, and the long-haul commuters who would pile eight or ten people into the back of a pickup truck for the drive to Columbus and back. What kind of a bonding experience was that? The factory anchored the community and arguably anchored workers to their community in ways that are difficult to achieve with data-based office jobs, and certainly with remote work.

With that said, I bring up all of these points to acknowledge that such discussions are taking place and that questions about meaningful employment, a healthy employer/employee relationship, and the role of manufacturing in the country are difficult to answer. In my research and in my writing, my goal has been to lay out the facts as I've found them, telling the story as straightforwardly as possible and withholding judgment as to who is right or wrong in any given conflict or which strategic decisions might have been made differently in hindsight. In most cases, the results speak for themselves over time, and to the extent they do not, the reader can decide on their own who was correct and what should have been done instead.

What's undeniable is that the legacy of Tom's really does remain today if one knows where to look. Obviously Tom's chips and pork rinds are still around, though they've become harder and harder to find in recent years. But it's the other, less obvious ways that I had in mind in titling this book *A Legacy in Peanuts*. That legacy lies in the myriad ways in which the rich history of Tom's as it existed between 1925 and 2005 still radiates. The company attracted community leaders and investment dollars to Columbus throughout that run. Tom Huston was brought to town by the already-established Columbus Iron Works, and from there every single one of the company's presidents moved in at least in part because of Tom's.

Walter Richards might never have returned from Daytona Beach if Tom's hadn't emerged as a promising new gig. J. W. Feighner might have moved elsewhere if opportunities for a young engineering graduate didn't exist in his girlfriend's hometown. Mike Tracy moved to Columbus for the explicit purpose of leading Tom's. Mike Dillon moved to Columbus in 1971 to launch the firm's marketing department, while Ron Divin came in 1995 for the CEO job and stayed until Tom's went bankrupt a decade later. These men not only led Tom's but also became involved in all sorts of community activities, with Richards and Feighner serving on the local school board and as the city's mayor, and Dillon, Tracy, and Divin contributing to less prominent but still significant civic affairs.

Perhaps more importantly, thousands of people over those eight decades found gainful employment, and many of them moved permanently to the city, because of the big peanut concern in town. Those people raised their children in Columbus, and thousands of them and their descendants are still there now thanks to those long-ago opportunities. The impact can be hard to trace directly, but by looking closely we can see it in the careers of a few executives in their post-Tom's careers. Though Tom's filed for bankruptcy in 2005, some of its top leadership began quietly leaving the company as early as the 1980s, when the firm first fell into trouble. Mike Dillon, for example, became the CEO of Columbus's Kinnett Dairies after leaving Tom's in 1995, and in 2004 he took a role with a Columbus-based business technology incubator to grow the next generation of employers.

Tom B. Black is another good example. He moved from Tennessee to Columbus in 1968 after his dad's chip business merged with Tom's, then stayed at the company as vice president and COO until 1986, when he took early retirement. But Black didn't leave town. He remained to operate a chain of Baskin-Robbins and Auntie Anne's stores in the area, then served as administrator of the Bradley-Turner Foundation from 1998 until 2006. Black played a major role in raising funds to build the RiverCenter for the Performing Arts and, before his death in 2014, helped bring a campus of the Mercer University School of Medicine to Uptown Columbus thanks to his status as a longtime trustee of the college. That medical school now has 240 future doctors enrolled at all times, and they no doubt will make their own impact on the community in the future.

The daisy-chain effect may be the ultimate legacy of the Tom Huston Peanut Company, as another link in the pattern of one industry begetting another. The presence of the Chattahoochee River led to the establishment of the city of Columbus on its banks, then to trade as a cotton port, and then to manufacturing as a cotton mill town using hydropower. That helped lure other businesses, including William R. Brown's Columbus Iron Works in 1849, which helped bring Tom Huston to the area seventy years later when he contracted with the firm to manufacture his peanut shellers. Once in town, Huston created a peanut snack food empire that drew in tens of thousands of employees who made their own contributions, including one who helped Columbus land its own medical school.

So while the Tom's factory site will enjoy a future in one form or another, its shuttering may prove to be just another step in the evolution of industries in Columbus and in Georgia, with assembly-line gigs replaced by jobs in growing sectors such as health care, information technology, and even film production. Like the cotton mills that once dominated Columbus, Tom's Toasted Peanuts were only a single step removed from the fields of agriculture. The crop was converted directly into a product, and a year with too much or too little rain could spell trouble in the factories. In this way, for better or worse, Tom's and its sprawling factory were a symbol of their time and place, representing an era when people left fields for cities in search of stable employment and new opportunities. That promise continues today through the descendants of those employees, and Tom Huston's impact is still felt every time someone rips open a bag of salted peanuts from the local convenience store.

NOTES

CHAPTER 1

9 *For Tom Huston*: Ruel McDaniel, "Made Millions with Peanuts," *National Nut News*, October 1929, 21.

9 *"It wasn't the goobers"*: "Tom's Peanuts," *Time*, August 25, 1930.

9 *"Many a night"*: McDaniel, "Made Millions with Peanuts," 21.

9 *Rather than feasting*: McDaniel, "Made Millions with Peanuts," 21.

10 *He didn't seem*: Tom Sellers, "Genius in Exile," *Sunday Ledger-Enquirer Magazine* (Columbus), August 29, 1965, 18–19.

10 *Huston's father ran*: "A Peanut Romance," *Candy*, October 1929, 10.

10 *The dreaded bug*: Powell, *More Than Peanuts*, 25.

10 *Peanuts, which are*: Smith, *Peanuts: The Illustrious History*, 3.

10–11 *Recent research has*: David J. Bertioli et al., "The Genome Sequence of Segmental Allotetraploid Peanut *Arachis hypogaea*," *Nature Genetics* 51 (May 2019): 877–84.

11 *Centuries-old gravesites*: Smith, *Peanuts: The Illustrious History*, 6–7.

11 *Some accounts have*: *25 Years of Peanut Progress*, 29.

12 *For example, early*: Smith, *Peanuts: The Illustrious History*, 12.

12 *The name comes*: *25 Years of Peanut Progress*, 29.

12 *largest peanut producer*: Raphael Warnock, "That's Nuts—Warnock for Georgia," campaign advertisement, posted September 30, 2022, by Reverend Raphael Warnock, YouTube, 30 sec., https://www.youtube.com/watch?v=FXJNRfhEwTQ.

12 *Peanuts could be*: Interview with Ben Smith, October 26, 2023.

12 *Peanut-fed hogs*: Crawford and Eberhardt, *Tom's: Back Home*, 4.

12 *There are several*: Smith, *Peanuts: The Illustrious History*, 13, 17, 64.

13 *Just as the*: Smith, *Peanuts: The Illustrious History*, 15.

13 *"He used to"*: Cleburne Huston, "Millionaire Peanut Man," *Stamford (Tex.) American*, July 23, 1929.

14 *His childhood is*: Sellers, "Genius in Exile," 18.

14 *The earliest reference*: Howard Valentine, "Remembering Our Past and How It Affected Our Present and Future," *Peanut Science*, July 1, 2019.

14 *Huston spent years*: "A Peanut Romance," 10.

15 *A sort of*: Smith, *Peanuts: The Illustrious History*, 48.

15 *Peanut butter began*: Smith, *Peanuts: The Illustrious History*, 30.

15 *Peanut butter was*: Smith, *Peanuts: The Illustrious History*, 30, 39.

15 *In 1915, while*: The patent numbers are 1,178,075 and 1,246,100.

15 *The first spate*: Crawford and Eberhardt, *Tom's: Back Home*, 5.

16 *There were two*: McDaniel, "Made Millions with Peanuts," 23.

16 *Columbus, as history*: Causey, *Red Clay, White Water*, 1–2, 6–8.

16 *Columbus, Georgia, is*: Causey, *Red Clay, White Water*, 7.

16 *At its founding*: John Hayes, "Federal Road," in *New Georgia Encyclopedia* (Georgia Humanities, 2004–), published February 10, 2003; last modified July 21, 2020, https://www.georgiaencyclopedia.org/articles/business-economy/federal-road/.

16 *Steamboat technology advanced*: Delfino and Gillespie, *Southern Industrialization*, 20–21.

17 *Eli Whitney's 1793*: Holt, *George Washington Carver*, 123–24.

17 *Most of the South's*: Causey, *Red Clay, White Water*, 19.

17 *The mills helped*: Causey, *Red Clay, White Water*, 1–2.

17 *Textile mills were*: Delfino and Gillespie, *Southern Industrialization*, 127.

17 *Almost as soon*: Causey, *Red Clay, White Water*, 19, 21, 58.

18 *The Civil War boosted*: Causey, *Red Clay, White Water*, 39.

18 *While Black citizens*: Coleman, *A History of Georgia*, 222, 248, 252, 257.

18 *There was innovation*: Causey, *Red Clay, White Water*, 126–29.

19 *The other story*: Causey, *Red Clay, White Water*, 23, 61, 212, 257–58; Scott Trubey, "Global Payments to Merge with TSYS in Tie-Up of Georgia Fintech Firms," *Atlanta Journal-Constitution*, May 28, 2019, https://www.ajc.com/business/economy/global-payments-merge-with-tsys-tie-georgia-fintech-firms/eq1DfaXdcBj75T243O5B8H/. *The Atlanta Journal-Constitution* will be abbreviated as AJC hereafter.

19 *William H. Young*: Causey, *Red Clay, White Water*, 59, 82.

19 *Yet even this*: Peter A. Coclanis, "More Pricks Than Kicks: The Southern Economy in the Long Twentieth Century," *Study the South*, May 26, 2020, https://studythesouth.org/more-pricks-than-kicks/.

19 "*The presumption that*": Delfino and Gillespie, *Southern Industrialization*, 16–17.

20 *Mill work was*: Coclanis, "More Pricks."

20 *The situation was*: Coleman, *A History of Georgia*, 320.

20 *For example, mill*: Causey, *Red Clay, White Water*, 93.

20 *As University of*: Coclanis, "More Pricks."

20 *Cotton and textiles*: Coleman, *A History of Georgia*, 257; Coclanis, "More Pricks."

21 *Indeed, in Columbus*: Causey, *Red Clay, White Water*, 93.

21 *Roughly 26.5 million*: USDA peanut survey, 1909–2023.

21 *"My train left"*: Rachel Kaufman, "In Search of George Washington Carver's True Legacy," *Smithsonian*, February 2019, https://www.smithsonianmag.com/history/search-george-washington-carvers-true-legacy-180971538/.

21 *the Southern cotton*: Kaufman, "In Search of."

21 *many Georgians suffered*: Coleman, *A History of Georgia*, 331–32.

22 *Carver was a*: Holt, *George Washington Carver*, 225–28.

22 *Because cotton was*: Kaufman, "In Search of."

22 *The scientist toured*: History.com Editors, "George Washington Carver: Facts, Inventions & Quotes," History.com, last updated June 30, 2025, https://www.history.com/topics/black-history/george-washington-carver.

22 *Domestic peanut farmers*: Smith, *Peanuts: The Illustrious History*, 16, 66–68.

22 *Tragically, this demand*: Lewis, *Slaves for Peanuts*, 190–91.

23 *The commercial use*: Smith, *Peanuts: The Illustrious History*, 53.

23 *Foreign import tariffs*: Anshu Siripurapu and Noah Berman, "What Are Tariffs?," Council on Foreign Relations, published May 16, 2019; last updated April 1, 2025, https://www.cfr.org/backgrounder/what-are-tariffs.

23 *In 1921, the*: Smith, *Peanuts: The Illustrious History*, 16, 91–92.

24 *Remarkably, Carver did*: Holt, *George Washington Carver*, 256–59.

25 *Carver found three*: Holt, *George Washington Carver*, 317–18.

25 *Georgia farmers lived*: Coleman, *A History of Georgia*, 263, 276.

26 *they'd learned through*: Causey, *Red Clay, White Water*, 87.

26 *Carver found kinship*: Powell, *More Than Peanuts*, 106.

CHAPTER 2

27 *By 1918 Huston*: Tom Sellers, "Genius in Exile," *Sunday Ledger-Enquirer Magazine* (Columbus), August 29, 1965, 18.

27 *Following up on*: The patent numbers are 1,412,614, 1,477,649, and 1,477,648.

27 *Huston found a*: Haisten Willis, "A Legacy in Peanuts: Columbus Says Goodbye to Tom's Foods Factory," AJC, April 6, 2021, https://www.ajc.com/life/a-legacy-in-peanuts-columbus-says-goodbye-to-toms-foods-factory/QWBEL3XRWVBARC73ZG54C4WNHA/.

28 *"quite simple in"*: J. T. Huston, hand peanut sheller, U.S. Patent 1,477,649, filed May 16, 1919, and issued December 18, 1923, https://patents.google.com/patent/US1477649A/en.

28 *In fact, by*: Powell, *More Than Peanuts*, 134; peanut sheller advertisement, *Montgomery Advertiser*, January 14, 1917, 35.

28 *"a further object"*: J. T. Huston, peanut-shelling machine, U.S. Patent 1,477,648, filed May 16, 1919, and issued December 18, 1923, https://patents.google.com/patent/US1477648A/en.

28 *For a time*: Interview with J. Madden Hatcher Jr., April 22, 2024.

28 *In 1923 he*: T. Huston, tractor plow, U.S. Patent 1,637,525, filed June 23, 1923, by C. R. Medley and issued August 2, 1927, https://patents.google.com/patent/US1637525A/en.

30 *Huston also tested*: Crawford and Eberhardt, *Tom's*: *Back Home*, 7.

30 *In 1924 this*: Powell, *More Than Peanuts*, 29–30.

31 *"Under conditions by"*: Ruel McDaniel, "Made Millions with Peanuts," *National Nut News*, October 1929, 23.

31 *it involved toasting*: Powell, *More Than Peanuts*, 30–31.

31 *On June 9*: The patent number is 1,603,207.

31 *"My invention relates"*: Tom Huston, paper bag and seal, U.S. Patent 1,603,207, filed June 9, 1925, and issued October 12, 1926, https://patents.google.com/patent/US1603207A/en.

35 *Medley, it turns*: Sellers, "Genius in Exile," 19.

35 *The shack could*: "Our Company," *Tom's Toaster*, November 25, 1933, 1.

35 *The Southern Peanut*: Crawford and Eberhardt, *Tom's: Back Home*, 7–10.

35 *"I started this"*: "Creator of 'Tom's Toasted Peanuts' Tells of Economy of Means," *The Broadcaster*, December 1929, 9.

36 *Huston moved out*: Crawford and Eberhardt, *Tom's: Back Home*, 3–4, 20.

37 *One existing method*: Sellers, "Genius in Exile," 19.

37 *The patent, filed*: The patent number is 1,603,954.

37 *"tiny billboard" that*: "Creator of 'Tom's,'" 9.

37 *"The object of"*: Tom Huston, display stand, U.S. Patent 1,603,954, filed December 4, 1925, and issued October 19, 1926, https://patents.google.com/patent/US1603954A/en.

37 *"I wanted to"*: "Creator of 'Tom's,'" 9.

37 *A final jewel*: Crawford and Eberhardt, *Tom's: Back Home*, 3–4, 27.

38 *He not only*: "Talkie Thanks Peanut Buyers," *Columbus Enquirer-Sun*, September 11, 1929, 2; "Tom's Peanuts 1928 advertising record by Mr. Tom Huston 'The Daddy of Tom's Toasted Peanuts,'" posted April 8, 2021, by Dan The Victrola Man, YouTube, 3 min., 29 sec., Tom Huston Peanut Company advertising record, https://www.youtube.com/watch?v=K46aHfLsYb4; "In Memory of Tom's Toasted Peanuts, Columbus, GA. Circa 1928," posted April 8, 2021, by Dan The Victrola Man, YouTube, 3 min., 13 sec., Tom Huston Peanut Company advertising record featuring Sam Lanin's Orchestra, with vocal refrain by Irving Kaufman, https://www.youtube.com/watch?v=JenmuQQhVXU.

38 *Yet another performer*: "Jack Rose, 'the Peanut Boy,' Entertains on Radio," *Fort Wayne (Ind.) Journal-Gazette*, June 9, 1929.

38 *At one point*: "Talkie Thanks Peanut Buyers," 2.

38 *Winners were initially*: This information was obtained from the Tom Huston Collection at Columbus State University, hereafter referred to as the Huston Collection.

38 *These were rotated*: Minnie B. Huston, "Tom Fed Peanuts to All, His Profits to Georgia," *Columbus Ledger-Enquirer*, April 30, 1978, S-29. The *Ledger-Enquirer* will be abbreviated as CL-E hereafter.

38 *Some scholars have*: Tad Brown, "In the Patented Bag: Peanuts, Packaging, and Intellectual Property in the United States, 1906–1932," *Enterprise & Society* 25, no. 3 (2024): 933–56, https://doi.org/10.1017/eso.2023.

39 *An entity called*: Huston Collection.

39 *an angry letter*: "Don't Be Narrow; Forget It," *Peanut Journal*, January 1929, 9.

40 *In 1928 a*: "Huston Peanuts Make Ad Scoop of News Event," *Times-Picayune* (New Orleans), June 24, 1929, 12.

40 *The* Times *asked*: "Ingenuities of Advertising," *New York Times*, June 6, 1928, 28.

40 *More seriously concerned*: "Peanut Pushers Merely a Joke," *Peanut Journal*, July 1929, 9.

40 *He was selling*: McDaniel, "Made Millions with Peanuts," 26.

40 *The program for*: Crawford and Eberhardt, *Tom's: Back Home*, 11.

40 *in late November*: Cromer-Cassel's, "Old Santa Arrives Saturday at Cromer-Cassel's" (advertisement), *Miami Daily News*, November 29, 1929, 5.

41 *Huston's unorthodox approach*: McDaniel, "Made Millions with Peanuts," 26.

41 *Among the crudest*: "A.P. Tells About Tom Huston," *Columbus Enquirer-Sun*, December 8, 1929.

41 *"And now we"*: "A Peanut Romance," *Candy*, October 1929, 10–11.

41 *What's more, Tom's*: "A Peanut Romance," 11.

42 *The first suit*: "Infringement Suit, Involving Millions, Filed by Tom Huston Co.; Action Aimed at Curtiss 'Chicos' Item," *Candy*, September 1929, 4.

42 *"peanuts have ceased"*: "Peanut Business Seventy-Five Million Affair," *Walhalla (S.C.) Courier*, August 14, 1929.

42 *"inviolable as any"*: "Infringement Suit," 4.

42 *Several other suits*: Brown, "In the Patented Bag."

42 *Ever the marketer*: Crawford and Eberhardt, *Tom's: Back Home*, 16–17.

43 *Other new offerings*: "Tom's Peanuts," *Time*, August 25, 1930.

43 *In 1929 Huston*: Tom Huston Peanut Company, bag filling apparatus, U.S. Patent 1,859,562, filed December 14, 1929, and issued May 24, 1932, https://patents.google.com/patent/US1859562A/en.

43 *Net earnings grew*: "Huston Peanut Report Shows Earnings Gain," *Columbus Enquirer-Sun*, October 22, 1929, 1.

43 *The company went*: "Tom Huston Co. Sought by New York Concern," *National Nut News*, July 1929, 63; "Tom's Peanuts," *Time*.

43 *In March 1928*: Hatcher interview.

43 *built a summer*: Mike Owen, "'Tom's Lake' Causes Problems for Snack Makers on 10th," CL-E, February 24, 2016, https://www.ledger-enquirer.com/news/local/news-columns-blogs/article61688437.html.

43 *Huston dabbled in*: "Local Youth in S. Dakota on Smithsonian Expedition," *Columbus Enquirer*, June 27, 1958, 12.

43 *The weapons, utensils*: Latimer Watson, "Boyhood 'Whittler' Now Takes Hobby Seriously," *Sunday Ledger-Enquirer* (Columbus), May 12, 1957, D-6.

44 *The biggest deal*: "Tom Huston Co. Sought," *National Nut News*, n.d.

44 *"The lowly peanut"*: "$4,000 Offered for Peanut Plant," *Atlanta Georgian*, October 27, 1929.

44 *Huston rejected the*: Crawford and Eberhardt, *Tom's: Back Home*, 10.

44 *Industry press approved*: McDaniel, "Made Millions with Peanuts," 26.

44 *had brought in*: Minnie B. Huston, "Tom Fed."

44 Time *marveled that*: "Tom's Peanuts," *Time*.

45 *The* Montgomery Advertiser: "A Great Industry in Columbus," January 5, 1929.

45 *And Tom's proved*: "Tom Huston Starts Move to Increase Peanut Yield," *Columbus Ledger*, January 2, 1929.
46 *In fact, Tom's*: Sellers, "Genius in Exile," 19–20.
46 *Sadly, as at*: Coleman, *A History of Georgia*, 237, 288.
46 *The Curtiss Candy*: Smith, *Peanuts: The Illustrious History*, 81–84.
46 *Closer to home*: "Our Story," Lance Inc., accessed March 23, 2024, https://www.lance.com/our-story/.

CHAPTER 3

50 *"Aside from any" . . . "Why don't you?"*: Powell, *More Than Peanuts*, 29–35, 67, 77.
53 *Domestic peanut production*: "Peanut Production Increases Greatly; Imports Smaller," *Indianapolis News*, February 1, 1930.
53 *Carver wrote extensively*: Powell, *More Than Peanuts*, 36–37.
53 *Though Tom's never*: Tad Brown, "In the Patented Bag: Peanuts, Packaging, and Intellectual Property in the United States, 1906–1932," *Enterprise & Society* 25, no. 3 (2024): 933–56, https://doi.org/10.1017/eso.2023.
53 *By September 1929 . . . "Agriculture behind them"*: Powell, *More Than Peanuts*, 40, 42, 44–50, 53, 55, 57–59, 68–72, 78–82, 86, 96–102, 108, 110, 123–24, 127–29, 131.
59 *Left unsaid, however*: Walter Richards, letter to Tom Huston, February 23, 1934, personal collection.
59 *Even so, the*: Powell, *More Than Peanuts*, 112–13, 133, 144–45, 151.
59 *Just as Tom's*: Holt, *George Washington Carver*, 293–94.
60 *It wasn't because*: Skip Connett, "Peanut Wizard-Peanut King: The Carver-Huston Connection," CL-E, March 26, 1989, E-1.
60 *"I, with others"*: Powell, *More Than Peanuts*, 105–6.
60 *Tom's was in*: Connett, "Peanut Wizard," E-2.
60 *But Carver was*: Skip Connett, "Carver Had Close Ties to Columbus and a Special Love for His 'Boys,'" CL-E, March 27, 1989, C-1.
60 *The Carver/Huston partnership . . . frozen peach venture*: Powell, *More Than Peanuts*, 46–47, 54, 71, 77, 98, 104–5.
61 *Charles Herty, who*: Germaine M. Reed, "Charles Herty," in *New Georgia Encyclopedia* (Georgia Humanities, 2004–), published September 30, 2005; last updated September 17, 2019, https://www.georgiaencyclopedia.org/articles/business-economy/charles-herty-1867-1938/.
61 *It was again*: Brown, "In the Patented Bag."
61 *Huston wrote to*: Powell, *More Than Peanuts*, 143.
62 *While retaining the*: Powell, *More Than Peanuts*, 147.
62 *Huston thus developed*: Tom Huston, *What Happened to Tom Huston? The Whole Story in a Peanut Shell*, pamphlet, n.d.
62 *One account holds*: "Tom's Sets Example" (advertising supplement), CL-E, January 6, 1974, 52.
62 *Huston set up*: Tom Sellers, "Dog Fleas to Dollars," *Sunday Ledger-Enquirer Magazine* (Columbus), September 5, 1965, 12.

62 *he never formally*: Huston, *What Happened.*

63 *When Huston first*: Crawford and Eberhardt, *Tom's: Back Home*, 9.

64 *Even his wife*: Minnie B. Huston, "Tom Fed Peanuts to All, His Profits to Georgia," CL-E, April 30, 1978, S-29.

64 *the latter offered*: Tom's 1938 sales manual, personal collection.

64 *a running greyhound*: Crawford and Eberhardt, *Tom's: Back Home*, 13.

64 "*Now that you*": Tom Huston, letter to stockholder, July 17, 1933, personal collection.

65 "*Back in 1929*": Richards, letter to Tom Huston, 1934.

68 *An unopened pack*: Rebecca Romanchuk, "The Accidental Artifact: Mint Julep Gum by Tom Huston," *Out of the Stacks* (blog), Texas State Library and Archives Commission, May 2, 2019, https://web.archive.org/web/20230610210123/https://www.tsl.texas.gov/outofthestacks/category/artifact-collection/.

68 *In a piece*: "Little Fellow's Baby," *Time*, March 19, 1934.

69 *Huston was certainly*: *Encyclopedia.com*, "Johnson, Hugh," accessed June 29, 2025, https://www.encyclopedia.com/economics/encyclopedias-almanacs-transcripts-and-maps/johnson-hugh.

69 *As a friend*: Tom Sellers, "Genius in Exile," *Sunday Ledger-Enquirer Magazine* (Columbus), August 29, 1965, 20.

69 *He moved there*: "Miami—the Magic City—as Seen by Tom Huston," *Miami Daily News*, July 16, 1939, 1–3.

69 *Otherwise, Huston kept*: Sellers, "Dog Fleas to Dollars," 10.

70 *The wares were*: Pal Pet Shop advertisement, *Concrete (Wash.) Herald*, March 19, 1960.

70 *He was paid*: Huston Collection.

70 *He tested fourteen*: Sellers, "Dog Fleas to Dollars," 12.

71 *It wasn't the*: Powell, *More Than Peanuts*, 150.

71 *Tom Sellers, a*: "Tom Sellers, Reporter; Exposed Corruption," AJC, February 26, 2006, E8.

71 *Sellers marveled at*: Sellers, "Genius in Exile," 18.

71 *Huston still held*: Sellers, "Dog Fleas to Dollars," 13.

71 *Huston separately funded*: Huston Collection.

71 *Time, Time tyrant*: Huston Collection.

72 "*Tom was a*": Minnie B. Huston, "Tom Fed."

CHAPTER 4

73 *Richards was a*: Carlton Johnson, "Richards' Tan No Sun-Lamp Job; Civic Chief Is Great Outdoorsman," *Sunday Ledger-Enquirer* (Columbus), March 27, 1949, C-3.

74 *Among them was*: Causey, *Red Clay, White Water*, 74, 77–78, 85, 91, 99, 103.

75 *The Gordon family*: R. Caligaris, "Historic Gordonido," *Southern Views Magazine*, November 10, 2020, https://soviewsmag.squarespace.com/homes/2020/11/10/historic-gordonido.

75 *Richards joined the*: "Walter Richards Dies; Civic, Business Leader," *Columbus Enquirer*, August 1, 1961, 1.

75 *He excelled in*: Causey, *Red Clay, White Water*, 123.

75 *In 1926 Richards*: Johnson, "Richards' Tan."

75 *Tom Huston, even*: Richards, letter to Tom Huston, February 23, 1934, personal collection.

75 *By all accounts*: Powell, *More Than Peanuts*, 54, 63, 73.

75 *A 1930 estimate*: "Frozen Fruit Plant Visited," *Columbus Ledger*, July 11, 1930, 20.

76 *Richards formally became*: "W. A. Richards to Head Tom Huston Company," *Atlanta Constitution*, January 28, 1932, 7.

76 *The company made*: Edwin T. Brinkley, "Peanut Industry Here Enjoys Business of $2,500,000 Annually," CL-E, November 22, 1936, 2.

76 *Its consulting partnership*: Tad Brown, "In the Patented Bag: Peanuts, Packaging, and Intellectual Property in the United States, 1906–1932," *Enterprise & Society* 25, no. 3 (2024): 933–56, https://doi.org/10.1017/eso.2023.

76 *Employees working on*: Powell, *More Than Peanuts*, 131, 136, 145.

76 "*Gentlemen: Received your*": Frank R. Burn, letter to Thomas Burkhard, Inc., September 26, 1933, personal collection.

76 *Tom's launched an*: Crawford and Eberhardt, *Tom's*: *Back Home*, 64.

76 *Richards often wrote*: Walter A. Richards, "John Usher," *Tom's Toaster*, July 2, 1960, 1.

76 "*We believe our*": "Our Company," *Tom's Toaster*, November 25, 1933, 1.

76 *Richards was certainly*: Crawford and Eberhardt, *Tom's*: *Back Home*, 22, 63.

77 *The factory labor*: L. Paschal Allen, "John Usher— a Straight Shooter," *Tom's Toaster*, July 2, 1960.

77 *General superintendent John*: "Mr. John: Ready, Able, and Willing," *Tom's Toaster*, July 2, 1960.

77 *The women in*: Brinkley, "Peanut Industry Here." This article, unfortunately, does not list men's wages or provide a comparison between men's and women's wages, nor does it list or compare Black employees' wages and those of white employees.

77–78 *Candy department foreman*: "In Memoriam," *Tom's Toaster*, December 20, 1952, 1.

78 *This led to*: Tom's 1938 sales manual, personal collection.

78 *Not everything worked*: "Tom's Big Chief Was Not a Big Hit," personal collection, n.d.

78 *Tom's briefly sold*: "Tom's First Foray into Potato Chips," personal collection, n.d.

78 *Along with its*: Tom's 1938 sales manual.

78 *Opposite from Big*: "Tom's First Penny Log Candies," personal collection, n.d.

78 *Richards dubbed it*: Crawford and Eberhardt, *Tom's*: *Back Home*, 1.

78 *Columbus called itself*: "Tom Huston Peanut Firm Founded 17 Years Ago," *Columbus Ledger*, July 26, 1942, 35.

80 *Later in 1939*: Crawford and Eberhardt, *Tom's*: *Back Home*, 70.

80 *Another celebrity spot*: Bob Hope photo, personal collection, n.d.

80 *An unofficial regional*: Curtis Clinard, "A History Lesson About the South: South Georgia, That Is," *Macon Telegraph*, August 18, 2007, 6A.

81 *The chart in*: Brinkley, "Peanut Industry Here."

81 *A major milestone*: Crawford and Eberhardt, *Tom's*: *Back Home*, 13.

81 *George Washington Carver*: "The Visit of Dr. Carver," CL-E, April 23, 1939, 6.

81 *valued at $750*: "Dr. Carver to Make Good Will Day Talk," *Columbus Ledger*, April 16, 1939, 5. The plaque apparently lost value between 1931 and 1939. It was originally part of a pair valued at $2,500, or $1,250 each.

81 *the same bust*: Skip Connett, "Carver Had Close Ties to Columbus and a Special Love for His 'Boys,'" CL-E, March 27, 1989, C-1.

81 *One account, written*: Amanda Rees, "Tom Huston Peanut Company," Columbus State University Archives and Special Collections, April 24, 2017, https://digitalarchives.columbusstate.edu/14-tom-huston-peanut-company.

81 *Carver spoke before*: Skip Connett, "Peanut Wizard-Peanut King: The Carver-Huston Connection," CL-E, March 26, 1989, E-1.

81 *"More and more"*: "Carver Tells of Way to Use South's Staple," *Columbus Enquirer*, April 24, 1939, 1.

81 *The crowd marveled*: "Carver Tells of Way," 3.

81 *Carver passed away*: Rees, "Tom Huston Peanut Company."

81 *Tom's got a*: Crawford and Eberhardt, *Tom's*: *Back Home*, 75.

82 *Richards led the*: "Walter Richards Is Named to Important Army Post," *Columbus Enquirer*, September 30, 1942, 6.

82 *The post added*: Walter Richards for city commissioner advertisement, *Columbus Ledger*, September 23, 1945, 15.

82 *Sales jumped as*: Causey, *Red Clay, White Water*, 166.

82 *Tom's delivery trucks*: Crawford and Eberhardt, *Tom's*: *Back Home*, 74–76.

82 *From September 1944*: *25 Years of Peanut Progress*, 26.

82 *Georgia remained 65*: Coleman, *A History of Georgia*, 257, 266–67, 269, 331.

82 *Tom's was now*: Causey, *Red Clay, White Water*, 149, 166.

82 *Tom's opened a*: *25 Years of Peanut Progress*, 26.

83 *He used the*: Dick Gruenwald, "Three Men Joined Hands to Make Center Possible," *Columbus Ledger*, March 1, 1955, 15.

83 *In any case*: Crawford and Eberhardt, *Tom's*: *Back Home*, 75, 77.

83 *A few of*: Crawford and Eberhardt, *Tom's*: *Back Home*, 27, 33, 35–36, 38, 49, 72, 78.

85 *When primary day*: "Bridges, Richards Winners in Primary," *Columbus Enquirer*, October 18, 1945, 1.

85 *In early 1947*: "Richards Elected Columbus Mayor," *Columbus Ledger*, January 6, 1947, 1.

85 *Richards's wife, the*: "Mrs. George Golden Succeeds Mrs. Walter Richards as Town Chairman of the Colonial Dames," CL-E, September 19, 1937, 17.

85 *When a new*: Johnson, "Richards' Tan."

85 *"I feel that"*: "Richards Declines to Seek Reelection to Commission," *Columbus Enquirer*, August 18, 1949, 1.

85 *However, the day*: "Richards Is President of Education Board," *Columbus Enquirer*, January 3, 1950, 4.

86 *number of people*: Coleman, *A History of Georgia*, 341.

86 *Tom's prepared a . . . "true to myself"*: *25 Years of Peanut Progress.*

88 *J. Fred Cleveland*: "John Frederick 'Fred' Cleveland Jr.," Find a Grave, accessed August 29, 2024, https://www.findagrave.com/memorial/29099638/john-frederick-cleveland.

88 *"T. C." Kendrick Jr.*: Kendrick's father was longtime Columbus High School principal T. C. Kendrick Sr., who died one year after his son. T. C. Kendrick High School in east Columbus was named for Kendrick Sr. in 1968.

88 *He was buried*: "Thomas Clarence Kendrick Jr.," Find a Grave, accessed June 12, 2024, https://www.findagrave.com/memorial/17558707/thomas-clarence-kendrick.

88 *Huston's letter was . . . toward the first*: Walter Richards, letter to Tom Huston, June 4, 1954, Huston Collection.

90 *In 1939 Richards*: "All Together," *Tom's Toaster*, February 18, 1939.

90 *for a time*: Front cover, *Tom's Toaster*, January 19, 1946.

90 *And in 1952*: Crawford and Eberhardt, *Tom's*: *Back Home*, 85.

90 *which was introduced*: "Silos Change Skyline of Columbus," Business and Industry section, CL-E, November 4, 1956, 12.

90 *"wholesome" Halloween candy*: Jim Bumpas, "A Great Month for Store Demonstrations: October," *Tom's Toaster*, September 26, 1958, 3.

90 *topped $20 million*: Crawford and Eberhardt, *Tom's*: *Back Home*, 85.

CHAPTER 5

91 *The first known*: Eric Jaffe, "Old World, High Tech," *Smithsonian*, December 2006, https://www.smithsonianmag.com/science-nature/old-world-high-tech-141284744/.

92 *gumball-style design*: Crawford and Eberhardt, *Tom's*: *Back Home*, 103.

92 *Such machines were*: Segrave, *Vending Machines*, 19, 31.

92 *Huston's "Tom's Talkie"*: "Talkie Thanks Peanut Buyers," *Columbus Enquirer-Sun*, September 11, 1929, 2.

92 *For a time*: Crawford and Eberhardt, *Tom's*: *Back Home*, 92.

93 *Born in 1898*: "William Shepherd Stricken, Dies," *Memphis Press-Scimitar*, July 31, 1954, 11.

93 *Vending machines were*: Segrave, *Vending Machines*, 32.

93 *Shepherd figured out*: Crawford and Eberhardt, *Tom's*: *Back Home*, 95.

93 *"The problem of"*: William F. Shepherd, vending machine delivery mechanism, U.S. Patent 2,738,102, filed March 27, 1951, and issued March 13, 1956, https://patents.google.com/patent/US2738102A/en.

94 *Shepherd's second patent*: William F. Shepherd, vending machine cabinet, U.S. Patent 2,738,049, filed April 25, 1951, and issued March 13, 1956, https://patents.google.com/patent/US2738049A/en.

94 *Along with a*: Crawford and Eberhardt, *Tom's*: *Back Home*, 94–95.

95 *the company established*: "Order Granting Charter," *Columbus Ledger*, April 4, 1951, 20.

95 *For example, the*: Douglas Larsen, "Coin Vending Machines Called Lure to 'Buying on Impulse,'" *Ithaca Journal*, July 31, 1947, 11.

97 *Fueled by rising*: Crawford and Eberhardt, *Tom's: Back Home*, 83.

97 *A grand opening*: "Tom Huston Firm to Celebrate 25th Anniversary of President," *Columbus Ledger*, April 16, 1953, 37.

97 *Tom's commissioned a*: Latimer Watson, "A Great Painter, a Dynamic Man—Robert Brackman," *Columbus Ledger*, January 21, 1953, 8.

98 *In October 1953*: "Condons Sued for $1,000 by Local Firm," *Cincinnati Post*, October 16, 1953, 14.

98 *The breach of*: "Million in Damages Sought in Patent Case," *Cincinnati Enquirer*, October 17, 1953, 14.

98 *Tragically, Shepherd died*: "William Shepherd Stricken."

98 *The Shepherd machines*: Back cover, *Tom's Toaster*, January 1, 1978.

98 *Total annual sales*: Bradford Mills, letter to J. W. Feighner, February 19, 1962, personal collection.

98 *A set of*: Ray Jenkins, "Presto! Goober Silos Change City's Skyline," *Columbus Ledger*, July 15, 1956, C-1.

99 *lowly Georgia peanut*: Coleman, *A History of Georgia*, 437.

99 *By the late*: "Silos Change Skyline of Columbus," Business and Industry section, CL-E, November 4, 1956, 12.

99 *Internally, the silo*: "Lee Grose Obituary," CL-E, April 16, 2005, https://www.legacy.com/us/obituaries/ledger-enquirer/name/lee-grose-obituary?id=21679910.

99 *who would join*: Crawford and Eberhardt, *Tom's: Back Home*, 85.

101 *creating, for example*: Front cover, *Tom's Toaster*, June 21, 1958.

101 *a Shepherd machine*: Crawford and Eberhardt, *Tom's: Back Home*, 94.

101 *one hundred different*: 1955 product catalog, Tom Huston Peanut Company.

101 *Stoltz was a*: George F. Bartsch, "Ex-Pennsylvanian to Bring Another Industry to Conway," *Northwest Arkansas Times* (Fayetteville), March 4, 1963, 9.

101 *so named because*: "Universal Former Officers Acquire Plant in Arkansas," *St. Louis Post-Dispatch*, March 2, 1962, 12A.

101 *Stoltz developed a*: Crawford and Eberhardt, *Tom's: Back Home*, 94–97.

101 *metal spirals, known*: Tina A. Richey, "There's Been a Time for Tom's for Almost 70 Years," *AntiqueWeek*, May 22, 1995, 41.

102 *In fact, it*: Crawford and Eberhardt, *Tom's: Back Home*, 94–97.

102 *A Shepherd D-60*: "Shepherd's Model D-60 Vendor by William F. Shepherd, Inc.," CardCow, accessed July 6, 2025, https://www.cardcow.com/513477/cincinnati-ohio-shepherds-model-60-vendor-by-william-f/.

102 *Pat Stoltz and*: Crawford and Eberhardt, *Tom's: Back Home*, 97, 99.

104 *The glass "Tom's"*: "The Telltale (Tom's) Jar," *Tom's Today*, Winter 2001, 17–20.

104 *"In the food"*: James W. Feighner, "Instant Food Will Comprise Menu of Future Diners," *Sunday Ledger-Enquirer* (Columbus), January 5, 1969, "Challenge 70" supplement, 23.

CHAPTER 6

107 *He was born*: Jim Green, "Feighner to Engineer Chamber During 1957," *Columbus Ledger*, January 6, 1957, 31.

108 *when Richards finally*: "Tom Huston Elevates Some Faithful Workers," *Columbus Ledger*, October 24, 1958, 4.

109 "*it has often*": James W. Feighner, "A Tom's Man Retires," *Tom's Toaster*, July 2, 1960.

109 *The first of*: Crawford and Eberhardt, *Tom's*: *Back Home*, 105–6.

109 *Black's plant at*: Betty J. Clay, "Tom Huston Plant Open House Held Here Friday and Saturday," *Corsicana (Tex.) Semi-Weekly Light*, December 3, 1963, 8. The address for the Knoxville plant can be found in the *Knoxville News-Sentinel* story "Tom's Foods Plant Moving to Karns," which ran on August 7, 1980. The address for the Salem plant can be found in a legal filing on page D6 of the February 15, 1985, issue of *The Roanoke Times*.

110 *A second new*: "Tom's Major League," *Tom's Today*, Spring 2003, 4.

110 *The other major*: "Walter Richards Dies; Civic, Business Leader," *Columbus Enquirer*, August 1, 1961, 1.

110 *Richards was buried*: "Rites Held for Richards," *Columbus Ledger*, August 2, 1961, 2.

110 *A middle school*: "Mrs. Richards, 74, Dies at Hospital," *Columbus Ledger*, August 13, 1970, 2.

110 *Feighner was named*: Crawford and Eberhardt, *Tom's*: *Back Home*, 110.

110 *Tom's grew at*: Bradford Mills, letter to J. W. Feighner, February 19, 1962, personal collection.

111 *In the summer*: "Tom Huston Company Buys McAfee, Inc.," *Macon News*, July 2, 1962, 3.

111 *Three years later*: "Huston Company Buys Additional Land Here," *Macon News*, September 2, 1965, 4.

111 "*We are pleased*": "Tom Huston Company Buys McAfee," 3.

111 *The factory would*: Gertrude Trawick, "Candy Profits Not as Sweet," *Macon News*, January 20, 1974, 8.

111 *Tom's executed a*: Legal notice, *Columbus Ledger*, November 10, 1962, 3.

111 *another new plant*: Clay, "Tom Huston Plant."

111 *The $750,000 plant*: "New Plants Spring Up over Texas," *Fort Worth Star-Telegram*, February 17, 1963, 52; Clay, "Tom Huston Plant."

111 *Big Tom's driver*: "'Big Tom's' Driver Keeps On Trucking," *Tom's Today*, Spring 1997, 8.

111–112 *Within a few*: "Tom Huston Company Markets Many Products from Corsicana," *Corsicana (Tex.) Daily Sun*, January 25, 1970, 89.

112 *In fact, when*: *Tom Huston Peanut Company Annual Report* (1965).

112 *By 1963, sales*: "Tom Huston Peanut Company Plans Future Progress," Business and Industry section, *Columbus Ledger*, November 17, 1963, 18.

112 *Total sales grew*: "Even Faster Growth in Sight for Tom Huston, Feighner Says," Business and Industry section, *Columbus Ledger*, November 6, 1966, 27.

112 *The company slogan*: Crawford and Eberhardt, *Tom's: Back Home*, 109.

112 *In February 1966*: "General Mills, Huston Peanut Co. Tentatively Agree on Merger," *Atlanta Constitution*, March 2, 1966, 41.

112 *General Mills had*: Crawford and Eberhardt, *Tom's: Back Home*, 113.

113 *General Mills president*: Raymond Massey, "'Tentative Agreement' Is Reached on Merger," CL-E, March 1, 1966, 20.

113 *Rawlings and Feighner*: "Even Faster Growth," 27.

113 *a product General*: Milton Moskowitz, "Taste Is In at General Mills," *Kenosha (Wisc.) News*, April 10, 1973, 18.

113 *On the back*: Crawford and Eberhardt, *Tom's: Back Home*, 113, 123.

113 *The Tom's board*: "Tom Huston's Stockholders to Meet Today," *Columbus Enquirer*, June 27, 1966, 1.

113 *Feighner was named*: Crawford and Eberhardt, *Tom's: Back Home*, 113.

113 *revenue of over*: Massey, "'Tentative Agreement,'" 20.

113 *in December 1966*: "Tom's Will Build Sandwich Plant; To Cost Millions," *Columbus Ledger*, December 15, 1966.

114 *an aggressive enforcer*: Lina M. Khan, "Amazon's Antitrust Paradox," *Yale Law Journal* 126, no. 3 (2017): 710–805, https://www.yalelawjournal.org/note/amazons-antitrust-paradox.

114 *In 1969, General*: "Food Firm OKs Consent Order in Proceedings," *Columbus Enquirer*, February 4, 1969, 19.

114 *For another example*: Burhans, *Crunch!*, 60–61.

114 *But the mid-sixties*: *Tom Huston Peanut Company Annual Report* (1965), 10.

114 *In some cases*: Tina A. Richey, "There's Been a Time for Tom's for Almost 70 Years," *AntiqueWeek*, May 22, 1995.

114 *On the personnel*: "Three Changes Are Announced by Tom Huston," *Columbus Ledger*, October 5, 1969, B-8.

114 *In 1970 Walter*: "Mrs. Richards, 74, Dies."

114 *Two years after*: Huston Collection.

114 *J. Madden Hatcher*: Crawford and Eberhardt, *Tom's: Back Home*, 116.

115 *Tom's was a*: Haisten Willis, "A Legacy in Peanuts: Columbus Says Goodbye to Tom's Foods Factory," AJC, April 6, 2021, https://www.ajc.com/life/a-legacy-in-peanuts-columbus-says-goodbye-to-toms-foods-factory/QWBEL3XRWVBARC73ZG54C4WNHA/.

116 *Led by paint*: Interview with Jernigan Gresham, August 13, 2024.

116 *Twice the Tom's*: Paul Cox, "Softball Meet Has 32 Entries," *Columbus Ledger*, March 22, 1970, C-4.

116 *Tom's also sent*: Paul Cox, "Local Team in WIBC Meet," *Columbus Ledger*, April 3, 1963, 21.

116 *Lillian Cox, whose*: Interview with Jack Warden, January 26, 2023.

116 *the average length*: Gresham interview.

116 *The children of*: Willis, "A Legacy in Peanuts."

116 *The company brought*: "Tom Huston Company Markets Many," 89.

116 *Feighner played an*: Charles Stafford, "Vending Machine Firms Get Foot in School Door," *St. Petersburg Times*, September 23, 1972, 16-A.

117 *There were roughly*: "Tom's Foods Will Operate Fresno Plant, Warehouse," *Fresno Bee*, November 24, 1970, 5-B.

118 *later opening an*: "Fresno Bank Gets Construction Loan," *Fresno Bee*, November 4, 1973, D12. The South Cherry Avenue address can be found under "Developments" on page E9 of the September 2, 2007, edition of *The Fresno Bee*.

118 *The Fresno facility*: Crawford and Eberhardt, *Tom's: Back Home*, 113, 123.

118 *The Fresno operation*: "Knight Named as Manager of Food Plant," *Columbus Ledger*, December 7, 1970, 10.

118 *Having a foothold*: Barbara Rivers, "Chip Plants Run a Quality Operation," *Tom's Toaster*, June–July 1987, 5.

118 *bags of chips*: Interview with Ben Smith, July 31, 2024.

118 *Reflecting this shift*: Crawford and Eberhardt, *Tom's: Back Home*, 114.

118 *Breadth of operations*: *Managing Your Tom's Distributorship* manual, 1973, personal collection.

118 *A mid-seventies sales*: *Discover Goodness* sales brochure, 1976, personal collection.

120 *However, Tom's Toasted*: Smith interview.

120 *By 1973 total*: *Managing Your Tom's Distributorship*. The 1940 and 1950 sales figures can be found in the 25 *Years of Peanut Progress* company history, while the 1960 figure can be found in the Tom's annual report for 1965.

120 *2,200 truck routes*: "Tom Huston Company Markets Many."

120 *The 1973 distributor's*: *Managing Your Tom's Distributorship*.

120 *In 1975 Tom's*: The updated logo can be seen in an advertisement that ran on page 5 of the *Columbus Ledger-Enquirer*'s annual "Junior Achievement" supplement on January 31, 1975. A similar ad that ran in the February 3, 1974, edition of the supplement features the older transitional logo.

121 *In a nod*: *Discover Goodness* sales brochure. Later product displays showcase the rounded logo on Tom's Toasted Peanuts.

121 *By 1974 the*: Trawick, "Candy Profits."

121 *Tom's had to*: Clark Hoyt, "Economic Controls Tighter in '72," *Tallahassee Democrat*, December 26, 1971, 4B.

121 *In 1978, with*: Rupert A. Triplitt, "Tom's 20¢ Line Well Accepted!," *Tom's Toaster*, February 1, 1978.

121 *During the 1976*: William Rowe, "Peanuts: The Salted, Oiled, Buttered Beans That Shaped the South," CL-E, April 30, 1978, S-4.

122 *Was Carter involved*: William Rowe, "Shelling Out $6 Million Is Peanuts for Tom's," CL-E, April 29, 1976, D-10.

122 *a high-yield breed*: "Peanut—Plant Breeding Program," UF/IFAS Programs and Projects, University of Florida, accessed July 10, 2025, https://programs.ifas.ufl.edu/plant-breeding/peanut/.

122 *Florunner quickly replaced*: "The 'Ground Nut' from the Ground Up," *Tom's Today*, Fall 2003, 17.

122 *the company reworked*: Crawford and Eberhardt, *Tom's: Back Home*, 7.

122 *During the transition*: Smith interview.

122 *Somewhat more noteworthy*: "Tom's in Washington," *Tom's Toaster*, January 1, 1978.

123 *Carter did have*: Causey, *Red Clay, White Water*, 212–14.

123 *at 235 feet*: "New Columbus Gov't Infrastructure to Cost Taxpayers $743 Million," *Muscogee Muckraker*, last updated February 14, 2023, https://www.muscogeemuckraker.com/articles/new-columbus-govt-infrastructure-to-cost-taxpayers-743-million.

124 *Earlier in the*: "Woolworth Co. Makes Meaningful Aid to Black Market," *Alexandria (La.) News Leader*, May 24, 1970, 4-C.

124 *In practice, there*: Crawford and Eberhardt, *Tom's*: *Back Home*, 121.

124 *returning $20 million*: Smith interview.

124 *Having led the*: Crawford and Eberhardt, *Tom's*: *Back Home*, 119.

125 *In 1982 Feighner*: "J. W. Feighner Obituary," AJC, January 3, 2005, https://www.legacy.com/us/obituaries/atlanta/name/j-w-feighner-obituary?id=51053257; Constance Johnson, "Feighner Leading Fundraiser," *Columbus Ledger*, September 7, 1982, B-1.

125 *He promised to*: Constance Johnson, "Mayoral Candidates Stress Need for New Industry," *Columbus Enquirer*, June 17, 1982, D-9.

125 *He could meet*: Gresham interview.

125 *He won the*: "Ex-Chief of Tom's Foods Is New Mayor of Columbus," *Macon News*, November 25, 1982, 2B.

125 *was sworn in*: Constance Johnson, "Feighner Plans Simple Inauguration," *Columbus Ledger*, December 27, 1982, B-1.

125 *Feighner implemented an*: Dean Barber, "Affirmative Action Proposal Expected to Be Approved," *Columbus Enquirer*, March 22, 1983, B-5.

125 *Feighner was later*: Jim Lynn, "Steele: City Must Set Hiring Goal," *Columbus Enquirer*, May 7, 1987, B-1; "Columbus All Talk on Hiring Women," *Columbus Enquirer*, May 11, 1987, A-6.

125 *In any case*: Constance Johnson, "Council Bids Feighner Farewell," *Columbus Ledger*, December 31, 1986, B-2.

125 *having stepped down*: Crawford and Eberhardt, *Tom's*: *Back Home*, 119.

CHAPTER 7

127 *Feighner explained that*: Nolan Walters, "Feighner Sees Local Flavor at Tom's After His Retirement," *Columbus Enquirer*, April 26, 1979, B-1.

127 *Tracy was born*: "Michael Loray Tracy," Find a Grave, accessed July 11, 2025, https://www.findagrave.com/memorial/6595356/michael-loray-tracy.

127 *was the star*: Ron E. Doggett, "Eulogy for Mike Tracy," *Tom's Toaster*, Spring 1989, 1.

128 *After graduation he*: Delane Chappell, "Northstar Industries President Michael L. Tracy Dies at 62," CL-E, April 17, 1989, 1.

128 *He sipped coffee*: Interview with Jack Warden, January 26, 2023.

128 *was known to*: Interview with Johnny Johnson, March 13, 2023.

128 *He was a*: Doggett, "Eulogy."

128 *Thus, "Tom Huston's"*: Walters, "Feighner Sees Local Flavor."
129 *Easter egg hunts*: "Easter Egg Hunt," *Family Weekly*, March 17, 1978.
129 *an employee's adoption*: "Altogether," *Family Weekly*, February 29, 1980.
129 *vice president Lee*: "Altogether," *Family Weekly*, September 11, 1980.
130 *In 1980, sandwich*: "Altogether," *Family Weekly*, March 7, 1980.
130 *Sometimes even former*: "Altogether," *Family Weekly*, January 20, 1978.
130 *Under Mike Tracy*: Chappell, "Northstar Industries."
130 *Tracy also established*: Crawford and Eberhardt, *Tom's: Back Home*, 82.
130 *In an era*: *Family Weekly*, September 11, 1980.
130 *Jack Warden learned*: Haisten Willis, "A Legacy in Peanuts: Columbus Says Goodbye to Tom's Foods Factory," AJC, April 6, 2021, https://www.ajc.com/life/a-legacy-in-peanuts-columbus-says-goodbye-to-toms-foods-factory/QWBEL3XRWVBARC73ZG54C4WNHA/.
131 *Just across the*: Michael J. Daniels, "Government Statistics Are Sometimes Misleading," CL-E, October 3, 1982, D-3.
131 *Rural folks not*: Jerome Walters, "If You've Got Vehicle, You're in Business," *Saturday Enquirer and Ledger*, July 4, 1981, A-3.
132 *On June 26*: Michael L. Tracy, "Invitation to J. W. Feighner Retirement," personal collection.
132 *Even at retirement*: Walters, "Feighner Sees Local Flavor."
132 *Rather, the natural*: "Our History," General Mills, accessed September 24, 2024, https://www.generalmills.com/about-us/our-history.
133 *peanuts as a*: Margareta Pagano, "Rowntree Buys into US for £140m," *Guardian* (UK edition), April 19, 1983, 20.
133 *"For over 55"*: Tom's advertisement, *Tampa Bay Times*, October 29, 1981, 6D.
133 *Developed in secret*: Interview with Glenn Seawell, March 1, 2025.
133 *For a premium*: *Tom's Great American Snacks* brochure, 1981, personal collection.
134 *Tom's had arguably*: Crawford and Eberhardt, *Tom's: Back Home*, 105–6.
134 *and certainly since*: *Tom Huston Peanut Company Annual Report* (1965).
134 *"Why do we"*: *Tom's Great American Snacks* brochure.
134 *Birmingham's Golden Flake*: Kelly Poe, "Golden Flake's Football, Community Legacy Won't Change Under Utz's New Ownership, Company Says," AL.com, July 20, 2016, https://www.al.com/business/2016/07/golden_flakes_football_communi.html.
134 *Charlotte's Lance Inc.*: Burhans, *Crunch!*, 37, 45, 76.
134 *major television advertising*: *Tom's Great American Snacks* brochure.
135 *Tom's completely rebuilt*: "Tom's Foods Plant Moving to Karns," *Knoxville News-Sentinel*, August 7, 1980, 28.
135 *It also built*: Martha Haynes, "Snack-Food Plant to Be Built in Perry," *Tallahassee Democrat*, July 18, 1979, 8.
135 *In yet another*: Crawford and Eberhardt, *Tom's: Back Home*, 116.
135 *In speeches, Tracy*: Warden interview.
136 *In Midwestern author*: Burhans, *Crunch!*, 76.
136 *Disturbing Polaroid pictures*: Warden interview.

136 *With only twenty-two*: Interview with Jernigan Gresham, August 13, 2024.

136 *Pat Stoltz, whose*: "Ban Upheld on State Pacts to Those Who Bribed," *Chicago Tribune*, November 11, 1977, sec. 5, p. 1.

136 *Stoltz died three*: "James Patrick Stoltz," Find a Grave, accessed July 13, 2025, https://www.findagrave.com/memorial/112483068/james-patrick-stoltz.

136 *his nine children*: Carrie Rengers, "Settling the Stoltz Family Feud," *Arkansas Business*, April 12, 1993, https://www.thefreelibrary.com/Settling+the+Stoltz+family+feud.-a013803934.

137 *American Canteen, the*: Segrave, *Vending Machines*, 188.

137 *Tom's even tried*: Warden interview.

137 *General Mills sold*: Pagano, "Rowntree Buys."

137 "*General Mills Chairman*": "General Mills to Sell Snack Operation," *Minneapolis Star Tribune*, April 19, 1983, 7B.

137 *It pledged not*: Pagano, "Rowntree Buys."

137 "*The British are*": Scott Shepard, "British Company Acquires Tom's Foods," *Montgomery Advertiser*, August 7, 1983, 3E.

137 *largest food industry*: Kevin Maney, "Nestle Will Acquire Carnation," *Reporter Dispatch* (White Plains), September 5, 1984, 14C; "Rowntree Seeks £36m to Finance US Takeover," *Manchester Evening News* (UK), June 14, 1983, 38.

137 *Tracy was allowed*: Shepard, "British Company."

138 *Tom's hosted a*: Crawford and Eberhardt, *Tom's: Back Home*, 123–24.

138 *This practice started*: Pat Quinley, "Tom's Foods to Add 50–60 Employees," *Columbus Ledger*, September 14, 1984, B-5.

138 *By late 1985*: Mary Brasier, "Rowntree Shrugs Off First Half Setback," *Guardian*, September 20, 1985, 27.

138 *which Tom's claimed*: Pat Quinley, "A New Tom's," CL-E, March 2, 1987, D-4.

138 *zesty ranch, spicy*: Jitney Jingle advertisement, *Yazoo (Miss.) Herald*, August 24, 1988, 28.

138 "*If you are*": Mike Dillon, "Only Salespeople Can Drive Up Sales for TOM'S," *Tom's Toaster*, October 1986, 2.

139 *Dillon had replaced*: Pat Quinley, "Top Executive for Tom's Foods Retiring After 40 Years Service," *Columbus Ledger*, January 9, 1987, 1.

139 *Dillon was born*: Delane Chappell, "Dillon Hopes Tom's Will Thrive in His Care," CL-E, April 29, 1991, D-3.

139 *Dillon was behind*: Crawford and Eberhardt, *Tom's: Back Home*, 125.

139 "*Tom's needs to*": Quinley, "Top Executive."

139 *Mike Tracy did*: Chappell, "Northstar Industries."

139 *remembered in Columbus*: "Tracy Served His City," CL-E, April 21, 1989, A-8.

139 *In the fall*: Ken Edelstein, "Tom's Food Workers Turn Down Union," *Columbus Ledger*, March 26, 1987, D-1.

139 *There were three*: Ken Elkins and Ken Edelstein, "Bakery Strike No Closer to Settlement," *Columbus Enquirer*, June 27, 1986, B-1.

140 *Dillon admitted that*: Ken Edelstein, "Union Bid Goes to Vote at Tom's," *Columbus Enquirer*, March 26, 1987, D-7.

140 *But a union*: Pat Quinley, "Tom's Facing Union Threat," CL-E, March 2, 1987, D-5.

140 *Paul Massey thought*: Priscilla Duncan, "Factory Job Teaches Respect for the People on the Line," *Columbus Enquirer*, March 25, 1987, B-1.
140 *A Tom's employee*: Edelstein, "Union Bid Goes."
140 *in the end*: Edelstein, "Tom's Food Workers."
140 *The unionization effort*: Roy Williams, "Hanging In There," CL-E, March 13, 1989, D-1.
140 *In April 1987*: "Tom's Foods in Salem to Lay Off 38 Workers," *Roanoke Times*, April 14, 1987, A8.
140 *"As you know"*: Mike Dillon, "TOM'S Faces Challenges Ahead," *Tom's Toaster*, June–July 1987, 2.
141 *On January 4*: Crawford and Eberhardt, *Tom's: Back Home*, 128.
141 *Tom's revenue did*: Tom Hallman, "Tom's Getting Back Its Hometown Flavor," AJC, May 31, 1988, 1E.
141 *Rowntree had other*: Mike Dillon, "The Sale of TOM'S FOODS INC. and What It Means to You," *Tom's Toaster*, August–September 1988, 3, 27; "Rowntree Accepts Bid by Nestlé," *New York Times*, June 24, 1988, D2.
142 *Dillon said the*: Dillon, "The Sale of TOM'S."
142 *The second was*: Burrough and Helyar, *Barbarians at the Gate*, 151.
142 *A leveraged buyout*: Will Kenton, "Leveraged Buyout (LBO): Definition, How It Works, and Examples," Investopedia, last updated June 8, 2024, https://www.investopedia.com/terms/l/leveragedbuyout.asp.
142 *Leveraged buyouts exploded*: Burrough and Helyar, *Barbarians at the Gate*, 140–41.
143 *Ron E. Doggett*: Michael Flagg, "GoodMark Files to Sell 1.6 Million Stock Shares," *News and Observer* (Raleigh), October 10, 1985, 6B.
143 *he wound up*: "Ron Doggett Obituary," *News and Observer*, October 7, 2021, https://www.legacy.com/us/obituaries/newsobserver/name/ron-doggett-obituary?id=25391679.
143 *Doggett described Tracy*: Doggett, "Eulogy."
143 *To do this*: Warden interview.
143 *In total, the*: Dillon, "The Sale of TOM'S."
143 *the deal closed*: Crawford and Eberhardt, *Tom's: Back Home*, 128–29.
143 *Employees were told*: Hallman, "Tom's Getting Back."
143 *A banner went*: Crawford and Eberhardt, *Tom's: Back Home*, 128–29. An order form sent to distributors listed the fifteen-dollar price for the history book, with a limit of ten book copies per order.
144 *"Tom's did a"*: Warden interview.
144 *Not only was*: Dillon, "The Sale of TOM'S."
144 *The Salem, Virginia*: Richard Lovegrove, "Tom's Foods Closing in Salem; 120 to Lose Jobs," *Roanoke Times*, October 16, 1988, B3.
144 *The Macon plant*: Stephanie Jordan, "Candy Makers Show Interest in Tom's Foods," *Macon Telegraph*, July 12, 1988, 6C.
144 *to five factories*: Dillon, "The Sale of TOM's."
144 *Tom's also sold*: Tom Murphy, "Tom's Foods Takes New Twist," *Rocky Mount (N.C.) Telegram*, March 25, 1990, 38.

144 *Columbus was mostly*: Lisa Eldridge, "Serff's Helping to Put Tom's Back on Track," CL-E, August 15, 1988, D-3.

144 *Tom's overall workforce*: Delane Chappell, "Carving Tom's Foods' Niche," CL-E, March 5, 1990, D-1.

144 *That figure included*: Chappell, "Dillon Hopes Tom's."

144 *Was Dillon stressed*: Hallman, "Tom's Getting Back."

146 *He created the*: Crawford and Eberhardt, *Tom's*: *Back Home*, 125, 128, 134.

146 *After the buyout*: Gresham interview.

146 *As Tom's vice*: "Stewart Lyman Returns to TOM'S," *Tom's Toaster*, Spring 1989, 22–23.

147 *But on the*: Interview with Sharon Sanders, March 1, 2023.

147 *Tom's was making*: Dillon, "The Sale of TOM'S."

148 *Dillon was named*: Chappell, "Dillon Hopes Tom's."

CHAPTER 8

149 *He launched a*: Crawford and Eberhardt, *Tom's*: *Back Home*, 135.

150 *Dillon looked into*: Pat Quinley, "A New Tom's," CL-E, March 2, 1987, D-1.

150 *Despite the debt*: Ken Elkins, "Cable Makes Commercials Affordable," CL-E, September 18, 1989, D-1.

150 *In 1990, Dillon*: Delane Chappell, "Dillon Hopes Tom's Will Thrive in His Care," CL-E, April 29, 1991, D-3.

150 *First, the entire*: Burrough and Helyar, *Barbarians at the Gate*, 514–15, 519. LBO firms rebranded themselves as "private equity" firms due to the backlash.

150 *By the end*: Burhans, *Crunch!*, 65, 69.

150 *it looked at*: Tom Hallman, "Tom's Getting Back Its Hometown Flavor," AJC, May 31, 1988, 1E. According to the story, Flowers Industries (later renamed Flowers Foods) of Thomasville, Georgia, also looked into buying Tom's.

150 *Most notably, Anheuser-Busch*: Burhans, *Crunch!*, 65–67, 73–74.

152 *It technically ended*: "Business Cycle Dating Committee Announcement December 22, 1992," National Bureau of Economic Research, December 22, 1992, https://www.nber.org/news/business-cycle-dating-committee-announcement-december-22-1992.

152 *helping Bill Clinton*: Chester Pach, "The 1992 Presidential Election and the Rise of Democratic Populism," Bill of Rights Institute, accessed July 17, 2025, https://billofrightsinstitute.org/essays/the-1992-presidential-election-and-the-rise-of-democratic-populism.

152 *There were lots*: Delane Chappell, "Carving Tom's Foods' Niche," CL-E, March 5, 1990, D-1.

152 *The push convinced*: Mary Rowland, "Franchises Attracting 'Corporate Dropouts,'" *N.Y. Times News Service*, March 10, 1991, E2.

152 *scholars refer to*: Peter A. Coclanis, "More Pricks Than Kicks: The Southern Economy in the Long Twentieth Century," *Study the South*, May 26, 2020, https://studythesouth.org/more-pricks-than-kicks/.

152 *In December 1991*: Jim Poole, "The Man of Vision at Heico," CL-E, May 15, 1993, 1.

152 *"The saddest day"*: Interview with Glenn Seawell, March 1, 2025.

154 *Born in Alexandria*: Richard Goldstein, "Michael Heisley, Who Rebuilt N.B.A.'s Grizzlies, Dies at 77," *New York Times*, April 27, 2014, https://www.nytimes.com/2014/04/28/sports/michael-heisley-who-rebuilt-nbas-grizzlies-dies-at-77.html.

154 *Heisley joined* RCA: David Baines and Mike Beamish, "Grizz Suitor Vows Team Will Stay in Vancouver," *Vancouver Sun*, January 25, 2000, 1.

154 *Suddenly there were*: Poole, "The Man of Vision."

154 *He often paid*: H. L. Murphy, "Food Firm Buyouts Altering Heico's Bottom-Fishing Diet," *Crain's Chicago Business*, May 17, 1993, 4.

154 *When he bought*: Delane Chappell, "Tom's Foods Sold," CL-E, May 15, 1993, 1.

154 *annual interest payments*: John Carroll, "Peter Rogers: Turnaround Expert Spices Up Tom's," CL-E, July 4, 1994, D6.

154 *Dillon and his*: Interview with Ben Smith, July 31, 2024.

155 *the 1988 deal*: Poole, "The Man of Vision."

155 *His last deal*: Murphy, "Food Firm Buyouts."

155 *"When I looked"*: Poole, "The Man of Vision."

155 *"Mike is very"*: Murphy, "Food Firm Buyouts."

155 *Dillon was allowed*: Chappell, "Tom's Foods Sold."

156 *Johnny Johnson, a*: Interview with Johnny Johnson, March 13, 2023.

156 *Even little changes*: Interview with Jack Warden, January 26, 2023.

156 *Rogers and Johnson*: Burrough and Helyar, *Barbarians at the Gate*, 16, 19, 35.

156 *listened to Winston*: Carroll, "Peter Rogers."

156 *Rogers's caretaker presidency*: "Tom's Foods Gets New Chief," CL-E, January 15, 1995, F1.

156 *Divin made his*: Russell Redman, "Hunt-Wesson Acquires Chun King," *Supermarket News*, May 8, 1995, https://www.supermarketnews.com/grocery-operations/hunt-wesson-acquires-chun-king.

157 *Chun King was*: Kevin L. McQuaid, "Chun King Corp. to Close Plant, Eliminate 173 Jobs," *Baltimore Sun*, April 4, 1995, 11C.

157 *"It was a"*: Interview with Ron Divin, March 10, 2023.

157 *"had to be"*: Divin interview.

158 *The U.S. government*: "Why the Low-Fat Diet Failed," *Health & Nutrition Letter*, Tufts University, last modified March 11, 2020, https://www.nutritionletter.tufts.edu/healthy-eating/why-the-low-fat-diet-failed/.

158 *Nabisco was first*: George Lazarus, "Elves to Chip Away at SnackWells," *Chicago Tribune*, August 19, 1994, sec. 3, p. 4.

158 *Rogers, a former*: John Carroll, "Former Executive at Nabisco Brands Is Named CEO at Tom's Foods Inc.," CL-E, June 14, 1994, 1.

158 *Divin created a*: "Targeting Health Nuts" (advertising supplement), CL-E, April 2, 1995, 18.

158 *It tried out*: Ed Driggers, "Lowly Peanut Joins Foods for Waist Line Watchers," *Dothan (Ala.) Eagle*, February 13, 1966, 1.

158 *it experimented with*: "New Products Coming Soon from Tom's," *Tom's Toaster*, Spring 1989, 4.
158 *Under Divin's guidance*: "Targeting Health Nuts."
158 *Items like the*: Warden interview.
158 *One was that*: Burrough and Helyar, *Barbarians at the Gate*, 527.
159 *Within a year*: Tony Adams, "Tom's Foods Takes a Slice out of the Snack Food Market," Business Quarterly section, CL-E, April 30, 2000, 6.
159 *On March 12*: Minnie Bullock Huston obituary, CL-E, March 16, 1996, B10.
159 *met with the*: Crawford and Eberhardt, *Tom's*: *Back Home*, 135.
159 *Minnie Huston's graveside*: Interview with J. Madden Hatcher Jr., April 22, 2024.
159 *Lance laid off*: Burhans, *Crunch!*, 69–70, 76–77, 82–83, 85–88.
160 ABC*'s Peter Jennings*: "Frito-Lay Accused of Monopoly in Grocery Stores," ABC *World News Tonight*, aired May 28, 1996, on ABC.
160 *Divin paid close*: Divin interview. He also mentioned the investigation in the president's letter in the Fall 1997 and Fall 1998 issues of *Tom's Today*.
160 *In its investigation*: Burhans, *Crunch!*, 87–88.
160 *Tom Bigham, a*: "Justice Department Ends Inquiry into Snack Food Maker Frito-Lay," *Dallas Morning News*, December 23, 1998.
160 *Peter Sprecher, president*: Jim Zarroli, "Justice Department Taking a Look at Frito-Lay," *All Things Considered*, aired June 3, 1996, on NPR.
160 *When it merged*: Burhans, *Crunch!*, 60–61.
160 *when General Mills*: "Food Firm OKs Consent Order in Proceedings," *Columbus Enquirer*, February 4, 1969, 19.
160 *By the 1990s*: Lina M. Khan, "Amazon's Antitrust Paradox," *Yale Law Journal* 126, no. 3 (2017): 710–805, https://www.yalelawjournal.org/note/amazons-antitrust-paradox.
161 "*What a number*": Zarroli, "Justice Department Taking."
161 *In 1997, Frito-Lay*: "Justice Department Ends Inquiry."
161 *It launched Gold*: "It's a Gold Rush," *Tom's Today*, Spring 1997, 10.
161 *a cookie brand*: "It's Crunch Time," *Tom's Today*, Spring 1997, 3.
161 *a Hispanic-focused line*: Products can be seen on the front and back covers of the Fall 2001 issue of *Tom's Today*.
161 *loaded spud chips*: Products can be seen on the front and back covers of the Fall 1998 issue of *Tom's Today*.
161 *zesty lime chips*: "Stock Up! Sell Out!," *Tom's Today*, Fall 2003, 11.
161 *Peanut Butter Logs*: "New Products—Hot, Gummi, Sunny, and Retro 'Cool,'" *Tom's Today*, Winter 2001.
161 *Tom's created fifty-one*: Ron Divin, "Past Success Levels Returning for Tom's," *Tom's Today*, Fall 1997, 1.
161 *It tested out*: "Tom's New Products Aim High for Quality and Customer Appeal!," *Tom's Today*, Fall 1998, 11–14.
161 *A new flavor*: Warden interview.
162 "*They just skimmed*": Johnson interview.
162 *Heisley owned twenty-six*: "Tom's Foods Gets."
162 *Divin pointed to*: Divin interview.

162 *But the problem*: Ted Gavin, "Top Five Reasons Why EBITDA Is a Great Big Lie," *Forbes*, December 28, 2011, https://www.forbes.com/sites/tedgavin/2011/12/28/top-five-reasons-why-ebitda-is-a-great-big-lie/.

162 *Sharon Sanders, who*: Interview with Sharon Sanders, March 1, 2023.

162 *In 2000 he*: Baines and Beamish, "Grizz Suitor."

163 *Unfortunately for the*: Goldstein, "Michael Heisley."

163 *"If making a"*: Baines and Beamish, "Grizz Suitor."

163 *By 1993, Total*: Causey, *Red Clay, White Water*, 241–44, 247–48, 256–59, 261.

164 *still employing 800*: Adams, "Tom's Foods Takes."

164 *The first "millennium"*: Mick Walsh, "Local Family Welcomes Millennium Baby," CL-E, January 2, 2000, B1.

164 *Phenix City, Alabama*: Peggy Martin retirement announcement, Tom's employee newsletter, 2001, personal collection.

164 *Tom's products even*: "Tom's Is in the Movies Again," *Tom's Today*, Fall 1998, 5.

164 *Tom's expanded its*: Abby Brach, "Tom's Expands Bakery Plant," CL-E, December 22, 1998, C8.

164 *By 2001 Tom's*: "Candy Plant—Busy Again!," Tom's Columbus operations newsletter, June 2001, 1.

164 *Even bigger was*: Adams, "Tom's Foods Takes."

165 *Tom's looked at*: Divin interview.

165 *Paducah, Kentucky, distributor*: Joe Walker, "Working for Peanuts," *Paducah Sun*, August 8, 1999, 1C.

165 *Tom's thrived increasingly*: Divin interview.

165 *Tom's brought in*: Carroll, "Peter Rogers."

165 *By 2002, revenues*: Tony Adams, "Desperate for a Buyer," CL-E, October 3, 2005, D1.

165 *In the early*: Bradford Mills, letter to J. W. Feighner, February 19, 1962, personal collection.

165 *But Tom Hill*: Julie Jargon, "Snack Maker's Loan Troubles Hinder Heico," *Crain's Chicago Business*, April 4, 2005, 14.

166 *On April 6*: Ashby Jones, "Tom's Foods Bites into Chapter 11," *Daily Deal/The Deal*, April 11, 2005.

166 *The accounting department*: Sanders interview.

166 *Before the sale*: Warden interview.

166 *In August 2005*: Tony Adams, "Pension Funds Falling to Wayside," CL-E, August 27, 2005, B7.

166 *By October, Tom's*: Adams, "Desperate."

CHAPTER 9

169 *Philip L. Lance*: "Our Story," Lance Inc., accessed July 20, 2025, https://www.lance.com/our-story/.

169 *first sandwich cracker*: Jared Misner, "The Cracker Kingdom's New Ruler: A Look at Lance, Then and Now," *Charlotte Magazine*, May 7, 2020, https://

www.charlottemagazine.com/the-cracker-kingdoms-new-ruler-a-look-at-lance-then-and-now/.

170 *Lance didn't get*: "Our Story."

170 *sold millions of*: Misner, "Cracker Kingdom's New Ruler."

170 *Tom's annual revenue*: Tony Adams, "Lance Buys Tom's Foods," CL-E, October 21, 2005, A1.

170 *Lance was an*: Stella M. Hopkins, "Snack Maker Has Lots to Chew On," *Charlotte Observer*, February 20, 2007, 1D.

170 *sponsor a* NASCAR: Reid Spencer, "Purvis Rejoins Forces with Finch," *Charlotte Observer*, November 7, 1997, 8B.

170 *Paul Stroup III*: Adams, "Lance Buys Tom's."

171 *The final purchase*: Tony Adams, "Snyder's-Lance Sells Its Private Brands," CL-E, July 2, 2014, A1.

171 *Industry analysts were*: Adams, "Lance Buys Tom's."

171 *Ron Divin, as*: Ron Divin, letter to Tom's employees, October 21, 2005, personal collection.

172 "*Everybody except the*": Rebecca Ferrar, "Quick Bite," *Knoxville News Sentinel*, October 22, 2005, C1, C6.

172 "*The period of*": Interview with Ben Smith, July 31, 2024.

172 *Jack Warden had*: Interview with Jack Warden, January 26, 2023.

172 *Thanks to the*: Tim Chitwood, "Plant Sending Message That Snacks Are '100 Percent' Safe," CL-E, January 31, 2009, A1.

172 *Lance created the*: Legal notice, CL-E, November 27, 2006, C5.

173 *Tom's Toasted Peanuts*: Smith interview.

173 *Despite initially keeping*: Tony Adams, "Lance to Shift Administrative Jobs to Charlotte," CL-E, November 16, 2005, C7.

173 *shut down the*: Bill Brewer, "Karns Snack Plant Closes," *Knoxville News Sentinel*, July 4, 2006, C1.

173 *sold off the*: "Developments," *Fresno Bee*, September 2, 2007, E9.

173 *The Columbus workforce*: Andrea V. Hernandez, "Lance Expansion to Add 70 Jobs," CL-E, May 23, 2009, A1.

173 *Cape Cod kettle*: Burhans, *Crunch!*, 97.

173 *Tom's alone was*: Emily Fredrix, "Choices Are Fewer," *Modesto (Calif.) Bee*, February 21, 2009, B5.

173 *Many former Tom's*: Interview with Jernigan Gresham, August 13, 2024.

173 *Lance made $600*: Amy Baldwin, "Net Income for Lance Rises Nearly 18%," *Charlotte Observer*, February 14, 2008, 2D.

173 *By 2008 it*: Fredrix, "Choices Are Fewer."

173 *and in 2009*: Joseph Deinlein, "Snyder's Announces Lance Merger," *Evening Sun* (Hanover, Pa.), July 23, 2010, 1A.

174 *Singer turned to*: Chitwood, "Plant Sending Message."

174 *Sales still took*: Kirsten Valle, "Lance Reports 1Q Earnings of $6.5 Million," *Charlotte Observer*, April 24, 2009, 2D.

174 *In May 2009*: Hernandez, "Lance Expansion."

174 *Michael McDowell in*: "2009 Nationwide (on Your Side) Series Preview," *Bleacher Report*, February 8, 2009, https://bleacherreport.com/articles/121489–2009-nationwide-on-your-side-series-preview.

174 *Marcos Ambrose in*: "JTG Racing, Ambrose Sponsor News," *Motorsport*, October 2, 2009, https://au.motorsport.com/nascar-cup/news/jtg-racing-ambrose-sponsor-news-2009–09–11/2352868/.

174 *Bobby Labonte in*: "JTG Daugherty Racing Announces 2011 NASCAR Sprint Cup Series Line-Up," *Auto Channel*, February 4, 2010, https://www.theautochannel.com/news/2011/02/04/517377.html.

175 *In November 2008*: Linda Martz, "Ownership Change Looms for Archway," *Mansfield (Ohio) News Journal*, November 19, 2008, 1A.

175 *The next year*: Kerry H. Singe, "Growing Lance Is Buying Stella D'oro Bakery Brand," *Charlotte Observer*, September 8, 2009, A7.

175 *called Late July*: Lily Gordon, "Food Network Unwraps at Lance," CL-E, June 2, 2008, A3.

175 *On July 23*: Deinlein, "Snyder's Announces."

175 *Frito-Lay, which brought*: Mike Armstrong, "Pretzel-Maker Saga Has Twist at the End," *Philadelphia Inquirer*, July 23, 2010, D1.

175 *Snyder's was the*: "Snyder's of Hanover Officially Acquires Jays Foods," *PotatoPro*, December 7, 2007, https://www.potatopro.com/news/2007/snyders-hanover-officially-acquires-jays-foods.

175 *Both Lance and*: Deinlein, "Snyder's Announces."

175 *Singer stood to*: "Lance OKs Merger with Snyder's," CL-E, December 3, 2010, A13.

175 *The combined company*: Celeste Smith, "2Q Loss for Snack Giant Snyder's-Lance Inc.," *Charlotte Observer*, November 20, 2011, 2B.

176 *That fall, Snyder's-Lance*: "Snyder's-Lance to Close Texas Manufacturing Plant," *Charlotte Observer*, November 11, 2011, 2B.

176 *After another sluggish*: Ely Portillo, "CEO Singer to Retire," *Charlotte Observer*, January 15, 2013, 2B.

176 *In 2014 Snyder's-Lance*: Adams, "Snyder's-Lance Sells"; Katherine Peralta, "Snyder's-Lance Buys Diamond in the Rough," *Corpus Christi Caller-Times*, October 29, 2015, 1B.

176 *Lee made a*: Katherine Peralta, "Campbell Soup to Buy Charlotte Snack Maker in $4.9 Billion Deal," *Charlotte Observer*, December 20, 2017, 8A.

176 *In the middle*: Lillian Reed, "Snyder's-Lance to Cut 250 Positions Company-wide," *Evening Sun* (Hanover, Pa.), July 27, 2017, A1.

176 *Campbell Soup Company*: Peralta, "Campbell Soup to Buy."

176 *Campbell already owned*: Harold Brubaker, "Campbell Soup Pays $4.9B for Snacks," *Philadelphia Inquirer*, December 19, 2017, A1.

176 *In May 2018*: Jim Walsh, "Campbell Soup Names New President and CEO," *Courier-Post* (Cherry Hill, N.J.), December 22, 2018, 10A.

177 *Clouse focused on*: Harold Brubaker, "Campbell's CEO Says No One Makes Soup Better," *Philadelphia Inquirer*, November 17, 2019, E4. Clouse left Campbell to become president of the Washington Commanders NFL team in February 2025.

177 *On January 13*: Joshua Mixon, "Campbell Soup Company in Columbus Announces It Will Close by Spring 2022," CL-E, January 14, 2021, 1A.

177 *The closure did*: Haisten Willis, "A Legacy in Peanuts: Columbus Says Goodbye to Tom's Foods Factory," AJC, April 6, 2021, https://www.ajc.com/life/a-legacy-in-peanuts-columbus-says-goodbye-to-toms-foods-factory/QWBEL3XRWVBARC73ZG54C4WNHA/.

178 *Columbus television station*: James Giles, "Campbell's Snacks Employee in Columbus Reacts to Plant Closing," WTVM, January 13, 2021, https://www.wtvm.com/2021/01/15/campbells-snacks-employee-columbus-reacts-plant-closing/.

SELECTED BIBLIOGRAPHY

Burhans, Dirk. *Crunch! A History of the Great American Potato Chip*. University of Wisconsin Press, 2008.

Burrough, Bryan, and John Helyar. *Barbarians at the Gate: The Fall of* RJR *Nabisco*. Harper & Row, 1990.

Causey, Virginia E. *Red Clay, White Water, and Blues: A History of Columbus, Georgia*. University of Georgia Press, 2019.

Coleman, Kenneth, ed. *A History of Georgia*. 2nd ed. University of Georgia Press, 1991.

Crawford, Sara, and Janis Eberhardt. *Tom's: Back Home Where We Belong; The Sixty-Five Year History of Tom's Foods Inc., 1925–1990*. Columbus Productions, 1990.

Delfino, Susanna, and Michele Gillespie, eds. *Technology, Innovation, and Southern Industrialization: From the Antebellum Era to the Computer Age*. University of Missouri Press, 2008.

Holt, Rackham. *George Washington Carver: An American Biography*. Doubleday, 1943.

Lewis, Jori. *Slaves for Peanuts: A Story of Conquest, Liberation, and a Crop That Changed History*. New Press, 2022.

Powell, Edith. *More Than Peanuts: The Unlikely Partnership of Tom Huston and George Washington Carver*. NewSouth Books, 2022.

Segrave, Kerry. *Vending Machines: An American Social History*. McFarland, 2002.

Smith, Andrew F. *Peanuts: The Illustrious History of the Goober Pea*. University of Illinois Press, 2002.

25 Years of Peanut Progress: The Story of the Tom Huston Peanut Company, Columbus, Ga. Privately published, 1950.

INDEX

www.ingramcontent.com/pod-product-compliance
Lightning Source LLC
LaVergne TN
LVHW091125061026
849616LV00030B/266